European Cities in Dynamic Competition

Horst Albach • Heribert Meffert •
Andreas Pinkwart • Ralf Reichwald •
Łukasz Świątczak
Editors

European Cities in Dynamic Competition

Theory and Case Studies on Urban Governance, Strategy, Cooperation and Competitiveness

Springer

Editors

Horst Albach
Center for Advanced Studies
in Management (CASiM)
HHL Leipzig Graduate School
of Management
Leipzig, Germany

Heribert Meffert
Center for Advanced Studies
in Management (CASiM)
HHL Leipzig Graduate School
of Management
Leipzig, Germany

Andreas Pinkwart
Stiftungsfonds Deutsche Bank
Chair of Innovation Management
and Entrepreneurship
HHL Leipzig Graduate School
of Management
Leipzig, Germany

Ralf Reichwald
Center for Leading Innovation
and Cooperation (CLIC)
HHL Leipzig Graduate School
of Management
Leipzig, Germany

Łukasz Świątczak
Center for Advanced Studies
in Management (CASiM)
HHL Leipzig Graduate School
of Management
Leipzig, Germany

ISBN 978-3-662-56418-9 ISBN 978-3-662-56419-6 (eBook)
https://doi.org/10.1007/978-3-662-56419-6

Library of Congress Control Number: 2018934846

Printed on acid-free paper

This Springer imprint is published by the registered company Springer-Verlag GmbH, DE part of Springer Nature.
The registered company address is: Heidelberger Platz 3, 14197 Berlin, Germany

Preface

Urbanization is next to globalization and digitization as well as neo-ecology, another megatrend that does and will shape life on earth. Global population reached the level of 7.5 billion people in 2017 and is constantly increasing (reaching 8.6 billion in 2030). At the same time, the world population is increasingly moving from rural areas to urban agglomerations. The importance of cities as centers of socioeconomic and environmental activity grows, but the actual performance of individual cities will significantly differ from each other depending on their capability of addressing the megatrends and utilizing new technologies. Not only firms and industries may shrink or disappear, if they are not sufficiently willing to change and to improve.

For centuries, the city has been a place for a variety of economic and social relations, the center of educational and scientific activities, as well as a central place of health care and cultural institutions. The quality of urban life and technical infrastructure are considered to be crucial to attracting and retaining a skilled and creative labor force as well as innovative and successful firms. The increasing concentration of people and their economic activities in urban areas results in the proximity advantage and magnetic effects. On the other hand, it also leads to negative side effects for ecology, housing, and mobility.

In recent years, such effects were mainly investigated on the example of megacities in emerging economies, while European cities did not receive adequate attention in the literature. Moreover, the development of urban centers is often examined in isolation, although cities compete with each other for talents, labor, and firms on a global level. Currently, suitable models for a better assessment of the megatrends on our cities are lacking. Nevertheless, we are able to build on pioneering concepts from urban dynamics and competition as well as from management theory.

At the beginning of the twenty-first century, Europe can proudly look back on a rich tradition of cities, but it also faces a great challenge of rediscovering opportunities of transformation and utilizing them to the renaissance of the city. Therefore, we decided to devote the present edited volume to European cities shaped by centuries of steady development and renewal which are currently confronted by disruptive challenges and permanent change.

The ideas and related methods from economic theory and business economics as well as from other disciplines underlying this volume were developed and discussed at the Center for Advanced Studies in Management (CASiM) and its international scientific meetings (especially CASiM Conference 2016). This volume brings together the expertise of the chairs and centers of HHL Leipzig Graduate School of Management with that of other research institutions and practitioners and devises new solutions to current socioeconomic challenges.

Each book publication is the result of a considerable collective effort, and the completion of an edited volume always requires additional coordination. We would like to use this opportunity to thank all the contributors collectively for their important contribution to this project. Some contributors we would like to praise individually. Specifically, we thank all the authors for their highly stimulating papers and all the reviewers for their critical and constructive feedback. This book project also benefited greatly from fruitful discussions with the members of the advisory board of CASiM. We would like to acknowledge their important support. Special thanks go to Prof. Dr. Thomas Gehrig (University of Vienna, Austria) and Prof. Dr. Peter Letmathe (RWTH Aachen University, Germany), who also acted as reviewers in the double-blinded peer-review process.

We would particularly like to thank the Mercator Foundation for the financial support of this project. Without this, the publication would not have been possible in its current form. Last but not least, we owe special thanks to Daniela Neumann who professionally managed this book project. She successfully coordinated all activities of the authors, reviewers, and editors and provided continuous editorial support.

We hope this publication will not only provide interesting reading but will also encourage further discussions and academic research on urban dynamics and competition of European cities. We welcome your feedback via casim@hhl.de.

Leipzig, Germany
June 2018

Horst Albach
Heribert Meffert
Andreas Pinkwart
Ralf Reichwald
Łukasz Świątczak

Contents

About the Editors

Horst Albach was born in 1931 in Essen, Germany. After a year of study at Bowdoin College in Brunswick, Maine, USA, he continued his studies of management and economics at Cologne University, Germany, where he received his doctoral degree in business economics in 1958. He taught at Darmstadt Technical University (1958–1960) and Kiel University (1960–1961), Germany, and Graz University (1960), Austria. He accepted an offer to become Full Professor of Business Economics at Bonn University in 1961, cofounded the private Coblence School of Management in 1984, and taught there on leave of absence from Bonn until 1987 when he became Professor of Industrial Economics at the Free University Berlin. After the unification of Germany, he became a Professor of Management Science at the Humboldt University of Berlin. Professor Albach holds honorary degrees from the Swedish School of Management in Stockholm, the Finnish School of Business in Helsinki, the universities of Kiel, Bielefeld, Cottbus, Graz, Alcalá de Henares, Waseda, Bowdoin College in Brunswick, ME, and the Russian Academy of Sciences. He is a member of the German Order Pour le mérite for Sciences and Arts and was its Chancellor from 2004 to 2009. From 2012 to 2016, Professor Albach was a member of the Executive Board of the Center for Advanced Studies in Management (CASiM) at HHL Leipzig Graduate School of Management, Leipzig, Germany.

In 2016, HHL Leipzig Graduate School of Management conferred the title of Honorary Senator to Prof. Dr. Dr. h.c. mult. Horst Albach.

Heribert Meffert studied business administration in Munich, Germany, and wrote his habilitation about flexibility in business decisions in 1968. In 1969, he was appointed to the Chair of Business Administration at the University of Münster, where he established the first institute of marketing at a German university. In 1981, he was a founding member of the Wissenschaftliche Gesellschaft für Marketing und Unternehmensführung e. V., an academic society for marketing and management. From 1995 until 1997, he was responsible for the academic management of HHL Leipzig Graduate School of Management in Leipzig, Germany. As an emeritus professor, Heribert Meffert was Chairman of the Board of Management of the Bertelsmann Foundation from October 2002 to December 2005. He received numerous awards as well as honorary doctorates, and he was active on a number of supervisory boards and advisory committees of international companies. As a marketing researcher he has published more than 300 scientific writings and over 30 monographs. As the initiator of the AMD-Net NRW, Professor Meffert has been working since 2008 in an honorary capacity toward the improvement of the healthcare situation for people with visual impairments. Professor Meffert was a member of the Executive Board of the Center for Advanced Studies in Management (CASiM) at HHL Leipzig Graduate School of Management from 2012 to 2016.

Andreas Pinkwart was born in 1960 in Seelscheid, North Rhine-Westphalia, Germany. After his professional training as a banker, he studied economics and business administration at the Universities of Münster and Bonn where he finished his Diploma in Economics and obtained his doctoral degree (*summa cum laude*) in 1991. Subsequently, Professor Pinkwart ran the office of the Free Democratic Party's leader of the parliamentary group in the German Bundestag from 1991 to 1994. In 1994, he became a Professor of Economics and Business Administration at the School of Public Administration in Düsseldorf from where he moved to the University of Siegen in 1997. There, his qualifications equaling those of a habilitation in business economics were attested, and he was appointed as a Full Professor to the Chair of Business Administration, especially small and medium-sized companies. Being on sabbatical leave, Professor Pinkwart was a Member of the German Bundestag (2002–2005) and the German Bundesrat (2005–2010) as well as Minister for Innovation, Science, Research and Technology and Deputy Prime Minister of the federal state of North Rhine-Westphalia (2005–2010).

After a research visit as senior research fellow at AICGS, Johns Hopkins University, Washington, in April 2011, Professor Pinkwart became the Dean of HHL Leipzig Graduate School of Management in Leipzig, Germany, and was appointed as Chairholder of the Stiftungsfonds Deutsche Bank Chair of Innovation Management and Entrepreneurship (currently on leave). From 2012 to 2016, he served as an Academic Director of the Center for Advanced Studies in Management (CASiM) at HHL.

At the end of June 2017, Andreas Pinkwart has been appointed as new Minister for Economic Affairs, Innovation, Digitization and Energy of the state of North Rhine-Westphalia and resigned his office as Dean of HHL.

Ralf Reichwald studied economics and business management at the universities of Bonn, Marburg, and Munich in Germany. From 1970 to 1975, he worked at Ludwig-Maximilians-Universität München as a research associate at the Institute for Industry Research (Prof. Edmund Heinen), where he received his doctoral degree in 1973. From 1975 to 1989, he was an Associate Professor of Business Management at the University of the Federal Armed Forces, Munich. In 1990, he was appointed to the Chair of Business Administration at Technische Universität München (TUM). From 1994 to 1996, he was Dean of the Faculty of Economics and Social Sciences at TUM and from 2002 to 2005 Dean of the TUM School of Management. During this time, he was also Founding Dean of the Faculty of Economics at the Technical University Freiberg, Saxony. In 1994, he received an honorary doctorate degree, and in 2013, he was awarded with the title Honorary Senator of the Technical University Freiberg. Professor Reichwald is Academic

Director and co-founder (2006) of the Center for Leading Innovation & Cooperation (CLIC) at HHL Leipzig Graduate School of Management. In 2010, he became a Professor of Management at HHL. From 2012 to 2016, he was a member of the Executive Board of the Center for Advanced Studies in Management (CASiM). Furthermore, he has been a permanent visiting professor at the University of Tunis, El Manar, which honored him for his work in research and teaching in 2006 with the title Professor honoris causa. Since 2005 Professor Reichwald has been serving as Chair of the Advisory Board of the Peter Pribilla Foundation at the Technische Universität München (TUM).

Łukasz Świątczak has been the Executive Director of the Center for Advanced Studies in Management (CASiM) at HHL Leipzig Graduate School of Management since 2013. He holds a master's degree in operations research from the Poznań University of Economics (Poland) and a doctoral degree (*summa cum laude*) in economics from HHL Leipzig Graduate School of Management.

His postgraduate research—awarded with several DAAD scholarships—was devoted to interdisciplinary developments in mathematical social sciences.

As a research associate at the Chair of Economics and Information Systems at HHL from 2005 to 2011, he dealt with questions at the intersection of economic and information theory.

Dr. Świątczak now works toward a postdoctoral lecture qualification (habilitation) and does research in the domain of applied economics and game theory. He is holding an assistant professor position and teaches courses on economics, game theory, and quantitative methods. He gained hands-on experience while working on a number of projects in management consulting.

Introduction

Horst Albach and Andreas Pinkwart

1 Knowledge Management and the City

In Europe, cities developed in the Middle Ages. In the eleventh century, a truly remarkable revolution started as a result of the confrontation of Christianity with the Arabic world during the crusades: the rediscovery of Arabic, Greek, and Roman knowledge. This led to a tremendous increase in knowledge. Men no longer accepted the old church doctrine "All knowledge comes from God," which implied that this knowledge is imbedded in the Bible. The study of nature led philosophers to look for answers beyond those given in the Old Testament. They discovered Aristotle and his knowledge of nature and the life of plants and animals. This increased information and knowledge significantly.

The question was how to handle this mass of information. Two institutions emerged for solving this problem: the monasteries and the cities. Cities were the institution that lowered the cost of information. Agglomeration of people in the cities lowered the cost of communication and thus attracted migrating teachers. The possibility for teachers to move which was granted by the Pope under the "right to teach everywhere" (licentia ubique docendi) reduced the willingness/necessity of the people to move. Improved supply of teachers increased the attractiveness of a city as a market place for merchants, crafts, and businessmen. But before Gutenberg, the books were hand-written or printed with very simple wood stocks. One should remember that writing a copy of the Summa Theologica by Thomas Aquinus required parchment from 75 sheep skins—a small fortune. After Gutenberg, the teachers settled down, formed schools and universities with libraries that stored knowledge.

H. Albach (✉) • A. Pinkwart
HHL Leipzig Graduate School of Management, Leipzig, Germany
e-mail: casim@hhl.de; Pinkwart@hhl.de

H. Albach et al. (eds.), *European Cities in Dynamic Competition*,
https://doi.org/10.1007/978-3-662-56419-6_1

The cities obtained market rights which not only facilitated the exchange of goods but also standardized the rules of exchange (weights, laws) and improved the control of violations of trade. The cities thus were institutions of knowledge in trading and jurisdiction. In the thirteenth century, important international trading houses were established in cities. They developed early forms of knowledge management: bookkeeping and recording all their trading partners and all money movements. The cities thus became centers of innovation.

Summarizing, one can say that cities developed as centers of information, competition, and innovation.

2 European Cities in Global Competition

2.1 Information, Innovation, and New Technologies

New technologies were developed in the twentieth and twenty-first centuries. Traffic infrastructures were improved thus lowering the cost of exchange of goods, and information infrastructures were improved thus reducing the cost of information and communication. Innovation cycles and the time for change are becoming shorter, the intensity of competition increases. Due to new technologies, people and places are moving closer together in a virtual way. As a consequence, globalization and digitalization have become concepts that many people call the "4.0-revolution". Economists might be inclined to talk about a fascinating economic evolution.

2.2 Regional Economics and Spatial Economics

Economists have a long tradition of studying "regional economics". More specially, they have developed a theory of the cities, the "urban economics". Karl-Heinz Paqué in the first contribution to this volume reports on these theoretical models. He sketches a dynamic theory of global (and European) economic growth with an explicit geographical dimension and analyzes the empirical evidence of the theories. Innovation is the key success factor for regional growth and for successful competition among cities.

Following Paqué, Haberstroh and Pinkwart stress the importance of regional innovation systems and analyze cities as local innovation systems. By using a new comparative method for so-called pathways to success on the European level, the authors argue that different innovation strategies with the same outcome exist, thus allowing cities to define appropriate policies in line with their specific preconditions. They present a survey of empirical analyses of European cities and their innovative capacity and identify 43 variables that reflect a local innovation ecosystem.

2.3 Cities and Direct Democracy

Cities are characterized by their legal structure and their financial structure. The legal structure consists of the city parliament and the administration. The financial structure comprises the current and the long-term expenditures. One of the most interesting aspects of this volume is the thesis that the traditional structures of cities have become obsolete. They do no longer meet the challenges that cities face in global competition.

Hilgers and Schmidthuber report in the second part of the volume that cities increasingly make use of modern technology to interact with citizens. They show that in the nineties of the last century the idea of "New Public Management" was developed. In the first decade of this century, digitalization, e-mail, Web site, direct citizen–government communication were combined under the concept of "E-Government," and the present decade is characterized by a "Mobile Government" resp. "Open Government". In this kind of city governance, the citizens become citizen-innovators.

A fascinating idea of modern city governance is the "smart city". The "Smart City Concept" was developed time in the nineties of the past century. The city of Leipzig is a project partner of the "HORIZON 2020 Smart Cities and Communities Project TRIANGULUM." Korzer, Ginzel, and Riedel report on the application of the smart city concept in Leipzig West. They stress the importance of the role of the Mayor of Leipzig. The city administration acts as coordinator, initiator, enabler, and partner for the civil society, science, and local businesses. Smart City groups of citizens not only have advisory functions, but also have decision-making rights.

The smart city concept of Leipzig is best understood if one reads the paper by Christian Albert Jacke on "Location Communication in Leipzig and Thoughts About Destination Management" concluding the part on city management. Jacke reminds the reader that Leipzig after the fall of the GDR had an unemployment rate of 35–50%. Even worse, the citizens of Leipzig had lost all hope for the future. The slogan "Leipzig up and coming" and the authentic activities of the administration, the citizens, and the companies became a sign of trust in the future. All the citizens of Leipzig came to love their city. And love of the city by all the citizens is a very important success factor for a city in global competition.

2.4 Success Factors in Global Competition

None of the papers in this book deals with the role of the city parliaments. This is easily understood: The new challenges of digitalization and globalization require long-term trust in the administration and in long-term strategies.

A very good proof of this thesis is the contribution by Bernadette Spinnen "Key Success Factors for City Marketing: An Example from Münster." Quote: "A city in which anyone feels entitled to work for or against governmental decisions and promote any given opinion needs a strong leitmotif, a vision! And this is exactly where I see our city marketing organization's niche: It is perfectly suited to lead a dialogue with the urban society about the city's future, its potential, and its opportunities. This is due to the fact that it does not consist of elected members, it is not liable for political promises, and it is not required to produce feasible solutions. It is rather concerned with the city's future, with the citizen's feelings and perceptions towards the city." Spinnen does not go as far as proposing direct democracy for cities, but criticizes political debates, "which are known to hardly ever offer any solutions nor provide any in-depth knowledge." Good citizen–governance relations are necessary for strategies for the future and for successful city marketing.

Also in Part III, Horst Albach presents a paper of similar critique of the actual legal structure of German city government. The members of the city council represent different parties. The parties usually cannot disagree on short-term issues, nor can they agree on long-term projects submitted by the Mayor. Companies which were willing to add financial support to projects become frustrated and withdraw from their financial promises. Albach suggests to apply management science tools to city management and develops strategies for the cities of Bonn and Trier.

Competition of cities is not limited to the borders of the European Union. Competition in these days is global competition. Therefore, it is important to study, e.g., cities like Chicago and Tokyo. Their legal structure is one of decentralization. Their wards, shis, and kus are cut so that ghetto structures are avoided. The aldermen of the wards, etc. have just one objective: to serve the interests of all citizens in their ward. The Mayor is responsible for the police, the fire department, and the infrastructure of streets and roads. Any party struggle is avoided. Attractiveness of the city improves competitiveness.

2.5 Complementarity Between Region and City

Centralization used to be the strategy for improving effectiveness of cities in former times. Experience has shown that centralization increases the distance between the citizen and the administration. Urbanization does not mean centralization. On the contrary, Hermann Tengler shows in the chapter on complementarity between region and city that the city grows because the region provides attractive housing for families with members that work in the city. And the municipalities in the region benefit from urban growth because the children of the families are an important foundation for society and their own future economic sustainability. Furthermore, the region attracts businesses of the tertiary sector which provide services for the companies in the city. Region and city gain from their complementarity. Tengler is convinced that unless German cities and regions do not grow faster than before and become *global cities*, they will lose their competitiveness in global competition. In order to avoid this problem, the "Ministerial Conference on Spatial Planning" began to define "Metropolitan Regions" in 1995. Global cities that are competitive on the world markets have to give up their obsolete legal structures and develop "economic governance" (Tengler).

Complementarity is also an important success factor in the retail trade. One can also talk of an *as-well-as strategy* in contrast to the *either-or-strategy* dominant in former times. Heinemann and Wenzel present a nice example of this strategy. If the local retailers do not add an online activity, they will fail. They demonstrate this success factor by the project "Mönchengladbach on eBay".

2.6 Cost Efficiency in City Management

This book presents the thesis that in order to remain competitive cities have to make fairly radical changes. But the contributions to this book do not specify where the changes should start from the present legal and financial structures of cities—perhaps with one exception—on a path of a successful future. But the last paper contains a warning: Kress, Meiswinkel, Nossack, and Pesch remind the reader that city managers should not forget the basics. Every city has to improve its tools for efficiency in the new environments of global markets.

Part I

European Cities in Global Competition

Dynamic Competition in Space: Theoretical Models, Empirical Evidence, Political Challenges

Karl-Heinz Paqué

Abstract

The paper delivers a brief summary of what growth and structural change of the global economy as well as technological and demographic trends mean for urban agglomerations and rural areas in Europe. It covers theoretical models, empirical evidence and political challenges. Its main conclusion is that, at least in Europe, the time of "natural" convergence of regions in geographical space is over as the knowledge-based economy of the future favors innovative centers over the periphery. As a consequence, competition between urban growth poles in space will become ever more intense, and a traditional egalitarian regional policy ever more difficult. This may raise the level of economic and political tensions within the European Union and within individual member countries. The debt crises of southern European countries, the rise of populist movements as well as the recent referenda in the United Kingdom—on Scottish Independence and Brexit—may be first cases in point. Therefore, a thorough redesign of regional policy tools is called for: away from physical to intellectual infrastructure that fosters innovative capacity.

1 Theoretical Models

In 1979, Herbert Giersch, then President of the Kiel Institute of World Economics, published a seminal paper in the Review of World Economics (Weltwirtschaftliches Archiv)—its title: "Aspects of Growth, Structural Change, and Employment—A

K.-H. Paqué (✉)
Faculty of Economics and Management, Chair of International Economics, Otto von Guericke University Magdeburg, Magdeburg, Germany
e-mail: paque@ovgu.de

H. Albach et al. (eds.), *European Cities in Dynamic Competition*,
https://doi.org/10.1007/978-3-662-56419-6_2

Schumpeterian Perspective" (Giersch 1979). In this paper, he sketched a dynamic theory of global (and European) economic growth with an explicit geographical dimension. At the time, nobody could guess that his ideas were to become forerunners of the endogenous growth theory that emerged a few years later, and the models of trade in monopolistic competition as well as geography and trade that were pioneered by Paul Krugman in the 1980s and 1990s. Even with the benefit of hindsight, only few people have recognized this although Herbert Giersch wrote in plain English, but unfortunately he did not couch his model in the strictly mathematical terms, which were becoming ever more fashionable in academia at that time.

What was Giersch's vision to re-appear in much of the later sophisticated modeling? It was first of all the simple recognition that world economic growth is not driven by an exogenous (i.e., not further explained) technological change, but rather by the knowledge churned out in the innovative (and almost exclusively urban!) centers of the developed industrialized world by deliberate research and development efforts. Once existent, this Schumpeterian knowledge flows "downhill" into the poorer parts of the globe through adaptation and imitation, like a lava stream that runs down the slopes of a volcano—destructive at first, but fertile and creative later. The conjecture of Giersch (and later others) was that adaptation and imitation is becoming ever easier than innovation. Two trends were suspected to support this: first, the decline of the cost of international technology transfer due to massively improving transport facilities and the virtual revolution in electronic communication that had just begun at the time of Giersch's writing; and second the rise of upfront costs that genuine inventions and innovations on ever higher technological levels required. Hence there were good reasons to expect a natural catching up of the poor to the rich—a wonderful harmonious vision, which by and large survived the huge wave of new insights that were provided by new models of sophisticated endogenous growth theory that followed in the decades after Giersch's pioneering ideas (as summarized in standard economic textbooks like Aghion and Howitt 2009; Acemoglu 2009; Barro and Sala-i-Martin 2003).

Of course, many different models in this Schumpeterian tradition were developed to describe the process of innovation and imitation, of integration and specialization, of industrialization and urbanization along these lines. Distilling a simple "stylized story" from all this, it may read as follows: a country or a region can "catch up" if it has

- a reasonably well-educated population that also stands ready to learn on whatever new industrial or service jobs,
- a set of reasonably stable institutions that ensure the rule of law and of market-driven economics,
- a reasonably open economy that allows as much free trade and free capital in- and outflows as possible.

If these requirements are met, a country will be able to participate in an increasingly fine international division of labor in which ever more manufactured goods are produced worldwide under conditions of monopolistic competition, with ever more horizontal and vertical product differentiation allowing heterogeneous firms all over the world to find fertile (and productive) niches. In this process, of course, the newly industrializing countries and regions change radically: They become highly urbanized, and it is these urban centers that are home to most of the newly gained innovative potentials—thanks in particular to the dominance of localized externalities and agglomeration effects (Krugman 1991).

2 Empirical Evidence

So much for the stylized story of modeling. What about reality? Did the developments of the last decades bear out these facts? Of course, reality is at least as complex as the world of modeling so that we can only sketch some very broad trends. To do this, it is convenient to distinguish the global, the European and the national level:

- On the global level, reality did to a large extent follow the predictions of the model, notably with respect to fast-growing (and huge!) Asian countries. In fact, China, India and Indonesia (plus quite a few others) did catch up, and they did so more or less in the way the models of monopolistic competition predicted—involving powerful processes of industrialization, product knowledge acquisition and urbanization. As a consequence, there was a massive catching-up in terms of per-capita income from poor to rich. In this sense, the world has become much more equal with a dynamic growth of what may be called a new global (and mostly Asian) middle class (Milanovic 2016). Note, however, that this catching-up process was achieved without a surge of capital imports. To the contrary, many Asian countries persistently ran current account surpluses thus financing their growth push and modern capital formation out of their own savings. Sure enough, this defies prior predictions of Herbert Giersch and many others. In fact, on a global scale, capital "flew uphill" into "old" industrialized countries (notably the United States) and not "downhill" into the fast-growing industrializing parts of the world. By this token, a global savings glut was fed by the fast growing countries that led to a global state of chronically low real interest, which virtually no sensible economist had predicted for the future to come.
- On the European level, two stages of development may be distinguished. Until the early years of the twenty-first century, it all looked like a standard catching-up story, which appeared to be quite similar—though clearly less speedy—than on the global scale. Southern and post-communist Central and Eastern European countries caught up in terms of per capita incomes as well as urbanization and industrialization. Clearly, however, the debt-crisis in the

South revealed that much of the prior growth push was mostly driven by a "bubble", i. e. an unsustainable domestic service expansion at the cost of external competitiveness—hence quite different from the standard Southeast Asian catching-up story. In Central and Eastern Europe, there was no such bubble bursting, but the catching-up process itself did slow down after the main efforts of transformation had been completed. Apparently, the process of finding new slots in the monopolistically competitive global and European division of labor became ever more difficult and partly grinded to a first halt. In a nutshell, one may speak of a "middle income trap": the European South and Central East reached a decent equilibrium of sophistication of products and processes as well as urbanization and industrialization, but they lacked the innovative capacity to fully catch up to the level of the innovative industrial core countries of Europe. Note that, contrary to early naïve expectations, the growth of the service economy did not really solve the problem because most professional services are complementary to industry.

– At least within larger European nations, the regional trends ran parallel to or even preceded the developments in Europe as a whole. Take Britain and Germany: In both countries, the economic growth of the last decades favored the innovative core regions vis-à-vis the "old" industrial clusters. In Britain, the shift was from the Midlands, the North of England and Scotland to the South East in and around the fully globalized metropolis London. In Germany, it was first the shift from the Northwest to the South and, after the completion of the post-communist economic transformation in eastern Germany, a further accentuation of these trends, with Berlin in most recent times emerging as a new start-up growth pole, which defies this trend, although from a relatively low level of per-capita income (by urban standards) (Paqué 2013). Note that, by and large, you can find similar developments within virtually all larger European countries: again and again, you see a concentration of growth away from the old-style industrial centers to the new innovative agglomerations. The ubiquity of this trend in industrialized countries is remarkable. In a stylized way, it may be considered as "the other side of the mountain" of the industrialization and urbanization that started in the nineteenth century: In that historical period, the now traditional-style industrial agglomerations were booming, and in the later period up to the present, it is the new innovative-style clusters.

So much for the trends. They convey a clear-cut message for Europe. Except for its very eastern fringe, the whole continent finds itself in the industrialized and urbanized part of the world, at least by global standards. Hence, we must fundamentally focus on what allows cities to enhance their economic growth in an age which makes growth depend—more than ever before—on innovative capacity (and not on traditional types of resources!). This focus is all the more urgent for an economic and a political reason:

- Economically, the big difference to earlier times is that, except for immigration, European population does not grow anymore. Hence any process of urbanization due to attractive innovative clusters goes at the expense of the rural and traditionally industrial areas—thus "sucking out" the life blood out of the lagging regions. This is fundamentally different from the migration from the rural to the urban areas in the nineteenth century when population naturally grew everywhere, even in the backward areas. Note that immigration of highly-skilled people, if anything, accentuates this picture because immigration is today strongly biased towards the growing innovative clusters, which offer attractive jobs to arriving people.
- Politically, the recently emerging right-wing populism that has held sway over Europe is typically concentrated in exactly those areas that have poor growth records by national or international standards. In most dramatic form, the cleavage between growing and stagnating or shrinking regions could be observed recently in the Brexit-referendum: within England, booming London was pro-EU while the North and the Midlands voted pro-Brexit. Similarly, various types of election results in countries like Austria, France and Germany confirm the broad pattern (if not the detailed structure) of these trends. Hence, in the long run, the stability of the European Union and the cooperative spirit all over the old continent may be at stake. Hence, politically, the enormous importance of the dynamics of European cities and urban areas should be beyond any doubt.

3 Political Challenges

What is to be done in view of these great political risks? Three major directions of policies can be identified: (1) promoting educational excellence; (2) enhancing innovative capacities; (3) reforming regional policies. The first two are to address urban growth wherever it might take place; the third one is to address the unequal growth potentials across regions.

3.1 Promoting Educational Excellence

In a world of almost exclusively knowledge-based growth, the most obvious policy answer is to foster educational excellence. The task stretches over all levels: from child care and pre-schooling over primary and secondary schools to colleges and universities. The task also stretches over all types of education—from general to technical skills, with a particular emphasis on technical education that is provided in combination of formal schooling and practical work on the job as is typically (and successfully) done in German-speaking countries via the apprenticeship system, which tends to keep youth unemployment at low levels. To be sure, education was always important for growth, but it has become ever more important over the last decades—compared to the more traditional growth push factors like physical infrastructure and natural resources.

Note that the demand for good education is ever less restricted to young people. With life expectancy increasing, populations ageing and job characteristics changing ever faster, education must become ever more "enabling"—in the sense of renewing once acquired skills and adjusting them to new demands. In a sense, there must be an ever stronger "merging" of work and schooling: not a stiff sequence of first schooling and then work for the rest of one's life, but an occasional change of status from worker to student and back, thus ensuring a better intertemporal matching of the changes in the demands of structural change and the skills on offer.

Clearly, educational excellence of this differentiated type is a natural potential characteristic of cities and possibly a huge locational advantage, if the necessary investment is forthcoming, which requires a sound tax base and a healthy local economy in the first place. To be sure, it will be practically difficult, if not impossible, for rural areas and economically weak urban regions to remain or become competitive as many locational "economies of scale" are involved—given the large variety of educational offers that are required. However, to preserve and foster the dynamics of the economy as a whole, this adverse distributional effect must not serve as a reason to renounce on a further strengthening strong cities with educational facilities, but rather to provide—as far as reasonably possible—regional investment support for the weaker cities and regions (see point 3.3 below).

3.2 Enhancing Innovative Capacities

While excellent education is a necessary condition for urban growth, it is not a sufficient one. It must be transformed into an innovative culture of economic activity, which again stretches wide fields: from the easy and non-bureaucratic foundation of start-ups notably in the realm of universities, research institutes and schools of applied science down to the continuous stream of product and process innovations on the plant level. More than anything else, this requires a tax system, which is innovation-conducive, and a public administration, which is as non-bureaucratic as possible. As a major "soft factor", it also requires an innovation-friendly social climate that appreciates entrepreneurial success as a genuine contribution to the public good and is not contaminated by a spirit of mistrust and envy. Clearly, these are very subjective elements that local politicians and civil servants should keep in mind, even if there are no easy recipes how they can be achieved.

Again, as with educational excellence, already successful cities may have a natural advantage in most of these respects—notably because already existing agglomerations provide open "windows of opportunity" as well as entrepreneurial spirits and expertise that are most helpful. However, experience shows that clever local city management with a focus on pushing aside all bureaucratic hurdles may be a major instrument to compensate for the lack of powerful agglomeration effects. This is notably so if a small or medium-sized city is geographically (and thus also economically) "not too far" from the main center of knowledge creation and innovation so that, with some smart moves, innovative investment can be locally redirected to the relatively close-by urban "off-shoot"—thus allowing off-metropolitan cities to thrive as a kind of "satellite" of the big growth poles.

Note that, in practice, this model of metropolitan spillover into rural areas is of utmost importance. E. g., the remarkably good growth performance of southern Bavaria in the three decades after World War II is to a large extent the consequence of the growth of its major metropolitan area Munich. On the other hand, the relatively disappointing growth of central and eastern Germany after German unification went along with a poor performance of Berlin (Paqué 2009), which has only very recently begun to develop a thriving start-up culture (Paqué 2013). In a sense, the regional division of labor around a metropolitan area is the most important key to politically initiate the growth of the surrounding areas—as a kind of mostly market-induced "knowledge expansion" from the city to the suburban outskirts down to the rural world.

3.3 Reforming Regional Policies

With these spillovers in mind, the general philosophy of modern regional policies is quite obvious: If the aim is to have as much growth as possible *everywhere*, the instruments of regional policy should be such that they do help more remote places to hook themselves up to the next best regional growth center whatever it may be. Thus a cascade of regional divisions of labor emerges in space and allows even quite far-off places to become thriving members of the growth network. This requires the emergence of a hierarchy of knowledge centers—from the genuinely metropolitan areas over the middle-sized centers down to the rural "lowlands".

Note that, in regional policies that are actually practiced, this concept of a knowledge cascade has so far played a very minor role. In fact, traditional regional policy—on the national or European level—has been much more focused on mechanically equalizing living conditions through transfers (so-called "cohesion funds") and on supporting the construction of physical infrastructure in remote places. While this makes to some extent economic sense (and may have made even more sense in the heyday of good old industrial society!), it is ever less well-targeted in the modern knowledge economies we live in. In a quite dramatic form, this could be observed in the European Union in recent years. While Greece, Portugal and Spain had received lots of EU infrastructure support for their most remote valleys, mountains and/or islands, no self-sustaining growth developed in these areas. The reason is simple: growth in these countries must nowadays also be knowledge-based if these countries are to have a good opportunity to catch up; and that type of growth can only be initiated in the respective national urban centers.

Hence we need a re-orientation of regional policy, notably (but not only) on the European level. Support should go to emerging poles of knowledge creation in the national urban centers and sub-centers—and not quite to the poorest areas, which can only catch up as "satellites" of some sort of urban agglomerations. In an economic sense, we are virtually all city dwellers today—if not physically in a city then in the sense of urban knowledge creation and spillovers to the rest of the economy. If that plain fact is recognized by policy, there may be a proper chance for getting back to a convergence path, with innovative performance in dynamic competition penetrating even the remotest parts of our continent.

To sum up, the role of cities is nowadays greater than it ever was since industrialization came upon us in the nineteenth century. Of course, there were earlier times when the role of cities was even more paramount—economically as the only vibrant places at all, politically as havens of freedom. These were the Middle Ages from roughly the twelfth century on, the great time of the much-admired city states like Florence and Venice in northern Italy and Bruges and Ghent in Flanders (Cipolla 1994; Lopez 1971). To be sure, these times will never come back so that, even in the future of a knowledge society, the political role of cities will be a bit more humble than in this proud past. And it will also be economically a bit different because the city will serve as the hub of a very wide-ranging division of labor, much wider indeed than in pre-industrial times. In this sense, one may say: cities are back on centre stage of economic history!

References

Acemoglu D (2009) Introduction to modern economic growth. Princeton University Press, Princeton

Aghion P, Howitt P (2009) The economics of growth. MIT Press, Cambridge

Barro RJ, Sala-i-Martin X (2003) Economic growth. MIT Press, Cambridge

Cipolla CM (1994) Before the industrial revolution. European society and economy 1000-1700, 3rd edn. W.W. Norton, New York

Giersch H (1979) Aspects of growth structural change and employment. A Schumpeterian perspective. Weltwirtschaftliches Archiv 115(4):629–652

Krugman P (1991) Geography and trade. MIT Press, Cambridge

Lopez RS (1971) The commercial revolution of the middle ages, 950-1350. Prentice-Hall, Englewood Cliffs

Milanovic B (2016) Global inequality. A new approach for the age of globalization. Harvard University Press, Cambridge

Paqué K-H (2009) Die Bilanz. Eine wirtschaftliche Analyse der Deutschen Einheit. Hanser, München

Paqué K-H (2013) Gewachsen, aber gefährdet. Eine wirtschaftliche Zwischenbilanz der Deutschen Einheit für Mitteldeutschland und Thüringen. http://apps.thueringen.de/de/publikationen/pic/pubdownload1458.pdf. Accessed 24 Jul 2017

Karl-Heinz Paqué was born in 1956 in Saarbrücken. He studied economics at the Universities of Saarbrücken and Kiel (Germany), and British Columbia (Vancouver, Canada). After his doctoral studies at the University of Kiel he worked as professor, research director and department head at the Kiel Institute for the World Economy from 1991 to 1996. Since 1996, he has been holding the Chair of International Economics at the Otto von Guericke University Magdeburg. From 2002 to 2006, he was Minister of Finance of the German federal state of Saxony-Anhalt; from 2006 to 2008 he was chairman of the liberal fraction in the Saxony-Anhalt parliament. In 2010, he took up office as the Dean of the Faculty of Economics and Management at the Otto von Guericke University Magdeburg. In 2012, he was awarded an honorary doctorate from the University of Miskolc, Hungary. Among many academic and political duties, he is chief editor of the Journal Perspektiven der Wirtschaftspolitik of the German Economic Association. Karl-Heinz Paqué is a member of the Free Democratic Party. Between 2003 and 2007, he was a member of the party's federal executive committee of which he again became a member in December 2013. Since 2014, he has been Vice Chairman of the Executive Board of the Friedrich Naumann Foundation for Freedom. In May 2017, he was elected Vice President of Liberal International.

Increasing the Innovative Capacity of European Cities: Making Use of Proven Concepts from the National Level

Marcus Max Haberstroh and Andreas Pinkwart

Abstract

Besides facing challenges like globalization, agglomeration, digitalization, and demographical change, a nation finds its growth and development to be strongly influenced by its innovativeness. Innovation emanates from interaction and knowledge flows, and countries' systems of innovation shape the manifold innovation processes. Cities are the focal point of these processes, as they serve as regional hubs that facilitate the interplay between all involved actors and the exchange of related knowledge. Consequently, cities as fonts of innovation are central to policymakers' concerns. Despite cities' high value as a unit of analysis, few studies have investigated strategies leading to a high innovative capacity in cities. However, much research has occurred at the national level. Among this, one study introduces an innovative methodology to identify so called pathways to success for European member states using a comparative method. As the national level is an aggregate of the lower levels, the authors assume that such proven concepts from the national level also apply to cities and claim that different innovation strategies with the same outcome exist, thus allowing cities to define appropriate policies in line with their specific preconditions. The few academic works on the determinants of innovative capacity of European (secondary) capital cities, as well as several practical studies in this field, provide first evidence of the truth of this theory. Drawing on these fragmented sources, the

A previous version of the article was published in Haberstroh, M. M.: National innovative capacity: an established concept revisited. Doctoral thesis. Leipzig, HHL Leipzig Graduate School of Management, 2017.

M. M. Haberstroh (✉) • A. Pinkwart
Stiftungsfonds Deutsche Bank Chair of Innovation Management and Entrepreneurship, HHL Leipzig Graduate School of Management, Leipzig, Germany
e-mail: marcus.haberstroh@hhl.de

H. Albach et al. (eds.), *European Cities in Dynamic Competition*,
https://doi.org/10.1007/978-3-662-56419-6_3

authors propose a consolidated set of 43 variables reflecting a local innovation ecosystem, thus setting the scene for a quantitative proof of the concept in the future.

1 Introduction

Innovation has been critical for the long-term competitiveness of nations since the Industrialization Revolution (Romer 1986, 1990). In recent decades a scientific field has emerged, aiming to explain, forecast, and modify this essential of economic success (Acs et al. 2016; Atkinson 2013; Albach 2006), with elements of growth theory, the "Schumpeterian school of thought" (Schumpeter 1939), and modern, systemic approaches to innovation forming the foundation of research. This literature is dedicated to studying the production and use of formal and informal knowledge regarding the creation and adoption of new products and services, improved processes, organizational forms, and business models (Fagerberg 2016; Lundvall 2010). Regardless of whether the application area is country comparison, R&D forecasting, or analysis of technological systems, the doctrine of innovation systems is centered on the triad of innovative capacity, innovation strategy, and innovation policy.

Innovative capacity makes the difference between countries' prosperity or stagnation (Marceau 2008b; Furman and Hayes 2004; Porter 1990) as it reflects the level of invention and the potential for innovation in any nation, geographical area, or economic activity (Villa 1990; Furman et al. 2002). Studies of innovative capacity have focused mainly on the national level and provide a "conceptual framework to theory that feeds [the] concrete practice" (Edquist 2009, p. 182) of generating useful insights about the focal points of *innovation strategy* (Sun and Grimes 2016; Porter and Stern 2000, 2001, 2004). Innovation strategies build upon the availability, intensity, and combination of certain economic elements, such as GDP or production factors like capital and labor, which on the whole reflect a country's innovation ecosystem (Edquist 2016). Together with organizational and institutional arrangements these elements naturally differ in terms of levels, and *innovation policies* aim to create respective regional, local and sectoral innovation areas (Couchman et al. 2008). In this regard, "sub-national entities, such as provinces, industrial districts, cities or 'Silicon Valleys' are becoming, or have already become, more important than the nation-state" (Freeman 1998). This importance especially holds true in view of the fact that the highest rates of visible innovation are found in and around cities (Athey et al. 2008). However, in an effort to aggregate the complexity of the various ecosystems at lower levels, innovation policies are largely set on the national level.

As drivers of innovation in the twenty-first century, the contextual factors of innovative capacity are focal points for urban planning and development (Kourtit and Nijkamp 2012; Dameri 2017; Briggs 2009). Surprisingly, cities as units of analysis are fairly under-researched from an innovative capacity perspective (Martin and Simmie 2008). Although research in this particular field is gathering momentum and a small body of academic literature deals with the key elements of innovation in European cities, no study presents a holistic picture of the determinants of cities' innovation ecosystems. Thus, condensing the fragmented characteristics of European cities or city environments that might foster a consolidated view of innovative capacity provides significant research opportunities (McCann 2004). Moreover, understanding the factors that shape the processes of innovation in cities might also be helpful in determining the extent to which problems related to city growth may be resolved (Johnson 2008).

As the dominance of cities continue to grow, potentially at the expense of national interests, it is important that we seek to gain a clear and shared, globally relevant view. While many see that [Stuttgart, London and Paris] are some of the leading innovation hotspots today, some ask if they will continue to be so in the future. If we are going to identify the emerging centres of future innovation early, we need to collectively know what to look for. Maybe, as new locations begin to play a vital role as hubs for talent, ideas, and capital, the leaders will change. As the shift of power turns away from the traditional western cultures perhaps innovation will turn too. Maybe the new ideas will come from cities like Bangalore, Nairobi or even Dubai? (Jones 2017).

Hence, this article contributes to literature in two ways, first by setting the scene for quantitative analyses by proposing a consolidated set of variables reflecting European cities' innovation ecosystems, and second by closing the gap between national and local innovation systems. Policymakers also benefit from this research as it aims to advance the mostly linear national innovation policies toward becoming more holistic instruments of city-specific state intervention (Edquist 2016).

2 Theoretical Foundation: About Innovation Systems and Cities

Research on innovation systems emerged primarily from the theory of political economy. Early attempts to explain the development and performance of nations trace back to the forefathers of the German school of economics, among them especially Friedrich List. Roughly 200 years ago, he paved the way for a lively scientific discourse (List and Colwell 1856), in literature now recognized under the notion of exogenous (Solow 1956) and endogenous growth theory (Romer 1990, 1986). From Romer on, the question of the determinants of the long-run growth rate of an economy and in particular the contribution of innovation began to dominate this field of research (Acs et al. 2016).

2.1 The Purpose of Innovation Systems Research

Motivated by high practical relevance for policymakers, innovation scholars from all over the world are producing a rich body of literature consisting of various strands (Sun and Grimes 2016). At the beginning, a four-pronged taxonomy prevailed, with its foci on national, regional, and sectoral innovation systems and, as an overarching analytic perspective, the innovative capacity view, which emerged in parallel, closely attached to the mentioned geographies (Teixeira 2014). What today is called the innovative capacity framework was initially "proposed as an index that could provide regular diagnostics of national performance in invention over time" (Villa 1990, p. 290) with the intention to show the influence of technological change on economical growth.

Meanwhile, a new plurality of studies evolved, introducing new dimensions along with new notions like "global," "local" and "technical" innovation systems (Klein and Sauer 2016). Nevertheless, the methodology behind innovation systems research and also the research questions remains largely the same, demanding suitable answers on both the "DNA" of a certain country-level or industry innovation ecosystem as well as the respective measures to maximize the outcome of innovation endeavors (Edquist 2001, 2009, 2013).

However, rather than merely creating innovation systems in literature, scholars try to understand them in order to improve them (Acs et al. 2016). In that regard, within all strands of innovation system research various studies propose certain strategies that might lead to high innovative capacity. Even though the determinants of innovative capacity differ across levels, "the 'rules of the game' are fixed" (Acs et al. 2016, p. 1) on the national level with policy measures. These measures are, for instance, institutional changes, changes in economic incentives, or the setting of new quantified targets. Their purpose is to transform sub-national perspectives into institutional arrangements that reflect and aggregate the parameters of a smoothly working innovation system—from the bottom (local level) to the top (supra-/national level) (Edquist 2016). To identify the right parameters, regional systems and the local sub-systems have to be analyzed.

2.2 Regional Innovation Systems

As part of a national innovation system, regional innovation systems describe the interaction of different sectors with regional governance, innovation support infrastructures, and the national-level system (Teixeira 2014). In this regard, the regional innovation system concept complements the national innovation system concept by adding an additional layer that heavily emphasizes institutions (Parto and Doloreux 2004) and focuses on aspects like the proximity between firms (Klein and Sauer 2016). Even though views are conflicting, some scholars consider the regional level to be the "preferred spatial level for regulatory intervention..., rather than the central state" (Klein and Sauer 2016, p. 14). This claim is predominantly promoted by Philip Cooke, the widely recognized pioneer and seminal author in this strand of literature (Cooke 1992, 2002; Cooke et al. 1997, 1998). Along with other scholars in fields of innovation, he justified the necessity and importance of a regional dimension within innovation systems research. Nijkamp (2016) recently contributed another landmark work in the context of regional innovation, presenting a novel framework intended to help low performers catch up. At its core, his theory builds upon regions' unique portfolios of development possibilities and shows how to optimize the combination of available resources and capabilities. Zitek and Klimova (2016) propose a slightly different framework that highlights and builds upon knowledge flows within and between organizations. The study aims to identify appropriate indicators as well as a methodology for determining the knowledge base of a region. In line with Nijkamp's conviction, Zitek and Klimova recommend considering the unique characteristics of the given region when implementing regional innovation policies. In summary, the strand of literature on regional innovation systems discusses a more or less independent and complex analytical framework generating the empirical foundation for innovation policy making (Parto and Doloreux 2004). In this regard, the special role of cities within regional innovation systems constitutes an important factor.

Freeman, well known in the context of innovation research (Freeman 1989, 2001, 2002) , stressed the importance of cities within regional innovation systems based on his far-reaching studies on the root causes of catching up and falling behind in Eastern and Central Europe (Freeman 1998). Further analyses on the role of cities for economic growth and development of countries has been done by Johnson (2008), whose research also tackles the question of which factors might shape the processes of innovation in cities and thereby pursues a systemic approach to analyze institutional, political, and technical innovation in cities. In this context he is among the first to apply the rarely used notion of local innovation systems. Later on, Breschi (2001) and Capello et al. (2012) headed in the same direction and strengthened the link between the presence of cities in the region and innovative performance, finding a notably high degree of innovation in regions hosting large urban areas and so-called dynamic agglomeration economies[1] as well as knowledge spillovers generated by cities. The most recent contribution of Viitanen (2016) follows up on this and draws on the case of Cambridge to identify "the key ecosystem elements that are necessary for building up a solid foundation for the innovative regions" (p. 6). On the basis of these key elements he presents a holistic approach to managing the innovation

[1]See European Commission (2016b, p. 62) for a detailed explanation of urban and dynamic agglomeration economies.

ecosystem of the Cambridge region under the notion of the "innovation hub framework."

2.3 Local Innovation Systems

As noted earlier, the local innovation systems approach is somewhat underdeveloped and of limited impact within the systems of the innovation research stream. The fact that the notion of local innovation systems (LIS) is almost never found independent from regional innovation systems (RIS) is evidence of this gap in literature.

The LIS strand is still in its infancy. Mainly, current LIS literature is promoted by a handful of experts who have contributed the few fundamental works to date (Martin and Simmie 2008; Marceau 2008a, b; Breschi 2001; Simmie 2001). However, not only academic literature addresses LIS. Large-scale international field studies, such as the Local Innovation Systems Project or the Regional Entrepreneurship Acceleration Program hosted by the Massachusetts Institute of Technology, also contribute valuable knowledge (Regional Entrepreneurship Acceleration Program 2017; Local Innovations Systems Project 2005).

The notion of LIS complements the concepts of national, regional, and technological innovation systems. According to Martin and Simmie (2008), each innovation system has a particular focus. LIS research aims to increase the understanding of how localized technological innovation operates in a global economy—that is, the dynamics of the global–local relationship and the different ways they interconnect (Kosonen 2005). In this context, LIS scholars attempt to determine the conditions associated with the development of a sustainable local innovation system, or the transition from one kind of system to another, as well as the role, behavior, and performance of local innovation systems during a period of increasing globalization (Sotarauta et al. 2004).

In a broader sense, LIS can be defined as spatial concentrations of businesses (firms of all industries) and associated non-businesses (institutions like education and science, authorities, specialist associations) that collaborate to generate new practical knowledge, including new products or services, and to commercialize this knowledge (Martin and Simmie 2008). Furthermore, the LIS literature argues that "local innovation systems are the key driving mechanism underlying change in spatial economies because they are the primary source of new commercially valuable knowledge" (Martin and Simmie 2008, p. 194).

True to the "morphological" nature of innovation studies, the notions of LIS, RIS, and sectoral innovation systems (SIS) are not always rigorously applied, which creates a further barrier to the emergence of a clear-cut LIS strand in innovation systems literature.

2.4 Cities

Cities are comprehensive local innovation systems, "composed of the same elements as regional or national systems but geographically much more concentrated" (Marceau 2008b, p. 137). Cities' innovation ecosystems and innovative capacity, as pivotal points within LIS, have also not been covered from academia in a satisfactory manner, an omission that is quite surprising since cities play an enormous economic role in countries' prosperity (Kogler et al. 2016). In the EU, 271 metro regions hold 59 percent of the population, create 62 percent of all employment, and generate 68 percent of GDP (European Commission 2016b). However, cities are far more than mere centers of population, economic activity, and employment. Almost all patents and other measures of new products and processes in business are produced in cities (Marceau 2008b). As nations' innovation hubs, cities are the engines of a knowledge-based economy, shaping technological change and economic growth (Johnson 2008; Kogler et al. 2016).

Besides elaborating on the economic role of cities and the "plain connection" between innovation and cities (Shearmur 2012), the vast part of current research is concerned mainly with the "smart city" and focuses on the entire economic role of cities. In this broader context, innovation is perceived as one of the three levers of cities' competitiveness (Sáez and Periáñez 2015) and therefore a main aspect of so-called "smart economies" (Dameri 2017). The smart economy concept and theory are the result of knowledge-intensive and creative strategies aimed at enhancing the effectiveness, environmental considerations, and innovative capacity of cities (Vinod Kumar and Dahiya 2017). In this regard, only a few studies have tested the isolated influence of single factors on the innovative capacity of cities. Predominantly, although not exclusively, these factors are:

- Globalization (Eger 2012)
- Agglomeration (Simmie 2001)
- Urbanization (Vinod Kumar 2017; Vinod Kumar and Dahiya 2017)
- Social dynamics of city regions and migrant and ethnic diversity (Andrew 2014);
- Availability of "hard" production factors and non-material production factors (Caragliu et al. 2016)
- Knowledge base of a city (Kogler et al. 2016; Zitek and Klimova 2016; Makkonen and Weidenfeld 2016)
- Creation, availability, and distribution of human capital (Cowling and Lee 2017; Kiuru and Inkinen 2017)
- Contribution of risk-loving and innovative individuals (Caragliu et al. 2016)
- University–industry–government relations (Couchman et al. 2008)
- Attractiveness for new businesses and investments (Sáez and Periáñez 2015)
- Innovation platforms (Anttiroiko 2016)
- Benefits from partnerships (Atkinson 2013)
- Specialization patterns of inventive activities (Kogler et al. 2016)
- Relevance of marketing systems (Briggs 2009).

In addition, further studies attempt to test the influence of various city characteristics on the innovative capacity of cities in the form of so-called innovation indexes. Wang and Gong (2016), for instance, propose an innovation evaluation index for Shenyang, a Chinese national innovation-oriented city. Derived from the European innovative scoreboard and the Silicon Valley index, it is composed of three interlinked dimensions (innovation system, innovation input, and innovation performance), with several so-called "third-level indicators" underlying each dimension. Sáez and Periáñez (2015) propose another index, the urban competitiveness index that benchmarks the competitiveness of European cities as locations for businesses and in terms of their ability to attract investment. This index also consists of three dimensions not exclusively dedicated to innovation measurement, although one dimension focuses on an innovation construct consisting of ten indicators.

Besides these "academically perceptible" indexes, some rather practical indexes are to be found throughout the internet, such as the Regional Innovation Index calculated by the European Commission. Its aim is to help European cities learn from each other by comparing the performance of cities based on 12 indicators taken from the Regional Innovation Scoreboard (European Commission 2016a). Another example of measuring the impact of regional innovation policy is the Innovation Report 2009 of the German federal state of North Rhine-Westphalia (Fertig et al. 2010). Starting from the set of indicators of innovation formerly introduced in the innovation reports 2006–2008, the Innovations Report 2009, in a first step, selected key indicators as subject for update and reinterpretation. The position of North Rhine-Westphalia was analyzed in comparison with the federal average as well as with the federal states of Bavaria and Baden-Wuerttemberg. The goal was to consolidate the whole collection of indicators into a manageable set of core indicators, for which contemporary data were indeed available, so that an updated summary and assessment of the genuine potential for innovation in North Rhine-Westphalia became possible. In so doing, North Rhine-Westphalia was engaging in an approach to regional innovation policy measurement not previously used in Germany.

3 Making Use of Proven Concepts from the National Level

However, all of these innovation evaluation indexes propose a calculation method for the innovative capacity of cities only. They do not provide the theoretical basis for setting the right innovation parameters within innovation policies. This step explaining the results on the basis of the knowledge gained from the theory of path dependence is rarely to be found in LIS literature. The research work done by Martin and Simmie (2008) tends in this direction and, in the first instance, helps in understanding the different historical economic trajectories followed by different cities. The authors hold that path-dependent development of new technologies or industrial sectors within urban economies happens in four phases, each of which depends on the nature and interactions of a city's local innovation system combined with the capacity to absorb new knowledge.

In keeping with the wish for understanding the factors that shape the processes of innovation in cities, we propose the transition of proven concepts on innovative capacity from the national level to cities, as they have already reached a high level of sophistication (Acs et al. 2016).

3.1 Framework: Underpinnings of the Proposition

Proksch et al. (2017) have proposed an innovative methodology for identifying the pathways to success for 17 European countries using a comparative method. As a result of their analysis, those authors identified different paths leading to a high innovative capacity on the national level by combining various determinants. For instance, one set of solutions for high innovative output emphasizes the availability of a high capital base (measured by GDP, a high share of government expenditure on education, the amount of venture capital and the general capital stock of a country). Another set of solutions highlights the combination of specialization in the high-tech industry and private funding. Thus, they were able to show each country's correspondence to either entire or partial success pathways. For example, the UK is strong in all areas except high-tech specialization. These paths were translated into innovation strategies. Rather than a single strategy, different strategies with the same outcome exist, thus allowing countries to choose the appropriate strategies on the basis of their preconditions. In addition, results also shed light on the role of single determinants, such as venture capital, high expenditure on education and high-tech specialization. However, the analysis of holistic strategies is preferable to focusing on single determinants.

The framework of Proksch et al. (2017) might be a good fit to city cases for the following reasons:

- It is a novel framework that does not focus on showing the significance of single determinants on innovative capacity but instead analyzes the combination of different factors.
- On the basis of the results (different strategies) recommendations for policy improvement can be expediently derived. The overall knowledge facilitates learning and benefitting from each other.
- The framework is based on the Furman et al. (2002) model of innovative capacity and its applicability has been successfully proven within various innovation studies (Sun and Grimes 2016).
- It is a robust model confirming the innovative capacity framework of Furman et al. (2002) with a rather small data set.
- It overcomes the limitations of regression analysis, which most of the empirical innovation capacity studies have to cope with.[2] As multiple complex antecedent

[2] As laid out in detail in Proksch et al. (2017, p. 4).

paths with high sufficiency might also exist for cities, a linear model would inevitably lead to information loss.
- It brings the advantages of fuzzy set qualitative comparative analysis (fsQCA) (Ragin 1987, 2000, 2008) to city studies.[3]

Thus, the article at hand builds the foundation for transferring the methodology used by Proksch et al. (2017) to European cities. For this purpose, understanding the fundamentals of the underlying Furman et al. (2002) model is crucial.

According to Furman et al. (2002), the innovation ecosystem of countries can be reflected and measured by determinants that can be grouped into three categories: the common innovation infrastructure, the cluster-specific environment for innovation, and the quality of their linkage. The authors hold that the interplay among the three categories reflects the overall innovative performance of an economy. Taking into account the so-called Porterian Cluster (Porter 1990) and also the Idea Production Function (Porter and Stern 2000), they define these categories as follows (Furman et al. 2002, pp. 905–907):

- *The Common Innovation Infrastructure* reflects the cumulative technological sophistication, human capital, and financial resources available for R&D activity, resource commitments, and policy choices (e.g., investments in education and training, intellectual property protection, openness to international trade, R&D tax policies).
- *The Cluster-Specific Environment for Innovation* focuses on the microeconomic environment present in a nation's industrial clusters, comprising cluster-specific circumstances, investments, and policies (e.g. R&D expenditures funded by industry; relative concentration of innovative output in high-tech patent classes).
- *The Quality of Linkage* represents the relationship between the common innovation infrastructure and industrial clusters (e.g., R&D expenditures performed by universities, venture capital investments). "The strength of linkages influences the extent to which the potential for innovation induced by the common innovation infrastructure is translated into specific innovative outputs in a nation's industrial clusters, thus shaping the realized rate of national R&D productivity" (Furman et al. 2002, p. 907).

According to Stern (2014, p. 47),

> clusters are the fulcrum around which a region [and its cities in the center of local innovation systems] realize the potential from its innovative and entrepreneurial capacity. Clusters shape the potential to develop and commercialize new technology and scale new businesses for global impact.

In this sense, clusters and linkages allow regions and cities to focus and prioritize innovation in terms of their comparative advantage. Hence, on that basis the validity

[3]Ibid.

of this taxonomy for city cases, notwithstanding the fact that it was formerly introduced by Furman et al. (2002) in a national context, can be considered as given.

The outcome of the whole construct is measured on the basis of patents as a consistent country-specific indicator of the level of commercially valuable innovative output. However, measuring the output of innovation on the basis of patent statistics has been quite controversially discussed in innovation science for decades (Acs et al. 2002; Griliches 1990; Pavitt 1988; Roper and Hewitt-Dundas 2015). Nevertheless, the suitability of patents as a valid measure of cities' innovation outcome has been tested and confirmed. According to Kogler et al. (2016, p. 1), "patents provide a wealth of information to analyse the knowledge specialization at specific places, such as technological details and information on inventors and entities involved ...." The European City Report argues along similar lines, stating that "the innovative capacity of cities is underlined by the number of patents per inhabitant" (European Commission 2016b, p. 61). Hence, we rely on patents as outcome measure and thereby ensure closeness to the original model and its transferability.

However, Proksch et al. (2017) and the original model differ regarding the *Contributing and Related Outcome Factors*. These were initially introduced to the model as "alternative output measures... that are less comparable across countries and likely to be less closely linked to the level of... innovative output" (Furman et al. 2002, pp. 912–913). In contrast to this approach, Proksch et al. (2017) consider these indicators as proxy-determinants within a quasi-fourth category, complementing individual determinants of the other three categories which capture contexts that are partially difficult to measure. For instance, the economic success of a city can be measured by the amount of GDP, a variable that is not in itself directly relevant but that serves in place of this hardly graspable condition. These complementing determinants (e.g., real GDP, number of scientific publications, non-residential capital stock) thus become part of the modeled innovation ecosystem, which is a far more constructive approach than using them as sensitivity measures against the outcome variable (patents). The proposed approach is in line with OECD standards for collecting and interpreting innovation data (OECD 2005).[4] Transferring the entire taxonomy to city cases results in the generic model depicted in Fig. 1.

3.2 Method and Data: The Search for Appropriate Determinants

Validating and enhancing the determinants per category from a city perspective is the critical criterion for the transferability of the innovative comparative methodology to identify the pathways to success. In this undertaking, not only the academic work of the past 20 years is scrutinized, but also several practical studies in this field.

[4]The applicability of the Oslo Manual is not limited to OECD member states, as it was jointly developed with Eurostats.

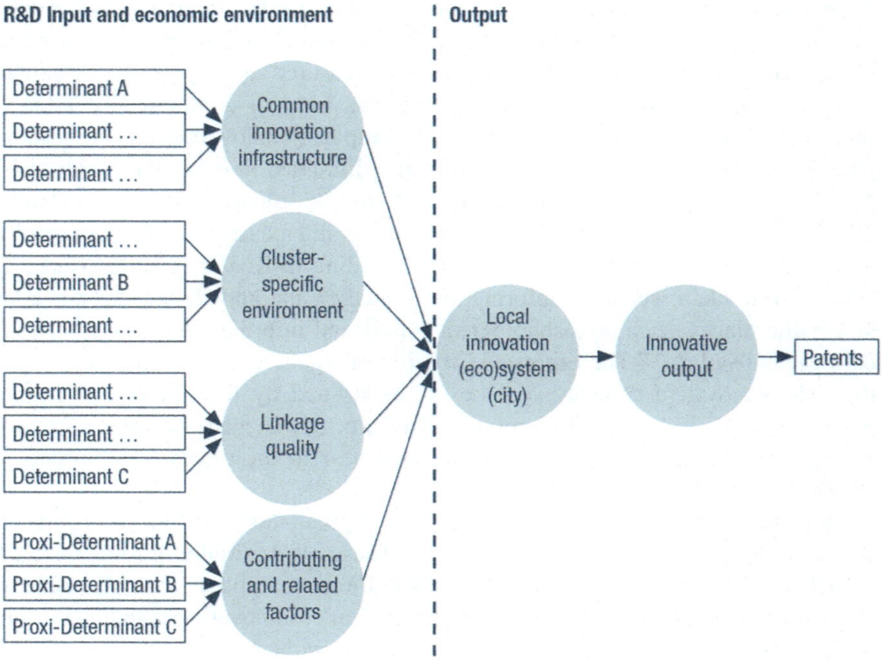

Fig. 1 Generic model: the innovative capacity framework (Furman et al. 2002) transferred to cities

Table 1 depicts the in scope European (secondary) capital cities and the respective academic articles which, at least to a certain extent, deal with the determinants of innovative capacity.[5]

In addition to these academic works, two practical studies are considered to be further knowledge sources with respect to the determinants of the national innovative capacity of the above-mentioned cities. These are the Regional Innovation Scoreboard (European Commission 2016a) and the European City Report (European Commission 2016b). These two studies provide a rich source of information based on time series and longitudinal data. Besides the comparison of certain variables, these reports also offer examples of policies that have worked. To this extent, all articles and reports together provide considerable information on cities' innovation ecosystems in general and, in more detail, on the economic and political dynamics as well as the policy regime inside the systems. Combining all these perspectives into an analysis allows for identification of the particular urban factors that support or impede innovative activity of cities, as they are critical to determining the pathways leading to a high innovative capacity.

[5]The scoping constraint was whether at least one study on the respective city's innovation ecosystem was available, regardless of their academic or practical backgrounds.

Table 1 European (secondary) capital cities, country assignments, and coverage included within articles

Country	City/region	Articles
Czech Rep.	Various	Zitek and Klimova (2016)
Denmark	Copenhagen	Makkonen and Weidenfeld (2016)
Estonia	Tallinn	Makkonen and Weidenfeld (2016)
Finland	Helsinki	Anttiroiko (2016) and Makkonen and Weidenfeld (2016)
	Oulo	Anttiroiko (2016)
	Tampere	Anttiroiko (2016)
France	Grenoble	Kogler et al. (2016)
	Marseille	Kogler et al. (2016)
	Paris	Pin and Galimberti (2016), Kogler et al. (2016) and Simmie (2001)
	Toulouse	Kogler et al. (2016)
Germany	Dortmund	Athey et al. (2008)
	Stuttgart	Simmie (2001)
Italy	Genoa	Dameri (2017)
	Milan	Pin and Galimberti (2016) and Simmie (2001)
Netherlands	Amsterdam	Dameri (2017), Simmie (2001) and Kogler et al. (2016)
	Eindhoven	Kogler et al. (2016)
	Rotterdam	Kogler et al.(2016)
	The Hague	Mayer et al. (2016)
	Wagenigen	Kogler et al. (2016)
Poland	Various	Nijkamp (2016)
Sweden	Malmö	Makkonen and Weidenfeld (2016)
Switzerland	Bern	Mayer et al. (2016)
United Kingdom	100 largest (ex. London)	Cowling and Lee (2017)
	Cambridge	Viitanen (2016)
	Coventry	Athey et al. (2008)
	Dundee	Athey et al. (2008)
	Leeds	Devins et al. (2016)
	London	Athey et al. (2008) and Simmie (2001)
	Newcastle	Couchman et al. (2008)
	Reading	Athey et al. (2008)
Various	Various	Capello et al. (2012) and Sáez and Periáñez (2015)

4 Results

On the basis of the aforementioned sources, we propose a consolidated set of 43 determinants reflecting cities' local innovation ecosystems. All determinants of this set are classified and categorized along the taxonomy of Proksch et al. (2017). Overall, these variables illustrate the interplay of firms, markets, assets, institutions, and networks within a systemic architecture designed for knowledge production, consumption, and commercialization. In this sense, most of the established determinants introduced by Furman et al. (2002), extended and updated by Proksch et al. (2017), are also valid for cities' innovation ecosystems. Only the *intellectual strength of protection for IP* and *openness to international trade* indicators seem to be conditions attributed solely to the country level and therefore not transferable to the city level.

Further determinants have been added to create an image as holistic as possible of cities' innovation ecosystems. At its core, the enhancement builds on both the basic characteristics of cities (spatial concentration and agglomeration) and major trends influencing a city's development (globalization, digitalization, and demographical change). Appendix, Table 2 offers a list of the proposed city-level determinants together with an in-depth explanation for each item. The influence of these determinants on the outcome variable (patents) needs to be tested, regardless of their treatment within other studies of national or sub-national innovation systems. The suggested comparative method (fsQCA) would provide such a test, as the resulting pathways consist of only those antecedent conditions that have had a measurable impact on the outcome condition (patents). In this context, respective data sources per determinant have to be identified. Even though data availability is a well known issue in innovation system research, scholars should exclude variables sparingly, as exclusion might lead to an undervaluation of the respective category within the whole construct.

4.1 Discussion and Implications

Although certain determinants can be used to reflect and understand a city's innovation ecosystem, the process of innovation in cities remains a complex phenomenon. Naturally, cities have evolved differently, and thus have different preconditions for future growth. However, regardless of their developmental trajectories, competitiveness and innovative capacity are somehow comparable among cities. Various benchmarking studies offer an elevated view of the innovative performance of cities, assigning them to well known groups such as innovation leaders, innovation followers, moderate innovators, and modest innovators (see, for example, European Commission 2016a; 2thinknow 2017). Consequently, development, or indeed non-development, is path-dependent. Different innovation strategies with the same outcome exist, allowing cities to define appropriate policies in line with their specific preconditions. Evolutionary economics argues that international knowledge exchange and the oligopolistic power exercised by firms are the cornerstones for unleashing innovative activity for the first time and defending innovation ecosystems from becoming locked into entrenched paths in the long run, thus maintaining the preconditions for a steady growth of all factors concerned with innovative capacity (Simmie 2001). In this sense, path dependence can be understood as means of explanation for different levels of innovative capacity. Following Porter (1990), one approach would be to "focus on the attributes that lead to the establishment of competitive industrial production clusters" (Simmie 2001, p. 42). Another approach, recommended by Krugman (2002), would be to emphasize "the importance of trade in producing external economies and agglomeration" (Simmie 2001, p. 42). In the end, no particular approach is right or wrong. Innovation emanates from both endogenous and exogenous factors, whose effect on innovative capacity is either increasing (e.g., the presence of key technologies) or decreasing (e.g., a lack of specialists owing to demographic change as well as unresolved questions of business succession). Innovative ecosystems of cities cannot be treated and analyzed hermetically, since no clear-cut innovation ecosystem exists in cities. As we know today, innovative capacity and entrepreneurial capacity are inextricably linked. Hence, the system's boundaries are dynamic rather than static. The objective, however, is to understand innovation in cities as a crucial economic power promoting countries' economic growth and development. Ultimately, institutional innovation, political innovation, and technical innovation are of equal relevance. To this end, partnerships between local places and the national government are critical prerequisites to inform the development of innovation policy from different perspectives, giving consideration to innovative inputs such as the concentration of knowledge workers as well as outputs such as new products, services, or even firms.

Fixing certain determinants to reflect a city's innovation ecosystem, even if they are broadly selected to capture the above-mentioned links, inevitably leads to the analysis of a *closed* system. However imperfect, such a system at least illustrates urban planning and evaluation processes attributed to innovative capacity and reveals the connections between different types of innovation. The results of a pathway analysis would enable policymakers responsible for urban development and sub-regional stakeholders involved in strategy implementation to identify promising areas of further knowledge development and smart specialization. Knowledge regarding the innovation trajectories for different city types (capital-metro, other-metro, non-metro) is critical to successfully transforming the parameters of all local innovation ecosystems within a country into institutional arrangements on the upper levels.

4.2 Limitations and Future Research

The above observations and the knowledge about the right city parameters lead to the conclusion that the framework proposed by Proksch et al. (2017) is transferable to city cases. Taking the proposed 43 parameters as a starting point, further quantitative research, ideally based on a comparative method, could determine the pathways leading to a high innovative capacity in cities. However, not all facets of innovation in cities can be reflected by variables. The well-known issues regarding patent statistics as a measure of innovative capacity are just the tip of the iceberg. Few studies offer fully tested determinants, and the academic quality of these works differs. Datasets largely build on estimations and algorithms, which from a methodical perspective do not result in reliable real-world observations. Hence, a major challenge for future quantitative research in this field will be finding appropriate data sources. A source comparable to Eurostats (Eurostats 2017) on the country level is not presently available for cities. However, the European Union has recently launched an internet-based Urban Data Platform (European Commission 2017) offering a rich load of determinants attributed to city comparison that might be a promising foundation for future research in this field. As similar resources may become available before long, covering different geographies (e.g., cities within OECD countries), the intelligence of this article might be expandable to pan-European settings soon.

5 Conclusions from a Mayor's Perspective

Innovation prowess is an important driver of economic growth and improves both social cohesiveness and environmental impacts. A lot of research work has been done to identify the most innovative countries, but consensus around the criteria used to identify an innovative city is still lacking.

Understanding what approaches are the most effective in leading locations requires an initial assessment which cities are the most innovative. For this purpose, cities' endeavors to drive innovation need to be analyzed, including challenges to the traditional technology and GDP output metrics, such as patents or share of exports. Tracking innovation prowess and impact of one location against another might be helpful in the search for an alternative view for measuring the best locations for innovation around the world. Coherently judging one location against another requires considering various perspectives - first, the country perspective which provides a rich review of country-by-country activity, second, the regional and local perspectives that are pivotal since innovation does not really happen at the national level, and third, the city perspective that reveals the most effective and efficient approach to innovation and also those approaches that work best, where and why.

Ultimately, views differ with respect to how innovation in cities should be measured. Unfortunately, presently no solid and consistent way of looking at this prevails, and assessing a myriad of indicators is only half the story. Understanding city-focused innovation will drive different approaches, depending on the city type. Predominantly 'black box processes' within cities drive improved innovation, extending to how groups of disparate people with varied expertise connect and collaborate and including the culture that supports this diversity across the communities. Civic-led change, city branding, social impacts and historical achievements might be interesting views that certainly provide a good starting point for mayors to explore and understand these innovative processes in depth (Jones 2017). It is only the understanding of a city's unique innovation system which renders possible the identification of the right parameters that have an impact on its performance.

Appendix

Table 2 List of the proposed city level determinants together with explanations

Variable name	Numerator	Denominator	Rationale	Included in Proksch et al. (2017)	Based on
Outcome variable					
International patents (per million inhabitants)	Patent applications to the European Patent Office by priority year, i.e. the year of the first international filing of a patent	Inhabitants (millions)	The capacity of firms to develop new products determines their competitive advantage. One indicator of the rate of new product innovation is the number of patents (European Commission 2016a). The innovative capacity of cities is underlined by the number of patents per inhabitant (European Commission 2016b).	Yes	Kogler et al. (2016) and European Commission (2016a, b)
Quality of the common innovation infrastructure					
GDP (per capita)	Gross domestic product (purchasing power parity)	Inhabitants	This is indicator denotes whether a city is more or less economically successful (Sáez and Periáñez 2015).	Yes	Makkonen and Weidenfeld (2016) and Sáez and Periáñez (2015)
Stock of international patents	Cumulative patents	Time period	This indicator reflects the state of the cities' knowledge economy and relatedly the intensity of knowledge linkages and networks within regions (Makkonen and Weidenfeld 2016).	Yes	Makkonen and Weidenfeld (2016) and Kogler et al. (2016)
Population	Total inhabitants per 1 January	Per year	Population is an attractor of company head offices and generally has important historical and cultural legacies that may affect an individuals' locational decision (Cowling and Lee 2017).	Yes	Cowling and Lee (2017)

(continued)

Table 2 (continued)

Variable name	Numerator	Denominator	Rationale	Included in Proksch et al. (2017)	Based on
People born abroad (percent)	Share of people born abroad (another country)	Inhabitants	This is a measurement of diversity and independency as part of socio-cultural (or societal) development (Makkonen and Weidenfeld 2016). Diversity is important in attracting talented workers who might prefer tolerant areas (Cowling and Lee 2017).	No	Makkonen and Weidenfeld (2016) and Cowling and Lee (2017)
Educational attainment rate (percent)	Share of inhabitants with tertiary educational attainment	Inhabitants	This is a general indicator of the supply of advanced skills. It is not limited to science and technical fields, because the adoption of innovations in many areas, in particular in the service sectors, depends on a wide range of skills (European Commission 2016a). The basic talent measure is simply the proportion of the adult population with an undergraduate degree and above (Cowling and Lee 2017).	No	Makkonen and Weidenfeld (2016), European Commission (2016a), Cowling and Lee (2017) and Sáez and Periáñez (2015)
Students	Number of enrolled students	Annual average	Additional measure of talent. Included are students across all types of tertiary education.	No	Cowling and Lee (2017) and Sáez and Periáñez (2015)
Public institutions that support innovation	Number of public institutions including science parks	–/–	A number of public institutions and actors support innovation—notably universities, individual change agents and some economic development agencies (Athey et al. 2008). As with science parks, there may be templates and exemplars that are promoted by policymakers, academics, and consultants but specific local configurations of institutions and governance relations lead to different outcomes (Couchman et al. 2008).	No	Athey et al. (2008) and Couchman et al. (2008)

Employment in medium-high and high-tech manufacturing and knowledge-intensive services (percent)	Share of employed persons in the medium-high and high tech manufacturing sectors	Total workforce including all manufacturing and service sectors	The share of employment in high technology manufacturing sectors is an indicator of the manufacturing economy that is based on continual innovation through creative, inventive activity. The use of total employment gives a better indicator than using the share of manufacturing employment alone, since the latter will be affected by the relative decline of manufacturing in some countries. Knowledge-intensive services can be provided directly to consumers, such as telecommunications, and provide inputs to the innovative activities of other firms in all sectors of the economy. The latter can increase productivity throughout the economy and support the diffusion of a range of innovations, in particular those based on ICT. (European Commission 2016a)	Yes	Zitek and Klimova (2016), European Commission (2016a) and Sáez and Periáñez (2015)
Aggregate R&D expenditures (percent)	Share of R&D expenditures, cross-sectors (government, higher education, business sector)	Gross domestic product	See *Private R&D Funding* and *Percentage of R&D performed by universities.*	Yes	Zitek and Klimova (2016), Makkonen and Weidenfeld (2016), European Commission (2016a) and Sáez and Periáñez (2015)

(continued)

Table 2 (continued)

Variable name	**Numerator**	**Denominator**	**Rationale**	**Included in Proksch et al.** (2017)	**Based on**
Non-R&D innovation expenditures (percent)	Share of total innovation expenditure, excluding intramural and extramural R&D expenditures	Total turnover (both innovators and non-innovators)	This indicator measures non-R&D innovation expenditure as percentage of total turnover. Several of the components of innovation expenditure, such as investment in equipment and machinery and the acquisition of patents and licenses, measure the diffusion of new production technology and ideas (European Commission 2016a).	No	European Commission (2016a)
Number of firms	Number of registered businesses	Annual net number	Firms are the key innovators, and cities support innovation by firms in a number of ways (Athey et al. 2008).	No	Athey et al. (2008)
Locational policy	Strength of locational policy	Score value based on survey	Strength of locational policy environment to support innovation, with regard to:	No	Mayer et al. (2016) Cowling and Lee (2017) and Viitanen (2016)
			• adapting national policy frameworks; • attracting funding (incl. council tax bill); • inducing cross-sectoral clusters; • incentivizing collaboration.		
Higher education share (percent)	Share of public spending on higher education	Gross Domestic Product	Measure of the intensity of human capital investment. A high level of *higher education share* creates a base of highly skilled personnel upon which ficre and other institutions across the economy can draw, both for formal R&D activities as well as other innovation-related activities (Furman et al. 2002).	Yes	Makkonen and Weidenfeld (2016)

Cluster-specific innovation environment					
Private R&D Funding (percent)	Share of R&D expenditures in the business sector	Gross Domestic Product	This indicator captures the formal creation of new knowledge within firms. It is particularly important in the science-based sector (pharmaceuticals, chemicals and some areas of electronics) where most new knowledge is created in or near R&D laboratories (European Commission 2016a).	Yes	Zitek and Klimova (2016) and European Commission (2016a)
Specialization degree (percent)	Share of high-tech patent applications to the EPO by priority year	Total patent applications to the EPO by priority year	An essentially positive relationship exists between specialization in high-tech sectors and innovation performance (Capello et al. 2012). Furthermore, specialization degree is a measure capturing an important consequence of cluster dynamics, the relative specialization of an economy in specific technologies fields (Furman et al. 2002).	Yes	Kogler et al. (2016) and Capello et al. (2012)
Head offices (percent)	Share of company headquarters	Number of registered businesses	The presence of company headquarters can be a lever of innovation, not only because of R&D departments but also because the filing address of patents is generally a company's head office, regardless patents' point of origin.	No	Sáez and Periáñez (2015)
Firms innovating in-house (percent)	Share of firms with in-house innovation activities	Number of registered businesses	This indicator measures the degree to which firms that have introduced any new or significantly improved products or production processes have innovated in-house. Innovative firms with in-house innovation activities have introduced a new product or new process either in-house or in combination with other firms. The indicator does not include new products or processes developed by other firms (European Commission 2016a).	No	European Commission (2016a) and Viitanen (2016)

(continued)

Table 2 (continued)

Variable name	Numerator	Denominator	Rationale	Included in Proksch et al. (2017)	Based on
Marketing or organizational innovators (percent)	Share of firms that introduced a new marketing innovation and/or organizational innovation to one of their markets	Number of registered businesses	The Community Innovation Survey mainly asks enterprises about their technological innovation. Many enterprises, in particular in the services sectors, innovate through other non-technological forms of innovation. Examples of these are marketing and organizational innovations. This indicator captures the extent that firms innovate through non-technological innovation (European Commission 2016a).	No	European Commission (2016a)
Product or process innovators (percent)	Share of firms that introduced a new product or a new process to one of their markets	Number of registered businesses	Technological innovation, as measured by the introduction of new products (goods or services) and processes, is a key ingredient to innovation in manufacturing activities. Higher shares of technological innovators should reflect a higher level of innovation activities (European Commission 2016a).	No	European Commission (2016a)
Specialization in technology (advanced manufacturing and knowledge intensive services) (percent)	Proportion of the total business stock that can be classified as operating in knowledge based industries	Number of registered businesses	Regions hosting large urban areas are the most innovative, and this statement is reinforced in regions characterized by specialization in knowledge-intensive services. The simultaneous presence of advanced manufacturing and knowledge-intensive service activities generates synergic effects, fostering innovative performance (Capello et al. 2012).	No	Cowling and Lee (2017) and Capello et al. (2012)

Commercial premises occupation (percent)	Occupancy rate of commercial premises	Area of commercial premises (sqm)	Business space is a critical urban asset in supporting innovation. Both underutilization and full utilization are important indicators with regard to factor availability and suitability.	No	Simmie (2001) and Athey et al. (2008)
Quality of linkages					
R&D performed by universities (percent)	Share of R&D expenditures in the higher education sector	Gross domestic product	R&D expenditure represents one of the major drivers of economic growth in a knowledge-based economy. Trends in the R&D expenditure indicator provide key indications of the future competitiveness and wealth of a region. Research and development spending is essential for making the transition to a knowledge-based economy as well as for improving production technologies and stimulating growth.	Yes	Zitek and Klimova (2016)
Venture capital Performance	Volume of venture capital investments	–/–	A given common innovation infrastructure results in a more productive flow of innovative output when there are mechanisms or institutions, such as . . . established funding sources for new ventures, which encourage the commercialization of new technologies in particular clusters. (Furman et al. 2002) Included are private equity transactions across these development phases: acquisition, preparation, founding and post-formation.	Yes	Simmie (2001)
New businesses registered (percent)	Proportion of new firms	Number of registered businesses	One measure of openness and vibrancy is the inflow of new entrepreneurial businesses as entrepreneurs start new firms to take advantage of perceived new market opportunities and gaps in the provision of goods and services (Cowling and Lee 2017).	Yes	Cowling and Lee (2017)

(continued)

Table 2 (continued)

Incubation environments per startup (percent)	Number of incubation environments (accelerators, incubators, idea labs, co-working spaces, brain trusts, etc.)	Number of new businesses registered	Another innovation ecosystem element is in the incubation environments, which provide essential, professional growth services for startups and growing SMEs. These incubation environments are physical locations where a selected group of young companies receive professional support for their management concerns. Included are all accelerators, incubators, idea labs, co-working spaces and brain trusts.	No	Own interpretation based on: Viitanen (2016)
Collaborative networks	Number of collaborative projects, programs or platforms (either digital or analogue)	–/–	Projects, programs or platforms promoting collaborative user-driven methods and tools for improving the real world development of products and services. Typical examples of these platforms include interconnected parts of user-driven cities, real-life experimentation sites on streets, open system platforms for developing mobile applications (with users), and internet-based, end-user beta-testing environments to engage users in an early-stage R&D process. (Viitanen 2016)	No	Anttiroiko (2016), Athey et al. (2008) and Viitanen (2016)
Internet users (percent)	Share of people who regular use internet	Population	The internet is a ubiquitous access point to innovation and creativity platforms as well as to economic opportunities.	No	Sáez and Periáñez (2015)
Public-private partnerships	Number of institutionalized innovation partnerships	–/–	These partnerships reflect the shared public/private interest of planning innovation activities to support the creation of intellectual property and cross-sectoral collaboration together (Viitanen 2016).	No	Viitanen (2016)

Innovative firms collaborating with others (percent)	Share of firms with innovation co-operation activities.	Number of registered businesses	This indicator measures the degree to which firms are involved in innovation co-operation. Complex innovations often depend on companies' ability to draw on diverse sources of information and knowledge, or to collaborate on the development of an innovation. This indicator measures the flow of knowledge between public research institutions and firms, and between firms and other firms. Firms with co-operation activities are those that have had any co-operation agreements on innovation activities with other enterprises or institutions.	No	European Commission (2016a) and Athey et al. (2008)
Contributing and related outcome factors					
Publications in academic journals	Number of scientific publications	Inhabitants (million)	Complement to *stock of international patents.*	Yes	Makkonen and Weidenfeld (2016) and Pin and Galimberti 2016)
			Scientific publications indicate the knowledge infrastructure (science base) of a city.		
High ranked universities	Number of high ranked tertiary education institutions	–/–	Complement to *educational attainment rate (percent).*	No	Makkonen and Weidenfeld (2016) and Cowling and Lee (2017)

(continued)

Table 2 (continued)

Variable name	Numerator	Denominator	Rationale	Included in Proksch et al. (2017)	Based on
			Research has highlighted considerable difference in labor markets between university and non-university cities. Some cities have universities that were founded hundreds of years ago and are woven into the culture of a city as well as being a major actor in the socio-economic system of a city (Cowling and Lee 2017). Especially cities hosting universities that enjoy a strong reputation in the offered scientific disciplines might be relevant for the acquisition of both new talent and high qualified labor (Makkonen and Weidenfeld 2016).		
Spoken languages	Number of foreign languages spoken	–/–	Complement to *educational attainment rate (percent).*	No	Simmie (2001)
			Language barriers restrict international labor mobility.		
Total workforce including all manufacturing and service sectors	Number of persons engaged	Annual average	Complement to *employment in medium-high and high-tech manufacturing and knowledge-intensive services*. Innovative capacity depends in part on the labor force of an economy.	Yes	Sáez and Periáñez (2015)
Job change rate	Mean length of stay in the same job	Time period	Complement to *firms innovating in-house (percent).*	No	Own interpretation based on: Simmie (2001)

			This indicator measures the duration of transferring exclusive knowledge among firms and organizations driven by job changes (i.e. the "rotation" of labor).		
Gross Domestic Product	Real GDP (purchasing power parity)	-/-	Complement to *GDP per capita.*	Yes	Makkonen and Weidenfeld (2016)
			Measure of economic development.		
Foreign direct investments	Non-residential capital stock	-/-	Complement to *GDP per capita.*	No	Makkonen and Weidenfeld (2016)
			Measure of economic development.		
Daily commuters (percent)	Share of daily commuters (inbound and outbound)	Total workforce including all sectors	Complement to *head offices (percent).*	No	Own interpretation based on: Makkonen and Weidenfeld (2016)
			This indicator signals how well the labor markets of the cities and regions are integrated.		
Dependency ratio (percent)	Share of people in age groups 0–14 and 65+	Population in the working age groups 15–64	Complement to *population.*	No	Makkonen and Weidenfeld (2016)
			This indicator is used to measure the pressure on productive population.		

(continued)

Table 2 (continued)

Variable name	Numerator	Denominator	Rationale	Included in Proksch et al. (2017)	Based on
Satisfaction	Level of inhabitants' satisfaction	Score value based on survey	Complement to *population.*	No	Simmie (2001) and Makkonen and Weidenfeld (2016), Cowling and Lee (2017) and Sáez and Periáñez (2015)
			Quality of life and place, aggregated measure consisting of the following sub-categories:		
			• Agglomeration economies (e.g., population density)		
			• Attractive environments (e.g., CO_2 emissions)		
			• High quality facilities (e.g., public transport)		
			• Cultural diversity (e.g., arts, cuisine, religion)		
			• Welfare (cost of living)		
			• Safety (crimes involving life and death)		
			• Healthcare infrastructure (e.g., hospitals)		
Ethnic groups	Number of different ethno-linguistic groups		Complement to *share of people born abroad (percent).*	No	Cowling and Lee (2017)
			The measure of diversity refers to the ethnic diversity of the population. (Cowling and Lee 2017)		

Market share (percent)	Share of exports in medium-high and high-tech manufacturing industries	Total exports	Complement to *specialization degree (percent).*	Yes	European Commission (2016a)
			The indicator measures the technological competitiveness of a region, i.e., its ability to commercialize the results of research and development (R&D) and innovation in the international markets. It also reflects product specialization. Creating, exploiting and commercializing new technologies are vital for the competitiveness of a region in the modern economy. Medium and high technology products are key drivers of economic growth, productivity and welfare, and are generally a source of high value added and well paid employment (European Commission 2016a).		
Sales of new-to-market and new-to-firm innovations (percent)	Share of total turnover of new or significantly improved products	Total turnover of firms (both innovators and non-innovators)	Complement to *specialization in technology (advanced manufacturing and knowledge intensive services)(percent.)*	No	European Commission (2016a)

(continued)

Table 2 (continued)

Variable name	Numerator	Denominator	Rationale	Included in Proksch et al. (2017)	Based on
			This indicator measures the turnover of new or significantly improved products to the firm as a percentage of total turnover. These products are not new to the market. Sales of new-to-the-firm but not new-to-the-market products are a proxy of the use or implementation of products (or technologies) already introduced elsewhere. This indicator is a proxy for the degree of diffusion of state-of-the-art technologies.		
Capital	Capital stock based on total financial assets	–/–	Complement to *VC performance* (funding sources).	Yes	Simmie (2001)

References

2thinknow (2017) Innovation Cities™ Program: making cities innovative. http://www.innovation-cities.com/indexes. Accessed 2 Jan 2017

Acs ZJ, Anselin L, Varga A (2002) Patents and innovation counts as measures of regional production of new knowledge. Res Policy 31(7):1069–1085. https://doi.org/10.1016/S0048-7333(01)00184-6

Acs ZJ, Audretsch DB, Lehmann EE, Licht G (2016) National systems of innovation. J Technol Transf. https://doi.org/10.1007/s10961-016-9481-8

Albach H (2006) Betriebswirtschaftliche Langzeitforschung. Z Betriebswirtsch 76(7–8):701–734. https://doi.org/10.1007/s11573-006-0034-8

Andrew C (2014) Seeking talent for creative cities: the social dynamics of innovation. In: Grant JL (ed) Seeking talent for creative cities. The social dynamics of innovation, vol 91. University of Toronto Press, Toronto, pp 227–228

Anttiroiko A-V (2016) City-as-a-platform. The rise of participatory innovation platforms in Finnish cities. Sustainability 8(9):922. https://doi.org/10.3390/su8090922

Athey G, Nathan M, Webber C, Mahroum S (2008) Innovation and the city. In: Marceau J (ed) Innovation and the city: Innovative cities, vol 10. EContent Management, Maleny, pp 156–169

Atkinson RD (2013) Innovation in cities and innovation by cities. In: Audretsch DB, Walshok M (eds) Creating competitiveness. Entrepreneurship and innovation policies for growth. Edward Elgar, Cheltenham, pp 26–53

Breschi S (2001) Knowledge spillovers and local innovation systems. A critical survey. Ind Corp Chang 10(4):975–1005. https://doi.org/10.1093/icc/10.4.975

Briggs MJ (2009) Innovation and the city. A macromarketing approach to industry development. Mark Intell Plan 27(2):233–245. https://doi.org/10.1108/02634500910945002

Capello R, Caragliu A, Lenzi C (2012) Is innovation in cities a matter of knowledge-intensive services? An empirical investigation. Innov Eur J Soc Sci Res 25(2):151–174. https://doi.org/10.1080/13511610.2012.660326

Caragliu A, Del Bo CF, Kourtit K, Nijkamp P (2016) The winner takes it all. Forward-looking cities and urban innovation. Ann Reg Sci 56(3):617–645. https://doi.org/10.1007/s00168-015-0734-5

Cooke P (1992) Regional innovation systems. Competitive regulation in the new Europe. Geoforum 23(3):365–382. https://doi.org/10.1016/0016-7185(92)90048-9

Cooke P (2002) Regional innovation systems. General findings and some new evidence from biotechnology clusters. J Technol Transf 27(1):133–145. https://doi.org/10.1023/A:1013160923450

Cooke P, Gomez Uranga M, Etxebarria G (1997) Regional innovation systems. Institutional and organisational dimensions. Res Policy 26(4–5):475–491. https://doi.org/10.1016/S0048-7333(97)00025-5

Cooke P, Boekholt P, Tödtling F (1998) Regional innovation systems. Designing for the future. CASS, Cardiff

Couchman PK, McLoughlin I, Charles DR (2008) Lost in translation? Building science and innovation city strategies in Australia and the UK. In: Marceau J (ed) Innovation and the city: Innovative cities, vol 10. EContent Management, Maleny, pp 211–223

Cowling M, Lee N (2017) How entrepreneurship, culture and universities influence the geographical distribution of UK talent and city growth. J Manag Dev 36(2):null. doi: https://doi.org/10.1108/JMD-03-2016-0043

Dameri RP (2017) Smart city implementation. Creating economic and public value in innovative urban systems. Progress in IS. Springer International Publishing, Cham, p 1

Devins D, Lodorfos G, Kostopoulos I, Webber DO (2016) Innovation and growth in the city region. Microeconomic evidence of asymmetries. Int J Innov Manag 20(02):1650032. https://doi.org/10.1142/S1363919616500328

Edquist C (ed) (2001) The systems of innovation approach and innovation policy. An account of the state of the art

Edquist C (2009) Systems of innovation. Perspectives and challenges. Afr J Sci Technol Innov Develop 2(3):14–43. https://doi.org/10.1093/oxfordhb/9780199286805.003.0007
Edquist C (2013) Systems of innovation. Technologies, institutions and organizations. Taylor and Francis, Hoboken
Edquist C (2016) The Swedish National Innovation Council. Innovation policy governance to replace linearity with holism
Eger JM (2012) Nurturing an innovation region. A new agenda for cities in the new economy. J E-Gov 35(3):129–132
European Commission (2016a) Regional innovation Scoreboard 2016. Belgium
European Commission (2016b) The state of European cities 2016. Cities leading the way to a better future. Publications Office of the European Union, Luxembourg
European Commission (2017) Urban data platform: data sharing and visualization platform for European cities and regions. http://urban.jrc.ec.europa.eu/. Accessed 14 Feb 2017
Eurostats (2017) Database overview. Databases by themes. http://ec.europa.eu/eurostat/de/data/database
Fagerberg J (2016) Innovation systems and policy: a tale of three countries. Stato e mercato (1):13–40. https://doi.org/10.1425/82941
Fertig M, Görlitz K, Peistrup M, Schmidt CM, Winter B, Grenzmann C, Kreuels B, Niehof B, Engel D (2010) Innovationsbericht 2009. Zur Leistungsfähigkeit des Landes Nordrhein-Westfalen in Wissenschaft, Forschung und Technologie. Endbericht-Januar 2010. Forschungsprojekt für das Ministerium für Innovation, Wissenschaft, Forschung und Technologie des Landes Nordrhein-Westfalen
Freeman C (1989) Technology policy and economic performance. Lessons from Japan, Reprint. Pinter, London
Freeman C (1998) Innovation systems: city-state, national, continental and sub-national. Nota Técnica 2:1–50
Freeman C (2001) A hard landing for the 'New Economy'? Information technology and the United States national system of innovation. Struct Chang Econ Dyn 12(2):115–139. https://doi.org/10.1016/S0954-349X(01)00017-0
Freeman C (2002) Continental, national and sub-national innovation systems—complementarity and economic growth. Res Policy 31(2):191–211. https://doi.org/10.1016/S0048-7333(01)00184-6
Furman JL, Hayes R (2004) Catching up or standing still? Res Policy 33(9):1329–1354. https://doi.org/10.1016/j.respol.2004.09.006
Furman JL, Porter ME, Stern S (2002) The determinants of national innovative capacity. Res Policy 31(6):899–933. https://doi.org/10.1016/S0048-7333(01)00152-4
Griliches Z (1990) Patent statistics as economic indicators. A survey. J Econ Lit 28(4):1661–1707. https://doi.org/10.3386/w3301
Johnson B (2008) Cities, systems of innovation and economic development. In: Marceau J (ed) Innovation and the city. Innovative cities, vol 10. EContent Management, Maleny, pp 146–155
Jones T (2017) Innovation hot-spot. How can we best identify the world's most innovative cities? ISPIM Junior Researcher Labs, Toronto. http://www.innovationmanagement.se/2017/03/27/innovation-hot-spots-countries-vs-cities/. Accessed 20 Apr 2017
Kiuru J, Inkinen T (2017) Predicting innovative growth and demand with proximate human capital: a case study of the Helsinki metropolitan area. Cities 64:9–17.
Klein M, Sauer A (2016) Celebrating 30 years of innovation system research. What you need to know about innovation systems. http://opus.uni-hohenheim.de/volltexte/2016/1287/pdf/dp_17_2016_online.pdf. Accessed 14 Feb 2017
Kogler DF, Heimeriks G, Leydesdorff L (2016) Patent Portfolio analysis of cities: statistics and maps of technological inventiveness. arXiv preprint arXiv:1612.05810
Kosonen K-J (2005) Strengthening the research and educational basis for regional development in less-favored regions. A local innovation system case study report. University of Tampere, Research Unit for Regional Development Studies, Tampere

Kourtit K, Nijkamp P (2012) Smart cities in the innovation age. Innov Eur J Soc Sci Res 25(2):93–95. https://doi.org/10.1080/13511610.2012.660331

Krugman P (2002) Geography and trade, [Repr.]. Gaston Eyskens lecture series. Leuven University Press, Leuven

List F, Colwell S (1856) National system of political economy. JB Lippincott, Philadelphia

Local Innovations Systems Project (2005) Industrial Performance Center. http://web.mit.edu/lis/papers.html. Accessed 1 Feb 2017

Lundvall B-Å (ed) (2010) National systems of innovation. Toward a theory of innovation and interactive learning. Anthem other canon series. Anthem Press, London

Makkonen T, Weidenfeld A (2016) Knowledge-based urban development of cross-border twin cities. Int J Knowl Based Devel 7(4):389. https://doi.org/10.1504/IJKBD.2016.080881

Marceau J (ed) (2008a) Innovation and the city. Innovative cities. EContent Management, Maleny

Marceau J (2008b) Introduction. Innovation in the city and innovative cities. In: Marceau J (ed) Innovation and the city: innovative cities, vol 10. EContent Management, Maleny, pp 136–145

Martin R, Simmie J (2008) Path dependence and local innovation systems in city-regions. In: Marceau J (ed) Innovation and the city: innovative cities, vol 10. EContent Management, Maleny, pp 183–196

Mayer H, Sager F, Kaufmann D, Warland M (2016) Capital city dynamics. Linking regional innovation systems, locational policies and policy regimes. Cities 51:11–20. https://doi.org/10.1016/j.cities.2016.01.005

McCann P (2004) Book review of Innovative Cities J. Simmie (Editor) London, Spon Press, 2001, ISBN 0415234042. Local Econ 19(1):89–90. https://doi.org/10.1080/0269094032000166912

Nijkamp P (2016) The "resourceful region". A new conceptualisation of regional development strategies. Investigaciones Regionales J Reg Res (36):191–214

OECD (ed) (2005) Oslo manual. Guidelines for collecting and interpreting innovation data, 3rd edn. OECD, Paris

Parto S, Doloreux D (2004) Regional innovation systems: a critical synthesis. UNU-INTECH Discussion Paper Series. http://EconPapers.repec.org/RePEc:unm:unuint:200417. Accessed 1 Feb 2017

Pavitt K (1988) Uses and abuses of patent statistics. In: van Raan A (ed) Handbook of quantitative studies of science and technology. Elsevier Science, Burlington, pp 509–536

Pin C, Galimberti D (2016) Making metropolis. Innovation and local governance issues in Paris and Milan. In: Cole A, Payre R (eds) Cities as political objects. Historical evolution, analytical categorisations and institutional challenges of metropolitanisation. Edward Elgar, Cheltenham, pp 197–217

Porter ME (1990) The competitive advantage of nations. With a new introduction. Free Press, New York

Porter M, Stern S (2000) Measuring the "ideas" production function. Evidence from international patent output. National Bureau of Economic Research, Cambridge

Porter ME, Stern S (2001) National innovative capacity. In: Porter ME et al (eds) The Global Competitiveness Report, 2002. Oxford University Press, New York, pp 102–118

Porter ME, Stern S (2004) Ranking national innovative capacity. Findings from the national innovative capacity index: Global Competitiveness Report, vol 2004. Oxford University Press, New York

Proksch D, Haberstroh MM, Pinkwart A (2017) Increasing the national innovative capacity: Identifying the pathways to success using a comparative method. Technol Forecast Soc Chang 116:256–270. https://doi.org/10.1016/j.techfore.2016.10.009

Ragin CC (1987) The comparative method. Moving beyond qualitative and quantitative strategies. University of California Press, Berkeley

Ragin CC (2000) Fuzzy-set social science, [Repr.]. University of Chicago Press, Chicago

Ragin CC (2008) Redesigning social inquiry: fuzzy sets and beyond, [Repr.]. University of Chicago Press, Chicago

Regional Entrepreneurship Acceleration Program (2017) A program of MIT Sloan Executive Education supported by the MIT innovation initiative. http://reap.mit.edu/. Accessed 1 Feb 2017

Romer PM (1986) Increasing returns and long-run growth. J Polit Econ 94(5):1002–1037. https://doi.org/10.1086/261420
Romer PM (1990) Endogenous technological change. J Polit Econ 98(5, Part 2):S71–S102. https://doi.org/10.1086/261725
Roper S, Hewitt-Dundas N (2015) Knowledge stocks, knowledge flows and innovation: evidence from matched patents and innovation panel data. Res Policy 44(7):1327–1340. https://doi.org/10.1016/j.respol.2015.03.003
Sáez L, Periáñez I (2015) Benchmarking urban competitiveness in Europe to attract investment. Cities 48:76–85. https://doi.org/10.1016/j.cities.2015.06.002
Schumpeter JA (1939) Business cycles. A theoretical, historical, and statistical analysis of the capitalist process. McGraw-Hill, London
Shearmur R (2012) Are cities the font of innovation? A critical review of the literature on cities and innovation. Cities 29:9–18. https://doi.org/10.1016/j.cities.2012.06.008
Simmie JM (ed) (2001) Innovative cities. Spon Press, London u.a
Solow RM (1956) A contribution to the theory of economic growth. Q J Econ 70(1):65. https://doi.org/10.2307/1884513
Sotarauta M, Kosonen K-J, Cooke P, Piccaluga A (2004) Strategic adaptation to the knowledge economy in less-favoured regions. A South-Ostrobothnian university network as a case in point. In: Cooke P, Piccaluga A (eds) Regional economies as knowledge laboratories. Edward Elgar, Cheltenham, pp 1–19
Stern S (2014) Investing in comparative advantage. Role of innovation and entrepreneurship in competitiveness and regional economic performance. Workshop: National Systems of Entrepreneurship, Mannheim. http://de.slideshare.net/TCINetwork/tci-2014 (20 Apr 2017)
Sun Y, Grimes S (2016) The emerging dynamic structure of national innovation studies. A bibliometric analysis. Scientometrics 106(1):17–40. https://doi.org/10.1007/s11192-015-1778-0
Teixeira AAC (2014) Evolution, roots and influence of the literature on national systems of innovation: a bibliometric account. Camb J Econ 38(1):181–214. https://doi.org/10.1093/cje/bet022
Viitanen J (2016) Profiling regional innovation ecosystems as functional collaborative systems: The case of Cambridge. In: McPhee C, Tukianen T, Leminen S, Westerlund M (eds) Smart cities and regions. Technol Innov Manag Rev 6(12):6–25
Villa LS (1990) Invention, inventive learning, and innovative capacity. Syst Res 35(4):290–310. https://doi.org/10.1002/bs.3830350404
Vinod Kumar TM (ed) (2017) Smart economy in smart cities. Advances in 21st century human settlements. Springer, Singapore
Vinod Kumar TM, Dahiya B (2017) Smart economy in smart cities. In: Vinod Kumar TM (ed) Smart economy in smart cities. Springer, Singapore, pp 3–76
Wang H-j, Gong S-y (2016) Research on the innovation evaluation indexes for innovation-oriented city. DEStech Trans Econ Manag (iceme-ebm). https://doi.org/10.12783/dtem/iceme-ebm2016/4205
Zitek V, Klimova V (2016) Identification of knowledge bases. The case of the Czech Republic. Eng Econ 27(5). https://doi.org/10.5755/j01.ee.27.5.14276

Marcus Max Haberstroh holds four academic degrees in business administration and law from international business and law schools. Before joining HHL Leipzig Graduate School of Management as a research associate at the Stiftungsfonds Deutsche Bank Chair of Innovation Management and Entrepreneurship, he was a management consultant with various consultancies. Currently his primary area of inquiry is the innovative capacity of nations, cities and industry sectors. In this connection, he is a regular contributor to books and relevant publications in academic journals.

Andreas Pinkwart was born in 1960 in Seelscheid, North Rhine-Westphalia, Germany. After his professional training as a banker he studied economics and business administration at the Universities of Münster and Bonn where he finished his Diploma in Economics and obtained his doctoral degree (*summa cum laude*) in 1991. Subsequently, Professor Pinkwart ran the office of the Free Democratic Party's leader of the parliamentary group in the German Bundestag from 1991 to 1994. In 1994 he became a Professor of Economics and Business Administration at the School of Public Administration in Düsseldorf from where he moved to the University of Siegen in 1997. There, his qualifications equaling those of a habilitation in business economics were attested and he was appointed as a full Professor to the Chair of Business Administration, especially Small and Medium-Sized Companies. Being on sabbatical leave, Professor Pinkwart was a Member of the German Bundestag (2002–2005) and the German Bundesrat (2005–2010) as well as Minister for Innovation, Science, Research and Technology and Deputy Prime Minister of the federal state of North Rhine-Westphalia (2005–2010).

After a research visit as senior research fellow at AICGS, Johns Hopkins University, Washington, in April 2011 Professor Pinkwart became the Dean of HHL Leipzig Graduate School of Management in Leipzig, Germany, and was appointed as Chairholder of the Stiftungsfonds Deutsche Bank Chair of Innovation Management and Entrepreneurship (currently on leave). From 2012 to 2016 he served as an Academic Director of the Center for Advanced Studies in Management (CASiM) at HHL. At the end of June 2017, Andreas Pinkwart has been appointed as new Minister for Economic Affairs, Innovation, Digitization and Energy of the state of North Rhine-Westphalia and resigned his office as Dean of HHL.

Part II

City Management and Direct Democracy

Open Government: Exploring Patterns of Mobile Interaction Between Citizens and Local Government

Dennis Hilgers and Lisa Schmidthuber

Abstract

Public sector organizations increasingly make use of modern technology to interact with citizens. Whereas communication between citizens and public employees was characterized by one-way (e.g., front-desk) or two-way transaction (e.g., e-mail) in previous times, advances in information and communication technology provide new possibilities for citizen-government interaction such as platform-based collaboration. Leveraging innovative channels facilitates many-to-many collaboration, and enables an increased level of government openness in terms of information and citizen integration.

In this exploratory study, we investigate the patterns of citizen-government interaction by focusing on an example of mobile open government. We examine which groups of citizens use the mobile application and why they are motivated to collaborate with local government. Furthermore, we analyze the interaction between mobile government users and public employees and shed light on users' perception of mobile government.

Survey findings provide evidence for a quite heterogeneous group of users in terms of age. However, the great majority of users are men. Users' motivation for communicating with local government via mobile phone is mainly driven by their interest in forwarding concerns easily and contributing to city improvement. Regarding users' activity in mobile government, results indicate that citizens with offline experience in communicating with public employees due to infrastructural defects write online reports less frequently than those without experience.

This chapter contributes to a better understanding about citizens' role in open government and about how individuals leverage mobile technology to

D. Hilgers (✉) • L. Schmidthuber
Institute for Public and Nonprofit Management, Johannes Kepler University Linz, Linz, Austria
e-mail: dennis.hilgers@jku.at; lisa.schmidthuber@jku.at

H. Albach et al. (eds.), *European Cities in Dynamic Competition*,
https://doi.org/10.1007/978-3-662-56419-6_4

collaborate with local government. To stimulate and design citizen participation more efficiently, we give some future research directions.

1 Introduction

Over the past few years, there has been a substantial change towards openness in government. Decreasing room for maneuver due to public debt, high levels of corruption and increasing mistrust in the system of public governance and its procedures all suggest the need for a new direction to be taken in public management. Promoting openness in the public sector is intended to counter these management and acceptance problems of the political-administrative system. An open government refers to an increased level of openness in terms of information and decision making. Next to access to government information, opening up governmental structures involves access to and integration of citizens in decision making (Evans and Campos 2013; Meijer et al. 2012). Open government is associated with a new form of collaborating with citizens and an innovative way of organizing public service delivery (Hilgers 2012).

Previous research has made efforts to conceptualize the phenomenon and provide field experience of open government initiatives. Linders (2012) develops a typology of citizen coproduction and outlines governments' possibilities for citizen integration. In a similar way, Hilgers and Ihl (2010) give an overview on how government can integrate citizens' knowledge, experience, and ideas in administrative processes. Nam (2012) concentrates on the design, performance, and impact of citizensourcing initiatives, and Mergel (2015) examines the process of open innovation by reviewing government initiatives. We contribute to research on open government by focusing on the role of citizens (Schmidthuber et al. 2017a, b; Wijnhoven et al. 2015). We aim at investigating the evolution of a new form of citizen-government interaction and at analyzing citizens' usage of modern technology to collaborate with local government. To explore patterns of citizen-government communication, we conduct a survey among users of an open government platform.

In this chapter, we first review the evolution of openness in the public sector and examine some of the core components of an open government. This is followed by a discussion on the changing patterns of citizen-government interaction which are influenced by technological advances and a government approach toward openness. For illustrating the evolution of a new form of collaboration between citizens and government, we take an example of an open government platform and analyze the users, their characteristics, and motivation to communicate with local government. We conclude with a discussion on the new mode of cooperation between government and citizens and open some avenues for further research.

2 Open Government and Citizen Innovators

2.1 The Evolution of Open Government

Open government as a "multilateral, political, and social process" (Wirtz and Birkmeyer 2015, p. 382) is widely understood as a concept that transforms governments (Hansson et al. 2015) and changes the relationship between government and the public towards a productive one (Schmidthuber and Hilgers 2015). Whereas Meijer et al. (2012, p. 11) associate open government with citizen's vision of "what is going on inside government" and voice in interactive terms, the term is related to governmental activities for the benefit of transparency, participative decision making, and collaborative activities between policymakers and citizens (e.g. Gavelin et al. 2009; Evans and Campos 2013).

Figure 1 illustrates the three pillars an open government is usually associated with. First, the public sector utilizes various ways to promote transparency of government action by providing free access to government data on open data portals. Beyond enhancing accessibility to government activities, second, an open government is intended to give citizens a voice by providing decision making possibilities. A famous example of citizen participation is participatory budgeting. By integrating non-elected citizens in the budgetary process, participatory budgeting aims at enhancing participatory democracy (Cabannes 2004; Sintomer et al. 2008). Whereas citizens have been integrated in budgetary processes since decades, new technology enables online citizen participation independent from time and location. Third, the integration of external factors such as citizens, businesses, or universities is promoted by leveraging modern information and communication technology (Linders 2012; Meijer et al. 2012; Nam 2012; Mergel 2015). Platform-based

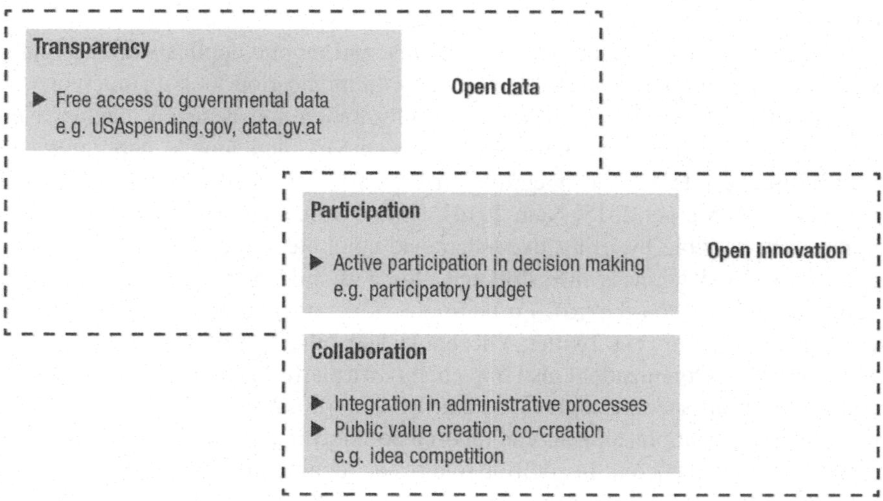

Fig. 1 Open government framework, modified from Schmidthuber and Hilgers (2017b)

collaboration allows externals to integrate their ideas or knowledge. For example, local governments utilize platforms to exchange with their citizens on urban planning, or to provide a channel for making requests and reporting defects on the public infrastructure (e.g., Schmidthuber and Hilgers 2017b). The cooperation between government and citizens as well as collaboration among citizens is supposed to increase public value creation and enhance citizen-government relationship.

2.2 The Role of Technology in Citizen-Government Interaction

The evolution of a more open and collaborative government was enabled by harnessing modern information and communication technology (Bertot et al. 2010; Jaeger and Bertot 2010). In terms of the New Public Management, public institutions try to improve customer orientation by providing citizens possibilities to get in touch with public employees. These traditional channels of government access are characterized by offline communication. For example, citizens visit or phone a government office to get government information or services. Citizens have to proactively search for information instead of getting informed, and public agencies only have few offline possibilities to inform the public, for example, about changed opening hours.

Continuous further development of information and communication technology and digitalization enable government to use Internet websites and electronic mails for information and service exchange. Municipalities increasingly use e-government and offer information and services 24/7 (Lee et al. 2008; Moon 2002; Norris et al. 2001). Technology enables public sector organizations to make information and services accessible to the general public, and citizens can access these data and services independent from location and time. Public employees can constantly update online information to keep citizens informed, and citizens are able to contact employees easily via mail.

The emergence of social media, platforms, and mobile applications has finally stimulated governmental use of innovative communication tools to interact with citizens and provide enhanced access to information and decision making. New digital media such as text messaging, social media, and mobile apps give new possibilities to interact and integrate citizens in government (Helbig et al. 2009; Linders 2012; Mergel 2015; Nam 2012). Online exchange with public employees is not only possible by using fixed-stationed computers, the evolution of mobile applications and wireless infrastructure allows mobile phone owners to contact public employees "on-the-go". Furthermore, governmental organizations are able to push information via Twitter, Facebook, and other social media channels to their followers. Organizations also implement own platforms for citizen-government collaboration on specific topics, see e.g. Linders (2012) and Nam (2012) for an overview. For example, citizens can report a pothole directly from the street in real-time via fixmystreet.com. In addition to citizens' communication with government and vice versa, these innovative and most technology-intensive channels enable many-to-many collaboration.

Table 1 Changing patterns of citizen-government interaction

	New public management	E-government	Open government
	Aucoin (1990) Hood (1991) Osborne and Gaebler (1992) Dunleavy and Hood (1994) Pollitt and Bouckaert (2004)	Layne and Lee (2001) Moon (2002) West (2004)	Lee and Kwak (2012) Meijer et al. (2012) Evans and Campos (2013)
Time	Since 1980s	Since 1990s	Since 2010s
Concept interface	Customer orientation front-desk, telephone, letter	Digitalization e-mail, website, short messaging service	Collaboration mobile apps, platforms, social media
Channel mode of cooperation	Offline one-way	Online dyadic transaction	Mobile one-to-many/many-to-many collaboration
Examples for citizen-government communication			
Citizens ➔ Government	• Visiting a public agency	• Writing a mail to public employees	• Installing mobile app and post a comment
	• Calling public employees	• Visiting government websites	• Follow/like public agency on Twitter/Facebook
Government ➔ Citizens	• Waiting for citizens to call	• Providing information online, answering to mails	• Post a tweet • Developing mobile apps

In general, we observe an increasing number of channels citizens can choose to communicate with government over time. Associated with these channel offerings, government provides an enhanced level of openness, possibilities to interact and to share information with a large number of individuals (see Table 1).

3 Mobile Government: The Case of Infrastructural Online Participation

As outlined in Table 1, mobile government represents a new possibility of citizen-government interaction. Communication via mobile phones is particularly interesting for governmental institutions, as citizens and other stakeholders can be reached anywhere and anytime. Additionally, citizens can access government information and services easily and without wasting time standing in the line. Furthermore, push messages allow real-time information and notifications (Ntaliani et al. 2008). Government organizations use mobile applications, for example, for parking fee payment, tracking systems, or alerting services (see e.g., Trimi and Sheng 2008). Additionally, mobile government is used for reporting infrastructural defects such as a broken streetlight or a pothole: For making such requests, in general, there are several ways for citizens to voice their problems. Next to traditional channels such as front desk, telephone, and mail, various cities have launched platforms where citizens are invited to post their requests. For example, the local government of Linz, the capital city of Upper Austria, offers platform-based collaboration in terms of infrastructural defects since 2013. Citizens can access the platform via computer, tablet, or mobile phone by downloading the mobile application. Similar to fixmystreet.com or seeclickfix.com, platform users are able to post their request on the platform and comment to other reports (see Schmidthuber and Hilgers 2017b).

As illustrated in Fig. 2, the platform was frequently used during the last years. Whereas the number of reports made via the platform has risen to more than 3500 in 2013 and 2014, the frequency of use of other channels (i.e. telephone, e-mail, face-to-face) remained constant over time, even after the implementation of online reporting. Consequently, the total number of reports made by citizens has increased after providing additional and digital channels for public service reporting.

Leveraging modern technology for communication has also contributed to an increased level of transparency. Whereas service requests made via traditional channels are not visible to other citizens, they are accessible in the online reporting platform. All users can read reports and their comments. In addition, the platform gives information on the proceeding status of the request.

An analysis of the reports posted on the online platform shows that the majority of reports are made on traffic issues. As illustrated in Table 2, users most frequently write contributions on traffic requirements such as road markings or road signs, on

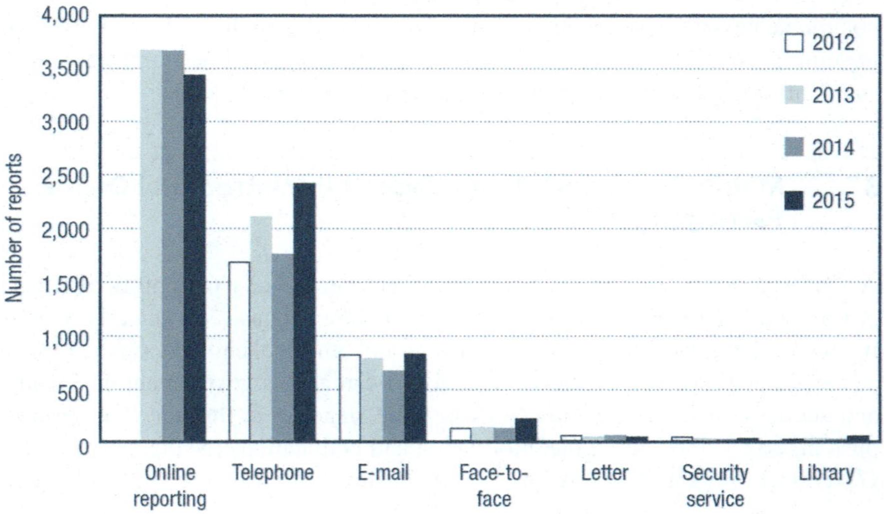

Fig. 2 Citizen reports by channel and year (Local Government of Linz 2016)

Table 2 Issues reported to government via online reporting platform since 2013 (Local Government of Linz 2017)

Category	Number of reports	Number/percent of problems fixed	
Traffic measures	2344	517	22.1%
Roads	1481	777	52.5%
Waste deposit	1376	916	66.6%
Traffic equipment	1359	891	65.6%
Street lighting	1342	1221	91.0%
Contaminants	1211	698	57.6%
Green areas	742	445	60.0%
Traffic lights	719	660	91.8%
Trees	614	424	69.1%
Cars	304	195	64.1%
Dogs	292	42	14.4%
Manhole cover	192	162	84.4%
Snow clearance	173	123	71.1%
Leaves	166	97	58.4%
Graffiti	102	50	49.0%
Other	2291	1091	47.6%
Total	14,708	8309	56.5%

waste deposits, and broken streetlights. In total, about 57% of all reports are fixed. However, more than 90% of problems with traffic lights can be solved.

4 Mobile Government Use

To shed more light on the patterns of modern citizen-government communication, we aim to investigate citizens interacting with government via their mobile phones. Consequently, we conducted a survey among all registered users of the online reporting platform of the city of Linz. One year after the platform implementation, we invited the users to fill out an online questionnaire to get information on their usage behavior, their motivation to use online reporting, and their satisfaction with the channel. We received 424 questionnaires from citizens who communicate with government via mobile applications to report infrastructural defects.

In the following sections, we illustrate mobile government use by pointing to respondents' demographics, their reasons for communicating with local government via their mobile phones, and their activities in mobile government. Furthermore, we examine the influence of experience in communicating with local government via traditional channels such as face-to-face, telephone, or mail on their usage behaviors in mobile government. Finally, we address users' perception of mobile government.

Table 3 Characteristics of mobile government users

Age group	Total		Male		Female	
<20	21	5%	18	5.9%	3	2.8%
20–29	94	22.5%	59	19.4%	35	32.1%
30–39	108	26.1%	85	28%	23	21.1%
40–49	88	21.3%	59	19.4%	29	26.6%
50–59	54	13%	41	13.5%	13	11.9%
60–69	41	10.2%	35	11.5%	6	5.5%
70 and older	7	1.9%	7	2.3%	0	0%
Total	413	100%	304	100%	109	100%

4.1 Users of Mobile Government

As illustrated in Table 3, there is a great gender gap in mobile government usage. While more than 74% of those who contact the local government via mobile application are male, about 26% are female. As far as users' age is concerned, about half of respondents are between age 20 and 39. The majority of male users are aged between 30 and 39 and most female contributors are between 20 and 29. The findings further indicate that citizen participation is relatively low below age 20, particularly among women. However, almost one quarter of users are aged 50 and older. Whereas primarily men use the mobile application to interact with local government, the characteristics of mobile government users refer to great usage diversity across age groups.

4.2 Reasons for Participating in Mobile Government

In addition, mobile users were asked about their reasons for interacting with local government via the platform (see Fig. 3). More than 80% of respondents strongly agree that the ease of forwarding their concerns to local government is a reason for participating in digital communication. The great majority further aims at contributing to city improvement by pointing to defects and enjoys the direct exchange with local government. Respondents additionally use the platform due to communication and interaction with other platform users. The commenting feature allows users to add their opinion and discuss on reports.

4.3 Activity in Mobile Government

As shown in Table 4, mobile government users have three possibilities for being active on the platform: First, users can read reports and comments written by other citizens. The great majority of respondents state to always or often read through the contributions on the platform. Second, individuals are able to comment on their own or other users' reports. This platform activity is done less frequently by respondents.

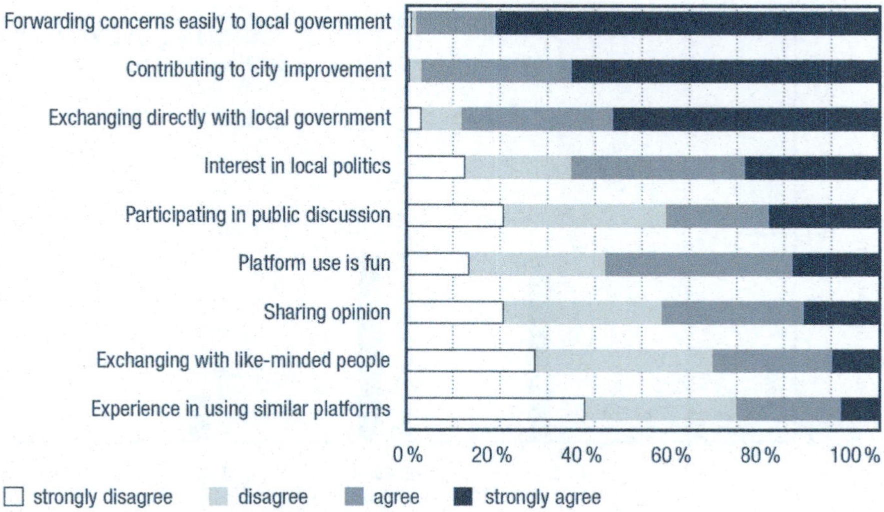

Fig. 3 Reasons for communicating with local government via mobile phone ($N = 404$–412)

Table 4 Activities in mobile government

Frequency	Reading through reports and comments		Commenting on reports		Writing reports	
Always	130	31.1%	0	0%	19	4.6%
Often	143	34.2%	8	2.0%	38	9.2%
Sometimes	74	17.7%	85	20.9%	165	40.1%
Rarely	53	12.7%	150	36.9%	151	36.7%
Never	18	4.3%	164	40.3%	38	9.2%
Total	418	100%	407	100%	411	100%

Third, after downloading the mobile application, citizens can write a report and inform local government about an infrastructural defect. About 14% always or often make a request when visiting the platform, 9% never write own reports. The findings indicate different usage behaviors of respondents. On the one hand, some follow the activities of other users by reading through reports and comments and show passive participation behavior. On the other hand, users proactively participate in mobile government by making requests or stimulate interaction between citizens by commenting on reports.

4.4 Reinforcement and Mobilization

In Fig. 4, we take a closer look at the reporting behavior of respondents and split the sample in two groups. The first group encompasses those individuals who have not contacted local government for pointing to defects before the implementation of

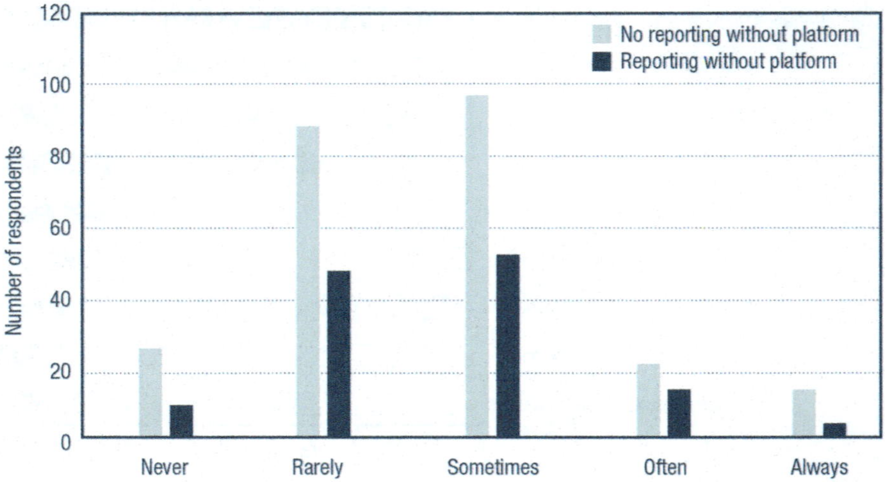

Fig. 4 Mobile government users with and without experience in communicating with local government ($N = 410$)

the platform. The second group includes respondents with experience in reporting via traditional channels such as face-to-face or phone. The figure illustrates the differences in frequency of reporting among the two groups, and shows that both groups share requests online. These results show that, first, the new channel for communicating with local government has attracted a new group of citizens. These individuals have not interacted with public employees in terms of infrastructural defects previously. However, the provision of a new digital channel activates them to contribute in terms of city improvement. Second, findings refer to a group of citizens who has already communicated with local government. These individuals have used traditional and offline channels for informing public employees about defects. The implementation of the platform has reinforced their participation in reporting defects, as they are also active online. Consequently, citizens with experience in reporting either changed the channel for interacting with local government or communicate via the platform in addition to traditional channels.

4.5 Mobile Government as Perceived by Users

Finally, mobile government users are asked about their satisfaction with the new communication channel. Figure 5 clearly shows that the broad majority of respondents perceive an improvement of citizen orientation of local government due to the possibility of interacting via the platform. Mobile government users are mainly satisfied with the reaction of public employees to citizens' reports: About 90% of respondents are pleased with the response time of local government. Between 80% and 90% of users agree that their concerns are taken seriously by public employees.

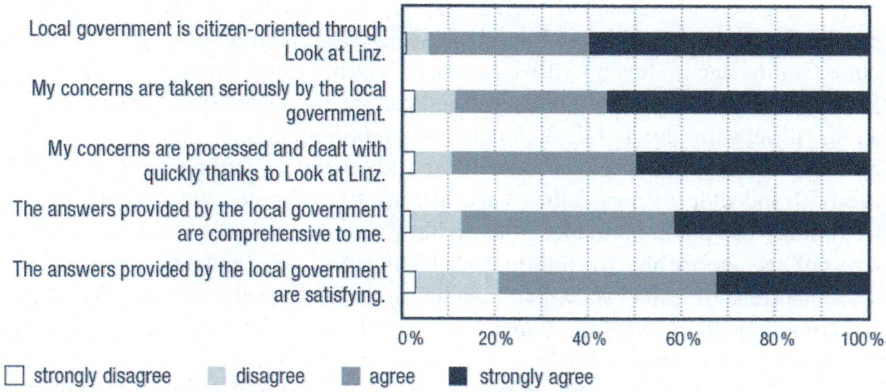

Fig. 5 Users' perception of mobile government ($N = 413–417$)

Public employees also comment to the citizens' reports and give information on the further processing of citizens' requests. This is particularly important when requests cannot be solved, for example, due to legal issues. Citizens state that these answers and comments made by public employees are mainly comprehensible and satisfying to them.

5 Discussion and Future Research

5.1 Discussion

In this chapter, we examined the evolution of a new government approach towards openness and investigated innovative forms of citizen-government interaction by leveraging modern technology. Advances in information and technology allow governmental organizations to provide an enhanced level of openness and access to government data and decision making processes. These new offerings for accessing government information and services are usually open to all citizens. To improve these open government initiatives and gear them to citizens' needs, we have to know more about their usage. As little research exists on citizens' usage of modern technology for citizen-government interaction, we took up this point. For illustrating the new and innovative mode of collaboration between citizens and government, we presented an example of a governmental-initiated and -led platform for communication between local government and citizens. Next to a web-browser, the platform can be accessed via mobile phone. In our exploratory study, we focused on mobile government users and investigated platform-based collaboration by studying users' characteristics, motivation to contribute, platform behavior, and perception of the new channel for communication.

The results of the survey conducted among mobile government users indicate a heterogeneous group of participants. Many studies on citizen participation via online channels discuss on a 'digital divide' by referring to the inequalities in providing access and using the Internet in society (Mossberger et al. 2007). Among other factors, age is shown to drive access to Internet and technology (Thomas and Steib 2003). Whereas our findings give indications for a gender gap, individuals of all age groups use the mobile application for reporting defects. The great majority of users are aged between 20 and 49 and about one quarter of respondents is aged 50 and older. Prior studies have already given some evidence that mobile technology has potential to close the digital divide (e.g., Wareham et al. 2004). In terms of age, we are able to confirm these results. As far as gender is concerned, this study and related results show that men are more likely to use mobile applications for communication, whereas female users prefer the web application (see also Schmidthuber and Hilgers 2017a).

The findings on users' motivation for communicating with local government via mobile phone demonstrate that citizens enjoy exchanging with local government in an easy and direct way while being able to improve the city. Although users are also pleased to share opinions and discuss with other users, interaction with local government comes first. The mobile application might be seen as a simple way to get in touch, as mobile phones are nearly always with the person and the provision of several wireless hot spots in the city and popular places faciliates using the mobile application. Leveraging mobile devices for interaction might also be relevant in other areas of administrative work. In accordance with Ntaliani et al. (2008)'s work in terms of agriculture, using mobile infrastructure is particularly suited for administrative activities, when

1. a large group of people should be reached (e.g., providing information to citizens via push messages),
2. information should be exchanged fast and real-time (e.g., due to emergency reasons),
3. location-based services should be provided (e.g., locating near public agency or location of infrastructural defect, fixmystreet.com),
4. administrative burden for public employees and citizens should be reduced (e.g., waiting times, paper), and
5. access should be provided with a low level of effort and thus for a heterogeneous group of people.

Furthermore, our study has shown that people who have previously not communicated with local government in terms of reporting defects participate in service improvement via the mobile application. Consequently, mobile technology gives government organizations the possibility to address groups of citizens who might not be mobilized by other channels. First, government organizations thus have to consider a multi-channel strategy when aiming for citizen participation and integration. Second, they should become aware of a new group of citizens and potential contributors. These individuals not previously engaged in administrative work might integrate new knowledge and ideas about how to improve public service quality.

Results on users' activities in mobile government indicate that respondents do not only visit the platform for making requests, they are also interested in other users' reports and comments. Furthermore, they participate in citizen-government interaction by making comments on reports. Whereas traditional and e-government channels provide one-way or dyadic communication, online platforms offer a new way of collaborating among a greater group of people. First, interaction between citizens and public employees is made transparent, everyone can read through the message exchange, the problem and reaction to local government. This open communication might stimulate other users' awareness of problems and their participation in reporting and commenting. Second, every user is allowed to actively participate in the discussion and add his/her knowledge or opinion on an issue. This possibility provides a new form of problem-solving mechanism, as more individuals are involved and can contribute to meet challenges and improve public services.

Finally, survey results suggest users' overall satisfaction with the platform and the processing of their requests. Prior research on citizen participation in open government highlights the importance of taking citizens' contributions seriously and giving reasons when a request or an idea cannot be considered by public organization (e.g., Wijnhoven et al. 2015). Public employees' feedback on the suggestion's processing cannot only influence citizens' continuous use of open government platforms, it could also have an effect on their perception of local government. Citizens' dissatisfaction with these new forms of services might then negatively influence their general satisfaction with and trust in the public sector and its institutions.

5.2 Limitations and Future Research

Of course, this study bears some limitations and raises questions calling for further research. First of all, we conducted an exploratory study, so that generalizability of our results is limited. We need more empirical examinations of open government use to make general conclusions about citizens' adoption of modern technology and their contribution behaviors. Second, in this study, we asked registered users of the platform about their motivation to communicate via mobile application with local government. For expanding our knowledge about citizen-government interactions, we should examine why citizens do not use modern technology for communicating with local government. These findings might be particularly interesting to learn about possible usage barriers and opportunities to facilitate access to a greater group of individuals.

In addition to stimulate research on citizens' use of modern technology and willingness to exchange with administration, we want to recommend future researchers focusing on public employees' role in terms of open government. By leveraging modern technology, an increased number of citizens has the possibility to communicate with local government. Studies could examine public agencies' benefits and costs of this new form of citizen integration. Next to public employees' attitudes toward utilizing new technology to exchange with citizens, research could investigate the outcomes of citizens' input in terms of financial and innovation performance of local government. First, it should be evaluated if the administrative burden for handling external input outweighs cost efficiency due to collaboration with externals. Second, the integration of citizens' experiences, ideas, and knowledge might positively influence public service quality and provide more innovative services. In addition, we need further evidence on citizens' perception of opening-up governmental structures and the influence on their attitudes towards the public sector (see e.g., Buell and Norton 2013; Grimmelikhuijsen and Meijer 2014; Grimmelikhuijsen 2012).

6 Conclusion

Digitalization and technological advances create new possibilities for government organizations to provide access to administrative activities and organize public service delivery. Beyond dyadic transactions between citizens and government, social media, online platforms, and mobile applications enable collaboration among a heterogeneous group of individuals. In this study, we concentrated on the role of citizens in open government and investigated their usage of mobile technology for citizen-government communication. The results offer insights into users' motivation, their participation behavior, and perception of mobile government. While the findings of our study improve the understanding of citizens' usage of open government offerings, they also reveal interesting and promising questions for future research.

Acknowledgments The authors thank Stefan Etzelstorfer (City Administration of Linz) and Thomas Gegenhuber (Johannes Kepler University Linz) for the support providing the data.

References

Aucoin P (1990) Administrative reform in public management. Paradigms, principles, paradoxes and pendulums. Governance 3(2):115–137

Bertot JC et al (2010) Using ICTs to create a culture of transparency: E-government and social media as openness and anti-corruption tools for societies. Gov Inf Q 27(3):264–271

Buell RW, Norton MI (2013) Surfacing the submerged state with operational transparency in government services. Harvard Business School Marketing Unit Working Paper, 14-034, pp 1–23

Cabannes Y (2004) Participatory budgeting. A significant contribution to participatory democracy. Environ Urban 16(1):27–46

Dunleavy P, Hood C (1994) From old public administration to new public management. Public Money Manage 14(3):9–16

Evans A, Campos A (2013) Open government initiatives. Challenges of citizen participation. J Policy Anal Manage 32(1):172–203

Gavelin K et al (2009) Open government. Beyond static measures. http://www.oecd.org/gov/46560184.pdf. Accessed 24 Jul 2017

Grimmelikhuijsen SG (2012) Linking transparency, knowledge and citizen trust in government. An experiment. Int Rev Adm Sci 78(1):50–73

Grimmelikhuijsen SG, Meijer AJ (2014) Effects of transparency on the perceived trustworthiness of a government organization. Evidence from an online experiment. J Public Adm Res Theory 24(1):137–157

Hansson K et al (2015) Open government and democracy: a research review. Soc Sci Comput Rev 33(5):540–555

Helbig N et al (2009) Understanding the complexity of electronic government. Implications from the digital divide literature. Gov Inf Q 26(1):89–97

Hilgers D (2012) Open government. Theoretische Bezüge und konzeptionelle Grundlagen einer neuen Entwicklung in Staat und öffentlichen Verwaltungen. Zeitschrift für Betriebswirtschaft 82(6):631–660

Hilgers D, Ihl C (2010) Citizensourcing. Applying the concept of open innovation to the public sector. Int J Public Particip 4(1):67–88

Hood C (1991) A public management for all seasons. Public Adm 69(1):3–19

Jaeger PT, Bertot JC (2010) Transparency and technological change. Ensuring equal and sustained public access to government information. Gov Inf Q 27(4):371–376

Layne K, Lee J (2001) Developing fully functional E-government. A four stage model. Gov Inf Q 18(2):122–136

Lee G, Kwak YH (2012) An open government maturity model for social media-based public engagement. Gov Inf Q 29(4):492–503

Lee H et al (2008) Research note: toward a reference process model for citizen-oriented evaluation of e-government services. Transf Gov People Process Policy 2(4):297–310

Linders D (2012) From e-government to we-government. Defining a typology for citizen coproduction in the age of social media. Gov Inf Q 29(4):446–454

Local Government of Linz (2016) Media service. http://www.linz.at/images/Bilanz-Beschwerdemanagement_2015.pdf. Accessed 15 Sept 2016

Local Government of Linz (2017) Statistics. http://schau.auf.linz.at/statistik/index.html?kategorie=-1&status=-1&stadtteil=-1&tage=31&norestriction=true. Accessed 17 Jan 2017

Meijer AJ et al (2012) Open government. Connecting vision and voice. Int Rev Adm Sci 78(1):10–29

Mergel I (2015) Open collaboration in the public sector. The case of social coding on GitHub. Gov Inf Q 32(4):464–472

Moon MJ (2002) The evolution of e-government among municipalities. Rhetoric or reality? Public Adm Rev 62(4):424–433

Mossberger K et al (2007) Digital citizenship. The Internet, society, and participation. MIT Press, Cambridge

Nam T (2012) Suggesting frameworks of citizen-sourcing via Government 2.0. Gov Inf Q 29(1):12–20

Norris DF et al (2001) Is your local government plugged in? Highlights of the 2000 electronic government survey. International City/County Management Association, Washington

Ntaliani M et al (2008) Mobile government. A challenge for agriculture. Gov Inf Q 25(4):699–716

Osborne D, Gaebler T (1992) Reinventing government. How the entrepreneurial spirit is transforming the public sector. Addison-Wesley, New York

Pollitt C, Bouckaert G (2004) Public management reform, 2nd edn. Oxford University Press, Oxford

Schmidthuber L, Hilgers D (2015) Open government in Österreich. Neue Wege zu kooperativen Verwaltungsinnovationen. Das öffentliche Haushaltswesen in Österreich (3/4):33–48

Schmidthuber L, Hilgers D (2017a) Browse or brush? An exploration of citizens' interaction with their local government. In: Proceedings of the 50th Hawaii international conference on system sciences. http://hdl.handle.net/10125/41449. Accessed 8 Jul 2017

Schmidthuber L, Hilgers D (2017b) Unleashing innovation beyond organizational boundaries. Exploring citizensourcing projects. Int J Public Adm. https://doi.org/10.1080/01900692.2016.1263656. Accessed 8 Jul 2017

Schmidthuber L et al (2017a) Shedding light on participation in open government arenas: determinants of platform activity of web and app users. In: Proceedings of the 50th Hawaii international conference on system sciences. http://hdl.handle.net/10125/41489. Accessed 8 Jul 2017

Schmidthuber L et al (2017b) The emergence of local open government: determinants of citizen participation in online service reporting. Gov Inf Q 34(3):457–469

Sintomer Y et al (2008) Participatory budgeting in Europe. Potentials and challenges. Int J Urban Reg Res 32(1):164–178

Thomas JC, Steib G (2003) The new face of government: citizen-initiated contacts in the era of e-government. J Public Adm Res Theory 13(1):83–102

Trimi S, Sheng H (2008) Emerging trends in M-government. Commun ACM 51(5):53–58

Wareham J et al (2004) Wireless diffusion and mobile computing. Implications for the digital divide. Telecommun Policy 28(5):439–457

West DM (2004) E-government and the transformation of service delivery and citizen attitudes. Public Adm Rev 64(1):15–27

Wijnhoven F et al (2015) Open government objectives and participation motivations. Gov Inf Q 32(1):30–42

Wirtz BW, Birkmeyer S (2015) Open government. Origin, development, and conceptual perspectives. Int J Public Adm 38(5):381–396

Dennis Hilgers is a German Professor of Public and Nonprofit Management at Johannes Kepler University Linz in Austria. Beforehand he worked as Assistant Professor of Public Management at the University of Hamburg and as a post-doc researcher at the Technology and Innovation Management Group at RWTH Aachen University. His research focuses on managing innovation and performance in public administrations. One of the phenomena of his particular interest is open government, the application of open innovation methods for innovation of services and offerings in the public sector. He has been a coordinator of several large-scale project consortia in this field, funded by the European Union and the German Academy of Sciences.

Lisa Schmidthuber is a doctoral researcher at the Institute for Public and Nonprofit Management at Johannes Kepler University Linz. Her research focuses on innovation management in the public and private sector. She investigates the use of modern technology such as online platforms, mobile applications, and social media and the emergence of new possibilities for organizations to integrate externals like citizens or customers in value creation. She applies quantitative research methods to study the role of citizens, customers, and employees in the innovation process. She graduated from Johannes Kepler University with a Master in Social Economics and a Joint Master in Social Sciences.

Building the Smart City: Leipzig

Tanja Korzer, Beate Ginzel, and Nadja Riedel

Abstract

Leipzig is one of the most dynamic cities in Eastern Germany, with approximately 580,000 inhabitants. After years of population decline and above-average unemployment rates, Leipzig has started to regain popularity in recent years. The number of inhabitants is continuously increasing. Population forecasts anticipate up to 720,000 inhabitants by the year 2030. Leipzig's economy is successfully turning from a post-industrial to a modern, knowledge-based structure.

In 2015, the city joined the HORIZON 2020 Smart city and communities project TRIANGULUM (www.triangulum-project.eu) as a Follower City. This was the starting point for a Smart City strategy for the City of Leipzig. The municipality is developing a Smart City implementation strategy by means of a broad participation process, involving the municipal utilities, the scientific institutions and the civil society. The case study is Leipzig West, a former industrialized area which has been turned into a lively and attractive neighborhood in recent years. The area has been one of the main focus areas for urban regeneration processes during its years of decline and high vacancy rates. With the help of national and EU subsidies the district became a role model for similar neighborhoods in Leipzig. Now, it will take on this role once again as it becomes the first district in Leipzig to develop a Smart City strategy.

T. Korzer (✉)
Institute of Urban Development and Construction Management (ISB), Leipzig University, Leipzig, Germany
e-mail: korzer@wifa.uni-leipzig.de

B. Ginzel • N. Riedel
Department of Urban Renewal Leipzig West, Office for Urban Regeneration and Housing Subsidies, Leipzig, Germany
e-mail: beate.ginzel@leipzig.de

H. Albach et al. (eds.), *European Cities in Dynamic Competition*,
https://doi.org/10.1007/978-3-662-56419-6_5

This article summarizes the current project activities. Special focus will be put on the governance structures that have been established and the co-creation processes between different stakeholders for the elaboration of the Smart City implementation strategy for Leipzig West.

1 Smart City: State of Research

The City of Leipzig is currently a project partner of the HORIZON 2020 Smart cities and communities project TRIANGULUM. Within the project the city started a participation process involving the municipality, the public utilities, scientific institutions as well as the civil society. For the coordination and scientific supervision of this process the Kompetenzzentrum für Öffentliche Wirtschaft, Infrastruktur und Daseinsvorsorge e.V. (Competence Center for Public Economy, Infrastructure and Public Services) of Leipzig University was engaged contractually.

1.1 Definitions and Elements of a Smart City[1]

The Smart City concept was developed in the 1990s in an attempt to highlight the new role that information and communication technologies (ICT) were starting to play within urban systems. This approach focused on developing supply and traffic facilities as well as communication and social infrastructures. The aim was to improve urban performance.

This former technology-based approach soon evolved into an integrated understanding of Smart Cities. In this context, the integration of urban sub-systems and its areas of application is as important as the inclusion of relevant systems and topics. Apart from that, sustainable urban development has gained an increasing importance. Smart urban networks must not only respond to current issues. Above all, they must be capable of reacting dynamically when it comes to coping with new challenges (Kaczorowski 2015). Smart City definitions focus on topics such as the sustainable input of resources, competitiveness, quality of life and participation of protagonists (Caragliu et al. 2011; Jaekel 2015; Portmann and Finger 2015). The current draft of a German Smart City Charter includes these definitions, addressing smart and sustainable urban development (BBSR 2017). In practice, Smart City projects intend to benefit from the opportunities and potentials that are seen between urban structures, sub-systems and key players. In this respect, applying new technologies is only a secondary goal. Apart from that, strengthening the urban competences of the key players is another important objective (Laimer 2014). Hence, citizens are to be more directly integrated into urban society (Beinrott 2015). The following objectives are addressed:

[1]The following chapter is partly based on the interim report of the Competence Center compiled by Stefan Geyler et al. (2016).

- creation of values by considering interfaces and their integration into the urban system **(strategic networking)**,
- supply of high-level infrastructural services at a sustainable cost level,
- increase of energy and resource efficiency in processes and buildings,
- promoting economic competitiveness and the creation of new economic business areas,
- increase of quality of life (incl. environmental protection)
- broad public participation and new forms of **governance**

The spectrum of pursued objectives delivers insight into the fields of action in the projects. Based on the analysis of primary and secondary data of 17 Smart City concepts, 19 areas of application can be identified (Geyler et al. 2016). Some of the most striking ones are presented below:

Energy and Environment belongs to the most important components within these concepts. This is strongly connected with the promotion of resource and energy efficiency and urban restructuring processes due to sustainability goals. The analysis reveals, that this module is explicitly specified in the majority of cases.

Most of the concepts consider **mobility** to be an autonomous area. Only Riemann and Leidel (2013) and Röding (2015) assign it to the field of infrastructure. Especially when it comes to e-mobility, a strong reference to the issue of energy can be identified in some case studies. Apart from that, transport also seems to be a relevant interface. Mobility is not only connected with the distance between A and B. It also implies new mobility needs due to changing forms of living, working and managing. In this respect, mobility is seen to be self-sufficient in the sense of representing an individual choice in the mode of transport which is available at any given time. Therefore, mobility need not be provided only by public authorities. New forms of mobility, such as sharing concepts, are addressed. Moreover, this area deals with technical problems such as the reduction of queue times and the synchronization of traffic flows and street lighting. This also contains the application of sensors integrated within modern networks, managing machine to machine communication (M2M).

Information and communication is regarded as a key area. As is commonly recognized, technical components of Smart City processes imply up-to-date ICTs. Keywords, e.g. digitalization, big data, cloud systems and the internet of things, are currently being discussed. Apart from the provision of broadband, topics such as information retrieval, conversion and real-time application are important. The underlying goal is the synchronization of technical systems as well as supply and demand, depending on individual performances.

Governance is the fourth module that is considered in nearly every one of the analyzed concepts. On the one hand, this is necessary since Smart City concepts cannot be realized without the local authority's support. On the other hand, outside of Smart City debates, administrations need to be modernized as a consequence of changing social, demographic and structural frameworks (Geyler et al. 2016).

1.2 Protagonists

The objectives and areas of application shown above illustrate the large number of participants involved. For the sustainable success of Smart Cities, it is of crucial importance that key players continue participating even after having completed conceptual processes. The following groups of players are identified:

- politicians (at least on a municipal and regional level),
- administration (including all functional departments),
- science, research and education,
- citizens—particularly private households,
- enterprises and economy (infrastructure providers and public-sector operations),
- credit services and financial institutions,
- private and public special interest/lobby groups (foundations, associations, unions etc.) and
- the media.

Smart City concepts have to be initiated by local authorities. Hence, mayors play a fundamental role. The transformation of a Smart City requires political attention. On the one hand, the development of visions, strategies and measures has to be managed. On the other hand, applying technical solutions and optimizing processes alone is not sufficient from an economic point of view (Kaczorowski 2015). And in terms of an integrated and cross-departmental approach, all administrative parts have to be involved. Technical innovations in cooperation with the economy are to be developed by science and research. For that reason, an exchange with practice partners is absolutely essential. This is particularly the case when it comes to user-friendliness, practice orientation, but also public acceptance. In order to be accepted, novel applications and technologies necessitate an appropriate level of knowledge. Thus, educational institutions can be regarded as significant participants. This is especially the case in the context of knowledge societies. The importance of civic participation and lobby groups is self-evident. Without user acceptance, such projects will not achieve the required effects (Mandl and Schaner 2012). The economy and enterprises take over manifold tasks and are situated between various players. Firstly, they are the developer of technologies. Secondly, enterprises assume the role of infrastructural providers that are to be linked and adapted. Likewise, they take efficiency into account. Furthermore, the economy takes over responsibility for the adoption of services for the public. Contrary to that, the credit services and financial institutions are supposed to fund innovations and new business areas. In this respect, new forms of funding for small and medium-sized enterprises (SMEs), start-ups and micro-ventures are identified as the key to new business areas and local economies. Moreover, the role of the media is not to be underestimated, since processes and strategies are highly dependent on broad discussions. Therefore, the relevant participants have to be addressed. Numerous case studies reveal that acceptance and participation fail due to a lack of cross-channel communication. If

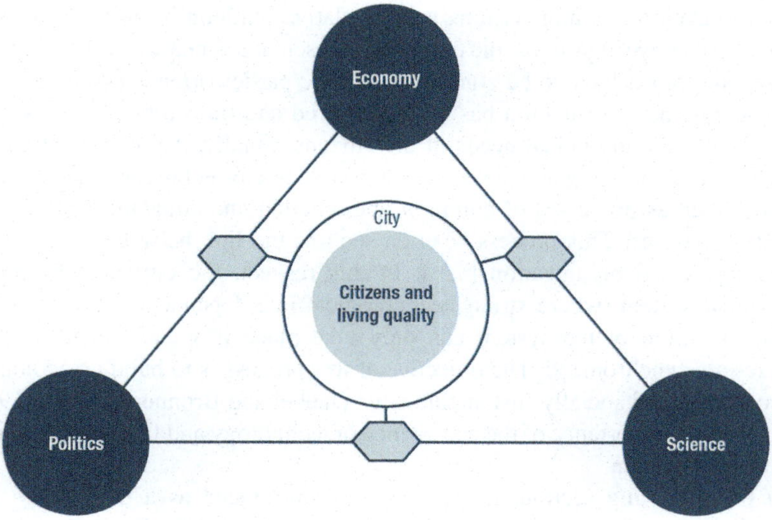

Fig. 1 Conceptual structure of the Smart City [based on Jaekel and Bronnert (2013)]

all key players are to be involved, the model presented in Fig. 1 has to be considered. Citizens and administrations are located in the center of Smart Cities. Apart from that, players with differing backgrounds are also able to lay the foundation for Smart City processes. Special attention should be paid to user's needs, in order to generate sustainable and long-term structures. "The core of the model consisting of citizen and administration is linked to other key players in the fields of the economy, politics and science via informational structures [. . .]. The platform itself is what can be described conceptually as Smart City" (Jaekel and Bronnert 2013, p. 17).

In order to put the developed strategy into practice by including the relevant key players, further requirements need to be met. Based on the analysis of 20 expert interviews, MANDL and SCHANER highlight the importance of technical, social and socio-technological conditions. *Technical prerequisites* are seen in "[. . .] the system integration via ICT and the creation of networks, e.g. between traffic, energy, supply and disposal in urban planning [. . .]. Basic technologies are area-wide broadband communication, a smart energy distribution grid, modern sensor networks [. . .] and a City Data Cloud as high-efficiency IT-structure which includes public, private and urban information [. . .]" (Jaekel and Bronnert 2013, p. 192). In this context, the authors emphasize that, first of all, Smart City concepts are a matter of social acceptance. Technology plays a minor role. In many cases, the technologies required are already provided—they just have to be completed or linked. Since the transformation of cities to Smart Cities implies a process of social change, some *social conditions* need to be met as well. "The main goal is an informed and smart public (Smart Citizens) that is prepared to take over (ecological) responsibility and shape the city in the function of its needs" (Jaekel and Bronnert 2013, p. 193). This requires change processes, sensitization and the willingness of decision-makers. In order to develop common visions and regulative guidelines, an interdisciplinary cooperation between politics, the economy and science is necessary. In this context, social frameworks have to be considered. Public participation is essential. Against that background, information has to be prepared and transmitted in a way which is adapted to the individual needs of the citizens. Finally, the identification of the citizens with their living area has to be supported. Socio-technological requirements are described as processes of common optimization and adjustment of social and technical systems. This process "can be seen as the link between human beings, technologies and organization [...]. In this respect, the city may be regarded as a social system, where strong technological interdependences are recognized. An optimization of the system can only take place if social and technological changes are synchronized. The objective of this process is to build an ecologically, economically and socially sustainable city" (Jaekel and Bronnert 2013, p. 194). At this point, the importance of the acceptance of technology and funding measures are revealed once again.

In the following section, Leipzig will be introduced as a case study. Based on analytical results, the city's process towards smart urban development will be presented.

2 Leipzig: A Dynamic Growing City in Central Germany

2.1 Current Developments

Leipzig is one of the most dynamic cities in Eastern Germany with approximately 580,000 inhabitants. After years of population decline and an above-average unemployment rate, Leipzig started to regain popularity in recent years. The number of inhabitants has continued to increase. Population forecasts anticipate up to 720,000 inhabitants by the year 2030. Thus, the reaction to the city's fast-growing population is one of the biggest challenges in Leipzig in regard to the provision of affordable housing, energy consumption, waste management and sustainable mobility. Smart and integrated solutions are crucial in facing the challenges of a growing city.

Leipzig's economy is successfully turning from a post-industrial to a modern, knowledge-based economy. The city's economic strategy focuses on five clusters: automotive and its related supply chain, healthcare and biotech, energy and environment, logistics and services, and media and creativity. SMEs form the backbone of the local economy. About two thirds of all employees work for firms with a workforce of less than 250. SMEs, as well as the new industrial locations of large companies of the automotive industry (Porsche, BMW) and logistics (DHL, Amazon) contributed to the employment increases of the past few years. Yet the unemployment rate still hovers at approximately eight percent (Bundesagentur für Arbeit 2017) and there is still a need to support and attract further SMEs, particularly in the inner-city areas. Leipzig has extensive experience in using EU and national funding for urban regeneration projects. Starting with the URBAN initiative and now the ERDF/ESF in combination with national subsidy programs are used for the regeneration of different districts. Investments in public spaces and institutions were made, but also projects with citizens' involvement and citizens' funds were initiated, as Leipzig has a long tradition of strong civil engagement. Therefore, including citizens and civil initiatives in urban regeneration processes has, up to this point, been one of the key success factors for Leipzig's positive development. This tradition shall therefore be continued in the development and implementation of Smart City strategies and projects.

2.2 Leipzig: Existing Urban Development and Smart City Strategies and Projects

The City of Leipzig has extensive experience in strategic urban development processes. The following chapters illustrate the existing urban strategies and concepts which are the basis for developing a Smart City strategy.

2.2.1 Integrated Urban Development Concept (INSEK) Leipzig 2030

In 2009, the city of Leipzig endorsed the Integrated Urban Development Concept "SEKo Leipzig 2020". The concept was elaborated on in a cooperative process in the years 2007/08. Not just members from very different departments of the city administration were involved. The civil society, scientific institutions and the local economy were also included in this process. The final concept contained 11 thematic concepts (e.g. for housing, energy and climate protection, social issues, the economy and employment) and highlighted specific focus areas for urban development and worked as a guideline for strategies and actions of the municipality.

The framework conditions in the city have changed rapidly since the enactment of the "SEKo Leipzig 2020" especially related to population development. In 2015, it was decided to revise the concept. The revision process included a broad public participation process and will be finalized by the end of 2017. By then, the INSEK Leipzig 2030 will function as a future strategy for the further development of the City of Leipzig. Aspects like digitization and other Smart City issues will also be included in the concept. It should be regarded as the result of the ongoing Smart City participation process in Leipzig, which is described later in this article.

2.2.2 Existing Smart City Strategies and Measures

Although the City of Leipzig has not yet endorsed an overall Smart City strategy for the whole city, several strategies and concepts tackling different Smart City innovation fields are already in place. Especially in the areas of climate protection and energy issues, the city has developed different concepts and strategies, e.g.:

- Participation of the City of Leipzig in the European Energy Award (2009),
- Adoption of the energy and climate protection program 2014–2020 (2014),
- Implementing the sectoral concept of energy and climate protection as part of the integrated urban development process (2015).

Apart from that, the measure and implementation concept "Leipzig—Stadt für intelligente Mobilität" (Leipzig—City of Intelligent Mobility) was developed in 2016/2017. Currently, the municipality is working on its own digitization and open data strategy.

Moreover, local public utility companies responsible for public transport, energy, heat and water supply, etc., have endorsed their Smart City concept called leipzig.leben.morgen. (leipzig.living.tomorrow.). The concept also includes various measures for the efficient use of resources with the help of innovative technologies and the possibilities of digitization.

2.3 Projects of the Smart City Leipzig

2.3.1 HORIZON 2020 Smart Cities and Communities Project TRIANGULUM

Since 2015, the City of Leipzig is a partner in the HORIZON 2020 Smart cities and communities project TRIANGULUM. The project is one of only three projects which were chosen for implementation within the first call of the funding program. In the framework of the project, as with the Czech capital Prague and the Spanish city of Sabadell, Leipzig assumes the role of a so-called "Follower-City". The Follower-Cities aim at developing individual Smart City strategies and encouraging the implementation of Smart City projects within the city. Therefore, the cities are linked with so-called "Lighthouse-Cities" which have already endorsed Smart City strategies for parts of or the whole city and implement concrete measures within TRIANGULUM. For TRIANGULUM, Eindhoven (NL), Manchester (UK) and Stavanger (N) were chosen as Lighthouse Cities. Those cities are developing and implementing strategies and measures in the fields of smart building, e-mobility and (renewable) energy as well as ICT. In total, the consortium consists of 22 project partners and is supported by 25 million EUR from the European Union.

For Leipzig, participation in the TRIANGULUM project offers the opportunity to develop a Smart City implementation strategy for the district of Leipzig West which reflects the specific framework conditions of the city and the district. The strategy will reflect the locally required actions with a special focus on urban infrastructure. Already existing strategies, subsidy concepts and measures on the district as well as the city level are included. First conclusions and recommendations of the elaboration process are included in the update of the Integrated Urban Development Concept (LEIPZIG 2030).

Within the TRIANGULUM project, the City of Leipzig pursues the following objectives:

1. aggregation of existing strategic plans and concepts, identifying relevant innovation fields and synergies or interfaces.
2. definition of local pilot projects for the development of a Smart City district Leipzig West through the involvement of relevant stakeholders.
3. specify pilot projects (financing, funding opportunities, relevant stakeholders) and initiate their implementation

In preparation for the "Smart City Implementation Strategy", research work on existing and relevant strategic plans and ongoing projects was carried out. In parallel, important representatives of science, politics, city administration and local enterprises have been identified and informed in order to support the development of the implementation plan.

2.3.2 Smart City Test Lab Leipzig West

In Leipzig, the activities within the TRIANGULUM project focus on the district of Leipzig West with a special focus on the premises of the Baumwollspinnerei (BWS, former cotton mill). The focal district Leipzig West includes the statistical districts of Lindenau, Neu- und Altlindenau, Schleußig, Plagwitz, Leutzsch and Kleinzschocher which form the historic part of Leipzig West. The area is dominated mainly by buildings from the Wilhelminian era and used to be one of Leipzig's most industrialized neighborhoods. After 1989, many industrial sites fell derelict and the vacancy rate of the housing stock rose. Leipzig West has therefore been one of the focus areas of urban regeneration with support from different EU and national funding programs. After years of decline the district is now one of the fastest growing areas in Leipzig (currently 78,000; 2030: 95,000 inhabitants), it is a "cultural and creative district" within the city and home of many innovative small businesses and start-ups. Today, the Karl Heine Canal, various attractive open spaces and a heterogeneous building stock contribute to Leipzig West's image as a vibrant housing area. Although several of the former industrial sites, such as the Baumwollspinnerei, Tapeten- or Westwerk have been in use again, mostly by cultural and creative industries or have been turned into housing (e.g. Buntgarnwerke, Globus-Werke), there are still derelict or under-used sites waiting for commercial or residential development.

In the past few years, being a home to start-ups and SMEs in the cultural field, Leipzig West has cultivated a supporting structure for innovation and development varying from business accelerators such as SpinLab, Social Impact Lab and the Business Innovation Center to co-working spaces. Multiple local subsidy programs of the city's economic development department aim at supporting innovation and promoting cooperation between different branches and enterprises. Especially the premises of the so-called Baumwollspinnerei (est. 1884, formerly one of the largest cotton-mills in Europe) has undergone an exemplary development from "cotton to culture". After the collapse of production following the change in 1989, most of the brick buildings (area of six hectares) fell derelict. In the early 1990s, a transformation process started and the premises became home to new users e.g. artists and galleries. Today, about 1000 people are working there and about 200,000 visitors come to the BWS every year. As the area faced the typical problems of deindustrialization, it has become a role model for other cities (see also INTERREG project SECOND CHANCE). Due to the existing structures, the past and on-going developments (e.g. the new Natural History museum will be located there as well as the establishment of a so-called Digital Hub in one of the buildings) the area will be one focal point for Smart City developments within Leipzig West (see also Sect. 3.3.3).

Implementing smart city solutions within a compact, partly historic and dense neighborhood presents different challenges. Framework conditions like protection of cultural heritage buildings, very heterogeneous ownership structures and a socially mixed population increase the challenges of Leipzig West to become an energy efficient and smart district. As large-scale interventions are often not possible it's the implementation and integration of small-scale measures that will help the area to face the challenges of a growing city, e.g. energy efficiency and climate protection, adaptation of traffic and innovation as an enabler for co-creation processes.

3 The Leipzig Smart City Approach and Participation Process

3.1 Smart City Working Structures Within the Municipality

The Office for Urban Regeneration and Housing Construction Subsidies (ASW) of the City of Leipzig is the main local project partner for the TRIANGULUM project. Through the project funding, the costs of a Smart City coordination unit responsible for the participation process as well as the development of the Smart City implementation strategy, etc. within the ASW are covered. Apart from that, there are no financial resources available for implementing Smart City projects. The coordination unit is in active exchange with other offices and departments within the municipality regarding Smart City topics (e.g. joint initiatives, prospective funding proposals). In addition to that, it works as a contact point for the public utility companies and their Smart City activities. Furthermore, the ASW represents the City of Leipzig in various Smart City initiatives on a national level. One is the so-called "Dialogplattform Smart Cities" (Dialogue Platform Smart Cities) initiated by the Federal Ministry for the Environment, Nature Conservation, Building and Nuclear Safety. In an extensive participation process (called "Dialogplattform Smart City"), representatives of different German cities, ministries, scientific institutions, NGOs and industry representatives developed the Smart City Charter Germany in 2016 and 2017 which was officially endorsed in June 2017.

The Smart City coordination unit at ASW is also responsible for the knowledge exchange with the international partners within the TRIANGULUM project.

3.2 Participation Process

Before the TRIANGULUM project, discussions on Smart City issues within the municipality mostly took place separately within the different departments and offices concerned, usually without involving other relevant stakeholders like the public utility companies, scientific institutions and the civil society. Therefore, a wide participation process on the Smart City topic, including different kinds of formats for involving various stakeholders, was initiated within the TRIANGULUM project. In general, the participation process uses top-down and bottom-up approaches to involve different stakeholder levels but also to represent the Smart City topic within the Leipzig West district (Fig. 2).

In order to accompany the participation process and to secure the exchange within the different formats the Competence Center for the public economy, the infrastructure and public services of Leipzig University were involved in the process.

The objectives of this participation process structure are:

- to involve a wide scope of Smart City stakeholders within the city,
- to discuss and develop a joint understanding and strategic approach for Smart City issues for Leipzig and conclude innovation fields that need to be addressed to become a Smart City,

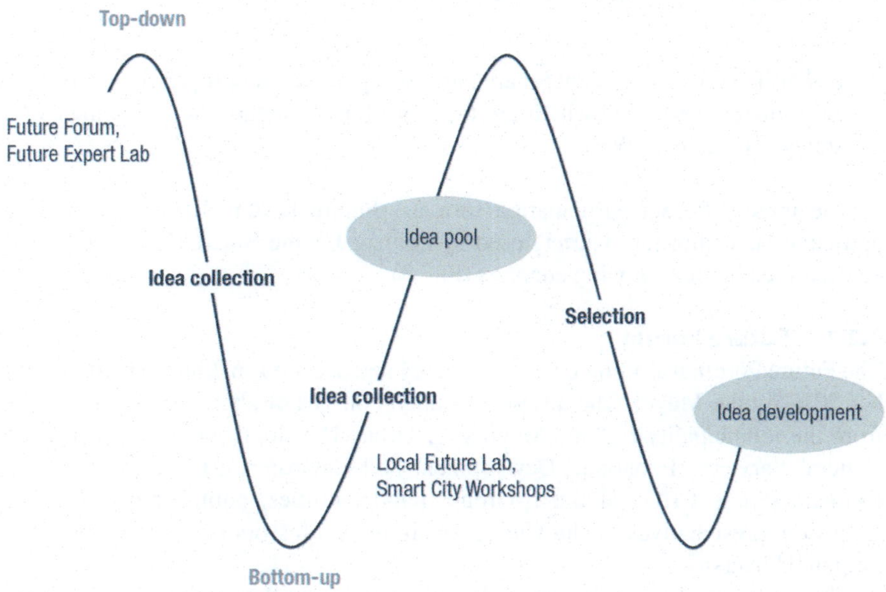

Fig. 2 Counter-current principle of participation

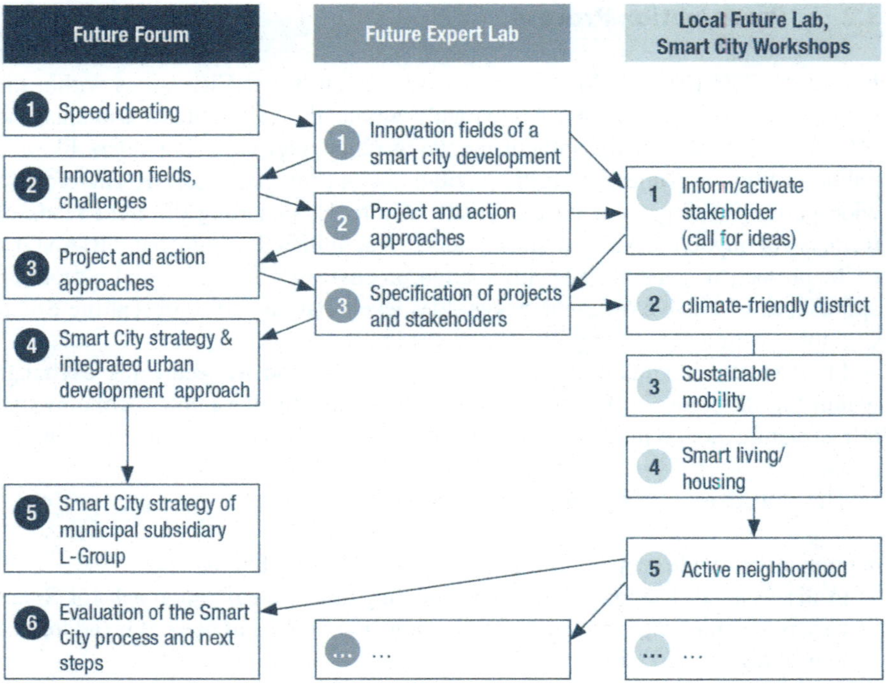

Fig. 3 Exchange between the different participation formats

- to identify and develop joint Smart City concepts and pilot projects on a city-wide and Leipzig West level which are the basis for the Smart City implementation strategy for Leipzig West.

The three different participation formats (Future Forum, Future Expert Lab, participation within the district) used in Leipzig for the Smart City process will be described in the following chapters (Fig. 3).

3.2.1 Future Forum

The Future Forum was initiated as an advisory and decision-making council in October 2015 by the Mayor. The advisory council consists of about 20 representatives from the municipality (i.e. the Mayors for Urban Development and Construction, General Services, Economic Development and Environment), the public utility companies (e.g. CEOs of the L-Group: public utilities, public transport, water supply), representatives of the City Council and professors of related subjects at Leipzig University.

The main objective of the Future Forum is to secure the (knowledge) exchange between the municipality and its public utility companies and to set the framework for joint Smart City strategies and projects. The Future Forum meets every three to four months. By April 2017, six meetings of the Forum had taken place. The topics of the meetings ranged from developing a joint Smart City understanding and common innovation fields, the introduction of the Smart City strategy *leipzig.leben.morgen.* of the public utility companies and the development of joint funding proposals. The Future Forum was also linked to the revision process of the INSEK Leipzig 2030 (see Sect. 2.2.1), i.e. to the workshop "Leipzig is growing sustainably—the digital city" in November 2016. In this workshop, approximately 50 participants from diverse backgrounds (civil society, science, the economy, city administration as well as other municipalities) discussed the opportunities and challenges of a "Digital City".

In the meeting of the Future Forum in March 2017, an evaluation of the progress of the Forum was discussed with its members. The participants concluded that, after working on a joint definition for Smart City Leipzig and more strategic aspects, the focus should be shifted toward concrete innovation fields and joint projects. Therefore, the format of the Future Forum will be adapted slightly in order to guarantee knowledge exchanges with the Future Labs and other participation formats.

3.2.2 Future Expert Labs

In addition to the "strategic" Future Forum, the "operative" Future Expert Labs were initiated in October 2015 to represent the working level of the different city departments involved, the public utility companies and representatives of the test lab Leipzig West.

Different workshops were held in which six thematic working groups (Energy, Housing, Water/Sewage/Waste, Businesses/Economy/Broadband, Mobility and Governance) each of which included about ten to twelve interdisciplinary experts discussing Smart City issues. As in the Future Forum, the first task was to develop a common Smart City understanding and identify relevant innovation fields. Furthermore, the working groups defined the challenges and opportunities of Leipzig West to become a smart district, developed initial project ideas for the district and identified synergies/interfaces between the different innovation fields. The Future Forum as well as the Future Labs have progressed during their various meetings. Some of the project ideas developed were evaluated as not applicable for implementation; others were discussed more in detail and led to funding proposals. To ensure the interlink to the Future Forum the setup of the Future Expert Labs will also be adapted slightly in the future as well.

3.2.3 Participation Process in the District

In 2016, the participation and communication process within the test lab Leipzig West was intensified. The objective is to involve the relevant local stakeholders, disseminate information on and explain Smart City developments and discuss possible pilot projects for the district. To kick it off, a Local Future Lab together with the Future Expert Lab took place in February 2016. About 70 interested citizens, businesses and local initiatives seized the opportunity to get to know the current Smart City developments in Leipzig West and discuss with experts their own project ideas for a smart district.

After this kick-off meeting a call for ideas was launched in March 2016. The objective was to elicit ideas for smart projects from the people directly affected by Smart City measures in the district. About 30 different project ideas coming from the different innovation fields (energy, housing, civil society) were submitted. Some of them were discussed and included in possible funding proposals, others will be incorporated into the Smart City implementation strategy for Leipzig West. The discussions during the kick-off meeting revealed the need for further information on Smart City issues but also for discussing the challenges and opportunities of digitalization. Therefore, various other participation measures were introduced to accommodate these demands.

In September and October 2016, a series of four thematic workshops took place. Each event was dedicated to one Smart City topic; Smart Energy, Smart Mobility, Smart Housing and Active Neighborhood Society. After an input speech by a member of the local TRIANGULUM team on Smart Cities and initial ideas for a "smart" district in Leipzig West, the participants got together in smaller groups. Visions and obstacles for the further smart development of the district were analyzed, but also new project ideas were discussed. The results contributed to the Smart City implementation strategy for Leipzig West. Additionally, the website *smartcity.leipziger-westen.de* was launched to document the Smart City Process in Leipzig West. It is constantly being updated with new information on events and other Smart City topics.

The ASW TRIANGULUM team also regularly distributes information about the Smart City process in the so-called Quartiersrat Leipzig West (District council Leipzig West). This council was set up through of the national urban development program Stadtumbau Ost. It represents the civil society of the district including building institutions, businesses, NGOs, social services, etc., and functions as a multiplier within the district.

Additionally, the local TRIANGULUM team works closely together with other partners to engage people in Smart City topics. In cooperation with the Institute for Urban Development and Construction Management of Leipzig University, the ASW contributes to the series of evening lectures HOT SPOTS :: DER STADTENTWICKLUNG in 2016/2017. The public lectures that take place in Leipzig West are presented by experts from different cities, scientific institutions, NGOs and other stakeholders to widen the view on Smart City related topics.

3.3 Key Findings of the Participation Process in the City of Leipzig

The Smart City participation process in Leipzig has been running since October 2015. So far it has illustrated that intensive discussions with various stakeholders on different levels form a good basis for Smart City development in Leipzig, i.e. to develop a sound implementation strategy and potential pilot projects. The following points will summarize the key findings of the participation process.

3.3.1 Smart City Definition

The starting point for all participation formats was to define what "Smart City" means for the City of Leipzig. It became clear that in Leipzig's understanding the term "smart" does not only refer to technology. Smart City also includes new ways of co-creation and cooperation as well as funding between the stakeholders within a city.

In summary, the following Smart City definition was described.

- Included in integrated urban development processes, the Smart City approach offers solutions for increasing quality of life and innovation to face the future challenges of a growing city, e.g. population growth and climate change.
- Opportunities occur through the implementation of connected ICT technologies and new forms of cooperation, co-creation and financing between city administration, (local) businesses, science and civil society.
- The city administration acts as a coordinator, initiator, enabler and partner for the civil society, science and (local) businesses to ensure integrated urban development.
- Smart City processes aim at building an adaptable, responsive, user-friendly and innovative city.

Apart from that, different innovation fields were defined that will be addressed in the Smart City strategy for Leipzig West (Fig. 4).

Moreover, guidelines for the development and implementation of Smart City projects were discussed during the participation process. They should be respected when it comes to detailing and prioritizing Smart City pilot projects:

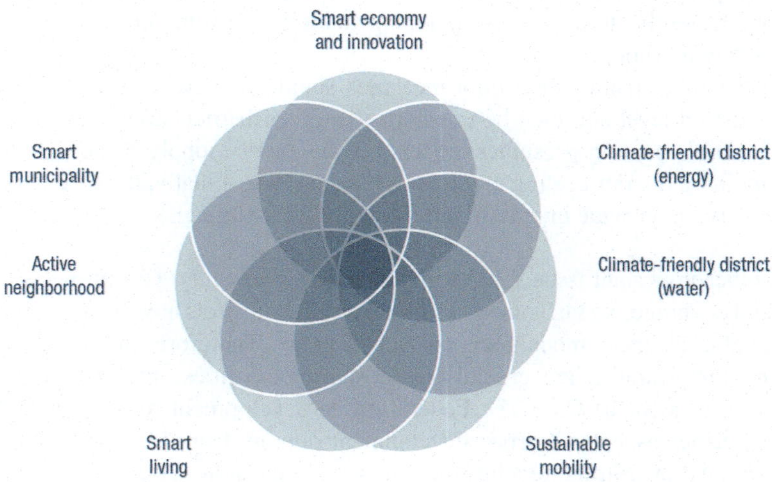

Fig. 4 Smart City innovation fields in Leipzig

- to act ecologically,
- to invest and finance innovatively,
- to use and connect Smart Data technologies,
- to create synergies by sharing processes and
- to impart and communicate knowledge and experience as well as to build community.

3.3.2 Challenges of Developing Smart City Pilot Projects

Smart City processes are complex. They include various thematic aspects such as mobility, energy, housing and governance and need to be developed, discussed and implemented by various stakeholders. Therefore, the development towards a Smart City cannot take place all at once. A series of steps are necessary. In this respect, pilot projects resulting from co-creation processes can contribute to combining action fields and making the output visible within the neighborhood. Smart solutions should aim to bring together different resources, offers and networks into the daily routine.

For some of the innovation fields, initial pilot projects in Leipzig West are defined and detailed (see Sect. 3.3.3). In discussing the measures, three key points can be identified when it comes to the pilot projects.

1. There are some innovation fields for a Smart City for which pilot projects can only be discussed and implemented for the entire city and not at a neighborhood level (e.g. developing a digitalization and open data strategy for the municipality).
2. In some cases, it is necessary to initially define city-wide strategies or concepts as a basis for neighborhood-based pilot solutions. For Leipzig, this could mean the development of a city-wide infrastructure catalogue on the municipality and data from the public utilities before planning and implementing Smart Grid measures in a neighborhood.
3. On the other hand, some pilot measures should first be implemented only at the district level and then be transferred to other districts after evaluating them (e.g. implementing prosumer models for the energy supply of households, i.e. combining district heating and renewable energies). Finally, the results of these projects can provide important input for city-wide strategies.

Another important issue for the implementation of Smart City projects is their financial coverage. So far, some of the possible pilot projects have a "test" character, i.e. suitable business models are not yet in place. Therefore, public and private funding opportunities are crucial for most municipalities, such as Leipzig, on their way to a Smart City. The Federal urban development funding in Germany covers various aspects of urban development ranging from housing development and technical infrastructure adjustment to social inclusion. Other funding schemes focus on single Smart City aspects (e.g. e-mobility, adaption to climate change, digitization). But a program focusing on integrated and smart urban development is not in place yet. The same applies to the funding opportunities at the EU level.

Therefore, it is the ASW's task within the Smart City process in Leipzig to look for the right funding opportunities for the pilot projects for Leipzig West. One example is described in the next chapter.

3.3.3 HORIZON 2020 Lighthouse Proposal: InnoLEVER

As part of its Smart City Implementation Strategy, the City of Leipzig answered the call for Smart Cities and Communities Lighthouse Projects (SCC-1-2016-2017) by the European Commission and applied in February 2017. In the InnoLEVER project proposal, the City of Leipzig joined forces with Dublin (Ireland) and Gdynia (Poland) to apply as a Lighthouse City. The consortium consists of 40 partners from ten countries including the Fraunhofer Society (Germany), the follower cities Ostrava (Czech Republic), Lviv (Ukraine), Tbilisi (Georgia) and other business and science partners.

In Leipzig, the proposal was submitted by the ASW which brought together a local consortium consisting of partners from the public utility companies, local SME's and local science institutions.

The core element of the project proposal is the so-called LivingLab Leipzig West: an experimental district in which innovative solutions will be developed with the active involvement of the civil society. This will continue and intensify the Smart City participation process started within the TRIANGULUM project. The planned co-creation process enables the active collaboration of multiple stakeholders; besides the municipality, local businesses, universities and citizens are included in the process.

Other measures within the InnoLEVER proposal address the areas of e-mobility, smart grids & energy storage, smart living and a comprehensive ICT reference architecture. The area of the Baumwollspinnerei (BWS) forms a sort of laboratory to test innovative solutions which can then be made available and scaled-up to the whole district. One example is energy storage consisting of second-life batteries. It will benefit the area and will be connected to the public grid. A corporate e-car sharing program will first improve accessibility of e-mobility at BWS and then extend to other locations in Leipzig West. Incorporating renewable energy resources in combination with smart building technologies will make the fabric of the historic building energy efficient without large scale interventions (e.g. windows, facades). The investments of InnoLEVER will supplement ongoing investments at the BWS (e.g. the new Natural History Museum) and in the energy infrastructure (e.g. extension of district heating) in Leipzig West. The local funding budget for the Leipzig consortiums reaches levels up to 4.8 million EUR, yet further private investment is necessary to implement the projects. A decision by the European Commission is expected in September 2017. But nevertheless, the developed project ideas will be part of the Smart City Implementation Strategy Leipzig West and, if necessary, other funding and implementation opportunities will be exploited.

4 Conclusion

The challenges Leipzig has to cope with represent all the German, European and global trends. In the context of a growing European City, the Smart City Strategy Leipzig addresses these challenges. The principal aim is to support sustainable urban development by means of smart approaches. This objective will be achieved if a pattern is created that takes into account needs and framework conditions allowing urban societies to participate and simultaneously offers sustainable and livable structures. On the one hand, this pattern is to be generated by considering all thematic sub-systems. On the other hand, participation of different key players guarantees the integration of all relevant needs into a Smart City Strategy Leipzig. In this respect, the consistent interplay between bottom up and top down processes can be identified as a unique feature of Leipzig's approach. Leipzig West provides the "scenery" for the first smart quarter in Leipzig. Based on integrated approaches, innovative modules are put to the test in a practical experiment (Reallabor). Against the background of linking innovative strategies with specific local requirements, the "smart house" and the "smart quarter" are terms for urban labs that have to be created and tested within future processes. The intensive participation process in Leipzig to become a Smart City may take more time to develop strategies and implement concrete measures than only a top-down oriented approach. Therefore, it is too early to give recommendations to other cities on how they should develop and implement Smart City strategies within their own individual context.

References

BBSR (2017) Bundesinstitut für Bau-, Stadt- und Raumforschung Smart Cities. Kommunen müssen Digitalisierung zur strategischen Aufgabe machen (press release of 27 Apr 2017). http://www.bbsr.bund.de/BBSR/DE/FP/ExWoSt/Studien/2015/SmartCities/SmartCities_node.html. Accessed 23 May 2017

Beinrott V (2015) Bürgerorientierte Smart City. Potenziale und Herausforderungen. Epubli, Berlin

Bundesagentur für Arbeit (2017) Arbeitsmarkt im Überblick. Berichtsmonat Juni 2017—Leipzig. https://statistik.arbeitsagentur.de/Navigation/Statistik/Statistik-nach-Regionen/BA-Gebietsstruktur/Sachsen/Leipzig-Nav.html. Accessed 27 Jul 2017

Caragliu A et al (2011) Smart cities in Europe. J Urban Technol 18(2):65–82

Geyler S et al (2016) Entwurf Zwischenbericht der Transferstelle des Triangulumprojektes Smart City Leipzig. Kompetenzzentrum für öffentliche Wirtschaft, Infrastruktur und Daseinsvorsorge e.V., Leipzig University (unpublished)

Jaekel M (2015) Smart City wird Realität. Wegweiser für neue Urbanitäten in der Digitalmoderne. Springer Vieweg, Wiesbaden

Jaekel M, Bronnert K (2013) Die digitale Evolution moderner Großstädte. Apps-basierte innovative Geschäftsmodelle für neue Urbanität. Springer Fachmedien, Wiesbaden

Kaczorowski W (2015) Smart City. Intelligent vernetzt, ökologisch und bürgerbezogen. Public Gov (Autumn):6–12

Laimer C (2014) Smart cities. Zurück in die Zukunft. Dérive: Zeitschrift für Stadtforschung 56 (July). http://www.derive.at/index.php?p_case=2&id_cont=1253&issue_No=56. Accessed 2 Feb 2017

Mandl B, Schaner P (2012) Der Weg zum Smart Cititzen. Soziotechnologische Anforderungen an die Stadt der Zukunft. In: Schrenk M et al (eds) Re-mixing the city. Towards sustainability and resilience? Tagungsband der 17. internationalen Konferenz zu Stadtplanung und Regionalentwicklung in der Informationsgesellschaft, pp 191–199

Portmann E, Finger M (2015) Smart Cities. Ein Überblick! HMD Praxis der Wirt-schaftsinformatik 52(4):470–481

Riemann A, Leidel K (2013) Klassifikation der Subsysteme von Smart City Konzepten. In: Bauhaus Universität Weimar, Fakultät Bauingenieurwesen (ed) 24. Assistententreffen der Bereiche Bauwirtschaft, Baubetrieb und Bauverfahrenstechnik, pp 101–108

Röding U (2015) Smart city. Europäische Städte smart in die Zukunft? Untersuchung des Smart City Konzepts am Beispiel Innsbruck. Master thesis at the Institute of Geography at Leopold-Franzens University Innsbruck. http://www.smartcities.at/assets/Uploads/Masterarbeit-Smart-City-15032015-UlrikeRoedig.pdf. Accessed 27 Jul 2017

Tanja Korzer has been the Executive Research Assistant at the Institute of Urban Development and Construction Management at Leipzig University since 2014. Her research activities focus on E-Commerce strategies and their implications on urban retail areas, cross-media based participation for integrated urban development planning processes and new concepts for affordable housing projects. Additionally, she is lecturer on urban management processes, methods and instruments. In 2012, she received her doctoral degree with the dissertation “Learning from shopping centers. Possibilities for retail development in small and medium sized cities”. She is a founding member of the “Wissensnetzwerk Stadt und Handel” (http://www.wissensnetzwerk-stadt-handel.de/).

Beate Ginzel has been Head of Integrated Urban Development and Housing Promotion Activities within the Office for Urban Regeneration and Housing Subsidies of the City of Leipzig since 2014. She is responsible for integrated urban development processes and all activities related to the smart city initiative. Additionally, within her scope of duties she is working on an affordable housing strategy and developing affordable housing projects. Previously, she was managing staff within the Institute of Urban Development and Construction Management at Leipzig University and was a lecturer for sustainable urban development. There she did her doctoral degree with the dissertation “The influence of local networks in urban development in the Global South”. For this, she was doing research in Tanzania. Originally, she worked as an architect for various projects in Eindhoven, The Netherlands, Tanzania and Germany.

Nadja Riedel has been a staff member within the Office for Urban Regeneration and Housing Subsidies since 2016 and the local coordinator for the SCC 1 project TRIANGULUM. Previously, she worked for different universities in the field of urban management and has led different international and EU projects and has extensive experience in transnational cooperation projects. She has been a lecturer on the topics of urban management, urban regeneration and urban economics. She holds a diploma in real estate economics and a master’s degree in urban management.

Location Communication in Leipzig and Thoughts About Destination Management

Christian Albert Jacke

Abstract

The first-hand report of the former Mayor for Economic Affairs, Real-Estates and Tourism of the City of Leipzig and present-day consultant and economic mediator covers the entire range from the beginnings of the reconstruction of the City of Leipzig via its successful repositioning in the 25 years after the German wall came down up to the establishment of a management and marketing concept for the development and institutionalization of rules in the corporate governance principles of the city as an enterprise. The "LEIPZIG KOMMT!" location campaign and its successor "Leipziger Freiheit" represent measures which in every aspect were successfully developed and implemented. This article portrays the development of the campaign, outlines the project structure and describes the principle of the marketing management process which has had the effect of creating consensus among the decision-makers of the region.

1 Mood in Leipzig in 1989/1990

Decision-makers and shapers (referred to hereafter as decision-makers) in the federal states and cities have been dealing with the challenges of location communication in the broadest sense for almost half a century now, for a variety of reasons, more or less systematically and with varying degrees of success. Especially

Dedicated to my "master of ceremonies" of many years—the distinguished Dr. jur. Hinrich Lehmann-Grube, Mayor of Leipzig (1990–1998) and honorary citizen of the city

C. A. Jacke (✉)
Hamburg, Germany
e-mail: caj@christianalbertjacke.de

H. Albach et al. (eds.), *European Cities in Dynamic Competition*,
https://doi.org/10.1007/978-3-662-56419-6_6

since the 1980s, a large number of standard reference works in the field of location communication by, amongst others, Meffert, Kotler and Kirchgeorg have become available and demonstrate methods for the development and implementation of strategies in the fields of location communication and location marketing (Kotler et al. 1994; Meffert et al. 2015). The situation in East Germany and specifically in Leipzig, forced decision-makers to face challenges which had not previously existed. This is not surprising. The fall of the Berlin Wall, German reunification with its subsequent system transformation and the reconstruction of the new federal states represented a historically unique process.

This article seeks to span the period from the early beginnings of location communication in Leipzig to thoughts on a modern city and destination management.

2 Can Leipzig Still Be Saved?

Despite the risk of the methodical approach of this account on the beginnings of location communication in Leipzig not being scientific enough, it is essential for there to be a proper description of the challenge of presenting the conditions and also the emotions of the people of Leipzig at the time after the wall came down in an authentic manner, also for the younger generation.

Shortly after the wall came down, a documentary entitled "Ist Leipzig noch zu retten?" ("Can Leipzig Still Be Saved?") was shot in the city, which was then broadcast on GDR television (Marquardt and Geist-Reithmeier 2010).

In referring to urban planning for the City of Leipzig, the film provides some key data (year 1989) on the housing situation in the city and the possible consequences of a lack of housing on the work force in the City of Leipzig in the foreseeable future. According to the data, about 104,000 apartments in the city dated back to before 1918. This was equal to 41% of all apartments. Approximately 70,000 apartments were so run-down that they could not have been saved. The plan was to build 3000–4000 new apartments and to demolish 1000 old apartments per year. Since 1987, however, more apartments were demolished than new ones built. Due to the lack of appropriate housing, a decrease in Leipzig inhabitants of 100,000 by the year 2000 was to be expected. Consequently, 70,000 fewer people would be available on the labor market.

The film is, in itself, a remarkable testament. Moreover, for the first time, GDR television showed an unembellished image of the economic disaster after 60 years of command economy (including the period of national socialism).

The film features the then Head of the Urban Planning Department of the City of Leipzig. The question regarding possible solutions to the housing problems was answered with the postulation that the state-operated building conglomerate in Leipzig should no longer be aligned with internal efficiency criteria but with the needs of the city. From a methodological point of view, this statement is of particular value. The officials were still caught up in the planned economy and wanted to optimize the process of state planning. They were still in the "glasnost" mindset, having not yet arrived at the transformation of the system.

When the film producers asked if Leipzig could still be saved, one woman replied, *"I hope so."*

It was hope which kept many Leipzigers from leaving their city and starting a new life somewhere else. The statement reflects the general mood of the early 1990s in East Germany. This aspect will be revisited when addressing the briefing for location communication.

3 Situation of the Economy in East Germany and Leipzig

Following the introduction of the D-Mark in East Germany, the exchange of goods and services with countries of the Council for Mutual Economic Assistance (COMECON) had to be conducted in a convertible currency. The national currencies of these states did not meet this requirement, which led to the exchange of goods and services being secured through counter purchases and/or government guaranties. At the same time, the Soviet Union fell apart as a sovereign nation. The successor states and the other Central and Eastern European countries fell into a severe recession which would last a long time. The markets for the East German economy basically crashed overnight. The author is hesitant to speak of "markets" in this context as the use of the term "market" would presuppose the existence of market mechanisms and free pricing (Piekenbrock 2017). The indicated changes strongly affected the field of mechanical engineering but also the chemical industry and plant engineering, and in particular the Leipzig state conglomerates severely. At the same time, the East German companies—operated as state companies by the Treuhandanstalt trust agency—had to compete in West Germany and the western markets against extremely successful West German companies. The West German economy held the title of Export World Champion; it was not a competition among equals. Over 100,000 industrial workers lost their jobs after 1990 in Leipzig alone. The development affected almost every family in Leipzig, covering the entire city and region in a negative mood like a dark cloud.

The economic situation in Leipzig in the early 1990s can be specified using the following key data (Stadt Leipzig 1995):

- Real unemployment was 35–50% (nominal unemployment adjusted for job creation schemes and qualification measures).
- Migration away from the City of Leipzig, which had already started before the wall came down, continued in a massive way, causing the number of inhabitants to fall significantly below 500,000 in 1991 (720,000 inhabitants in 1930).
- Private property owners had been expropriated in the territory of the German Democratic Republic from 1945 onwards, following the establishment of the Soviet command economy with central leadership and all production means owned by the government. The process had been handled particularly thoroughly in the former District of Leipzig. The City of Leipzig received 39,936 applications for the reconveyance of property, which was equal to 76% of all real estate in the City of Leipzig. The legal principle of "restitution before compensation"

stipulated in the German Reunification Treaty deprived this real estate of its marketability. Due to the unresolved ownership of the property, no investments could be made there. Also, it could not be mortgaged to collateralize investments. Economic activity in Leipzig almost came to a complete standstill, with only very few exceptions, for a period of almost 2 years between January 1991 and January 1993.

- The stipulations of the German Unification Treaty (Unification Treaty 1990) delivered almost 32,000 employees to the City of Leipzig in 1990. The city repeatedly found itself on the verge of insolvency.
- Despite the well-attended trade fair in spring, there were only 400,000 overnight stays in 6000 uncategorized hotel beds in Leipzig in 1991.
- A total of just 275,000 flight passengers and 366 tons of air cargo were registered at Leipzig/Halle Airport in 1990.

4 Glimmers of Hope

The situation of businesses could be described as concerning to hopeless; people were in low spirits. At the same time, important decisions made in mid-1991 brought some certainty to the city's future:

The Quelle Group would move to Leipzig and build the most modern dispatch center in the world, with an investment volume of over DM 1.0 billion. The factory was going to provide employment for over 4000 people. The construction of the new trade fair center and the creation of one of the most modern trading locations in Europe, directly next to the Quelle premises, for over DM 1.3 billion was also agreed upon (Marg 1997). The federal government and the Free State of Saxony pledged investments in the infrastructure in the upper nine-figure range for the northern areas of Leipzig alone. Major investments by Siemens, Mannesmann and Telekom were being prepared. Central German Broadcasting (MDR), Germany's second largest regional public broadcaster, was to come to Leipzig and bundle its television production at the Leipzig site (moving from Berlin and Dresden). The volume of these investments reached a scale far beyond DM 10 billion over a period of 5–6 years.

The decision-makers in the city administration, in the council and the trade associations recognized the challenge of having to reassure people in the city and offering orientation to the stakeholders. At the same time, the decision-makers in the urban administration were aware of the special importance of reliability and authenticity after decades of disappointment and deceit. They had to complete an unusual communicative task.

5 Project Organization, Quantitative Surveys and Agency Briefing

The Mayor enlisted a communications expert from Munich, who was quite experienced in the field of location communication, to accompany the project. Several discussion groups; both within the city administration and with the council, the decision-makers from the trade associations, the district administration, the universities and cultural institutions, were established. In addition to generating broad acceptance for the project, the focus was on sparking ideas and taking in suggestions. Exclusive meetings were organized to win over sponsors and the partner companies were included in the "Initiative Leipzig e.V." circle. An internal committee working in the area of operations for the mayor and the deputy mayors prepared trendsetting decisions.

This internal committee was responsible for preparing and evaluating representative surveys, developing a task breakdown for an agency competition ("briefing"), completing competitions, financing, and later campaign management, transmitting projects into the administration and monitoring the project. The project structure was consciously chosen as to have an effect on all project stakeholders so that it would create consensus.

Representative surveys were conducted in Leipzig/East Germany and West Germany seeking to obtain a reliable assessment of public awareness of Leipzig, the reasons for the awareness and possible strengths and weaknesses of the city.

Although no detailed representation or evaluation of the results can be offered within the framework of this article, the most important findings of the surveys can be summarized as follows:

Leipzig was extraordinarily well-known in Germany's new federal states. The Leipzig Trade Fair was of outstanding importance for the popularity of Leipzig. Karl Marx University and major sporting events ("Spartakiads") ensured a high level of awareness. Leipzig was also described as very appealing by the people surveyed in East Germany. The persona of Walter Ulbricht and the topic of air pollution and stench were given as negative aspects.

The respondents from West Germany attested to a rather average level of awareness of Leipzig, which was almost exclusively based on the Leipzig trade fairs. The appeal of Leipzig was rather low. Many respondents had bad memories of their visit to the Leipzig Trade Fair, if for no other reason than the harassment when entering the former GDR. People also associated Leipzig with a run-down city, extreme air pollution and a foul odor. At least there was an indication of openness towards information on Leipzig.

Besides the findings from the survey among people from East Germany and Leipzig ("self-perception") and West Germany ("external perception"), many older people in West Germany remembered Leipzig pre-1945 (and also pre-1933, of course) as well as its outstanding position among the most important cities in Germany and Europe. The history of the city had to be respected in an attempt at perspective positioning of the City of Leipzig. History greatly influences the self-perception of people from a certain city. The following list includes the institutions and historical qualities of the city (marketing strategists like to talk about "big points" of a destination) at the beginning of the 1990s which were mentioned in the surveys:

- Oldest trade fair in the world
- Fourth largest city in Germany
- Second oldest university in Germany (1409) which produced 30 Nobel laureates
- Site of the Battle of the Nations
- World city of books and home to the German National Library
- Seat of the German Publishers and Booksellers Association and Deutsche Welle, Germany's public international broadcaster
- Seat of the highest German Imperial Court of Justice
- Birth place and home to outstanding composers and writers
- Founding city of the German Football Association (DFB)
- Home to over 140 Olympic and Paralympic medalists
- Seat of the trade and stock exchange
- Founding city of the Schreber garden movement

Comparing the qualities of the City of Leipzig before 1933 and those in 1991 was rather concerning. When looking for a perspective positioning for Leipzig, many questions had to remain unanswered initially (Price Waterhouse GmbH, Institut für Marktforschung GmbH 1993).

What would Leipzig like to stand for?
Which companies will survive the system transformation?
Which clusters can develop in the future?
What role will the former Karl Marx University play?
How many people will live in Leipzig by 2030?
Would it rather be 700,000 people like at the beginning of the twentieth century?
Or rather 330,000 people—like in Bielefeld?

So many questions and no answers.

Under these circumstances, a location marketing concept was out of the question. However, it was still possible to prepare a clear briefing for the development of a communication campaign:

Leipzig would experience a dynamic process with extraordinary major public and private investments for many years. These projects could serve as beacons shining their light far beyond the new federal states. The willingness to act and the speed of action demonstrated by the city administration and politics could be evident from the approval procedures for projects; there were references (exactly six months passed from initial contact with the executive board of Quelle AG to the decision of the city council on the contract about the opening of the site). Soon, the city would have the most modern communication and transportation infrastructure in the country. The statements of the campaign would have to be immediately verifiable; they would have to be authentic.

6 LEIPZIG KOMMT! Location Campaign

In the agency competition, Serviceplan from Munich was chosen. Serviceplan had completed the task as follows:

"LEIPZIG KOMMT!" ("LEIPZIG UP-AND-COMING!") was at the core of the word and figurative signature. The lettering was underlain with a picture of the project that was up- and-coming—for instance, the building crane on the construction site of the Quelle dispatch center or a specific investment project by Siemens AG in Leipzig. The campaign conveyed the message of a vibrant, growing Leipzig and the underlaying of the capital letters with images showed what the specific project was. The authenticity of the statement was increased even more by a testimonial and photo of the person responsible for the respective project. The implementation of the ideas behind the campaign can be shown using Siemens AG and Stadtwerke Leipzig GmbH as an example. Further examples cannot be provided, as, apparently, the records were never digitalized and entered into the archives (Figs. 1 and 2).

The campaign was launched in 1993 and continued to 2000 with large-scale posters in the public sphere in the Leipzig region as well as select locations all over

Fig. 1 LEIPZIG KOMMT! Insert and poster campaign, example of Siemens AG (Despite intensive research possible owners of the image rights could not be identified. For clarification of legal claims, we ask any rights holders to contact the publisher)

Fig. 2 LEIPZIG KOMMT! Insert and poster campaign, example of Stadtwerke Leipzig GmbH (Despite intensive research possible owners of the image rights could not be identified. For clarification of legal claims, we ask any rights holders to contact the publisher)

Germany. Thanks to full-page inserts in daily newspapers and business journals, the campaign reached a wide audience and was further supported through editorial contributions. As the campaign progressed and the offered content increased, image brochures to advertise Leipzig as a business location, a destination for tourism and congresses as well as a city of music, were produced.

7 Exchanging Experiences as a Discovery Procedure

The discussion groups with the involvement of the departments of the city administration, the council, trade associations, universities and cultural institutions developed into a discovery process for the shaping of challenges and the recognition of opportunities in the best possible sense, according to Hayek (Freitum 2010). Many ideas went into a pool and were subjected to an analysis of their urgency, estimated effort and expected benefit. This procedure will be addressed again in the context of the thoughts regarding systematic destination management. Here, two projects will be used to demonstrate the principle of successful location development:

Very soon after the German Unification Treaty came into effect, the extent of the desolation marking Leipzig's inner city became increasingly concerning. Stores, cafés and restaurants closed down for various reasons. Even on the weekends, there were hardly any people in the city center, which appeared very lively whenever a trade fair took place. An abundance of administrative obstacles, which constrained the development of entrepreneurial activities, became apparent in the dialogue between trade associations, the special departments of the city administration and property owners (if known). With the subject heading of "Deregulation of Local Law“, the city parliament adopted an administrative draft to eliminate these obstacles, set deadlines and legitimize temporary solutions. In a very short amount of time, new bars, restaurants and stores were opened, creative artists and musicians played on the market square and Leipzig's city center soon became a magnet in the wider region for people of all ages. The appeal of the inner city also positively affected the business of trade fairs and congresses in Leipzig.

The city administration and its companies, even more so the businesses from West Germany, found it overly difficult to find both qualified and young people to work for them. For a certain amount of time, mainly people who had obtained their professional qualification and experience in the West were considered for some tasks. The potential employers were turned down repeatedly by suitable applicants who themselves, or whose partners, could not imagine a life in Leipzig. The acceptance of the decision to move to Leipzig improved following a small separate campaign, a communication mix targeting female decision-makers and with the help of an image brochure focusing on the aforementioned target group of decision-makers.

8 Real Estate Ownership: The Knots Unravel

The "LEIPZIG KOMMT!" campaign with its beacon projects was initially designed to mark the beginning of a new era and therefore to spread hope. As described previously, numerous smaller projects, which were tangible for the people in the city, were to be developed very soon.

At the same time, the blockage of real estate for commercial and residential purposes as outlined above also prevented a broadening of the basis for investment. Only tedious renegotiations by the mayor and those in authority with the federal ministries responsible for justice, urban development and housing, finance and economic affairs made it possible to transfer a larger number of lots back into private ownership, following the adoption of the Investment Priority, the Real Property Validation and the Registration Procedure Acceleration Act (note the exceptionally wordy terms). Additionally, an agreement was concluded with the Conference on Jewish Material Claims Against Germany (Claims Conference) which allowed for a mobilization of such real estate which had previously been owned by Jewish citizens. There used to be an abundance of Jewish stores, workshops and companies, especially in the city center, up to the 1930s.

In the first 7 years after the German reunification more than 2500 investment priority transactions for investments of any type and scale were legally concluded and more than 5000 properties were returned to the market through various distribution channels in Leipzig. For institutional investors with a long-term investment horizon, this was an opportunity to invest in commercial and office real estate in a prime inner-city location after reunification. The Treuhandliegenschaftsgesellschaft mbH (TLG) commercial real estate company, the Free State of Saxony, the Federal Property Office and the City of Leipzig offered property in exclusive locations within the framework of public notices, adopting the highest bidder procedure. By and by, it was not just large-scale investors but also private ones who participated in the reconstruction of the city, attracted by the favorable tax conditions for investments in real estate in the new federal states. For investments in commercial property, the City of Leipzig developed approximately 500 hectares of new industrial estates for its own purposes or the purposes of municipal project development companies and initiated a large part of the infrastructure investments made in modern operating sites, workshops and factories. Moreover, the City of Leipzig offered (and offers to this day) mainly residential real estate in the city's Wilhelminian-era neighborhoods through a public property exchange, after predetermining the market value of the property. This opened up concrete investment opportunities for private investors and investors from the city itself in their own home town. Also, with the goal of capital accumulation in East Germany, owners of single-family homes in Leipzig were able to purchase a corresponding plot with a size of up to 500 square meters based on the so-called "Modrow Act" (decision of the People's Chamber of the GDR, dated March 7, 1990), at the land prices charged in the GDR, which would have been DM 5–7 per square meter, depending on location.

With these measures, the economic upturn and reconstruction in Leipzig were established on a broad footing. The announcement "LEIPZIG KOMMT!" started to develop into a self-fulfilling prophecy. The upturn spread out into the entire urban region.

Dr. Jürgen Schneider, a project developer from Frankfurt, who had a strong media presence in the early 1990s and who was later sentenced to several years in prison for fraud had four projects under construction in Leipzig during the time of his arrest. This remark classifies Dr. Schneider's contribution to the reconstruction of Leipzig (Fig. 3).

9 Efficiency of the Campaign

The images of the desolation of East German cities, the extent of the destruction of the natural livelihoods and the horrible news about the downfall of the industry had been crammed into the heads of people from West Germany and the western world. Therefore, the "LEIPZIG KOMMT!" slogan made waves and attracted attention. The attention garnered as part of the communication mix of the campaign was multiplied by (free of charge) media reports, going far beyond the original effect. The impact of the campaign in West Germany and other western countries, all the way to North America, was exceptional (Randal et al. 1995; Schwelz and Kull 1995).

Fig. 3 Property issues resolved, Wilhelminian-era neighborhood Waldstraßenviertel Leipzig (Andreas Schmidt 2017)

The citizens of Leipzig themselves were glad to see the increasingly favorable reports in the media about their home town. The campaign started to produce the desired effect of raising spirits and excitement about the future.

The business journals reported about the "Boomtown Leipzig" and more than 250 building cranes were counted at one time in the mid-1990s above the rooftops of the city (Heinker 2004). While a more in-depth examination would seem worthwhile, a report on the multiplying and accelerating effect of the campaign would go beyond the scope of this article.

The fact that the discussion rounds with the stakeholders from the city sparked consensus has already been mentioned. The activities of Initiative Leipzig e.V., which organized the campaign, were also an immense success from a financial perspective. The committee of sponsors included about 20 companies, contributing a minimum of DM 250,000 each. Campaigns are generally deemed successful if they can achieve a 2:1 ratio between private and public funding. Campaigns with a 3:1 ratio are considered to be highly successful. "LEIPZIG KOMMT!" was able to achieve a ratio of 3:1; and at times, even 4:1. Therefore, it can be considered a particularly successful contribution from the field of destination communication from a commercial point of view as well.

10 The Bridge From "LEIPZIG KOMMT!" to "Leipziger Freiheit"

At the end of the 1990s, the "LEIPZIG KOMMT!" campaign had served its purpose. It was foreseeable that Leipzig would continue to undergo positive development. After a lean period of 5 years (the German industrial companies were facing the challenge of globalization), industrial investments gained momentum as well. Leipzig experienced dynamic development with employment increasing significantly. Leipzig had made great progress and it was time for a new communication campaign designed to find a modified approach to support the positive development.

Many Leipzigers had mustered all the courage they had in the fall of 1989 and took massive risks to overthrow an outdated system. These people had directly fought for their own freedom (and indirectly for the freedom of the people in the neighboring countries of Central and Eastern Europe) and learned to use this personal freedom they had gained after the wall came down. Continuing to tell Leipzig's story of success, offering a platform for the depiction of the living freedom and inviting others to use the freedom that Leipzig has to offer, this was and is the prime concern behind the approach for the "Leipziger Freiheit" ("Leipzig Freedom") campaign. Just like its predecessor, the "Leipziger Freiheit" campaign also uses the opportunity to provide an announcement and the evidence in one image. Testimonials combined with pictures of the active people continue to be used as well. This campaign is also based on credibility and verifiability.

Personalities such as Kurt Masur, Music Director of the Gewandhaus Orchestra at that time and honorary citizen of the City of Leipzig, or Professor Emmerich, the founding father of biomedicine in Leipzig and his team talk about how they have used "Leipziger Freiheit" for their purposes, for the unfolding of their life and goals as part of this campaign. Students from all over Germany learn about how living in Leipzig can be beautiful and, at the same time, reasonably priced if they furbish their rooms in a shared apartment (Figs. 4, 5 and 6).

11 Sustainability in City and Destination Management

Using Leipzig as an example, the establishment of various dialogue platforms for the inclusion of the stakeholders of a city or region during the development of location communication was demonstrated. The connecting element for those involved in the project was the goal of achieving a turnaround for the city and the region. Many concerns and forms of egoism were subordinated to this objective. This explains how the administration, politics and the regional administrative authorities worked together, showing great determination and pace in their decision-making. Word of the quality of this location had quickly spread among the leaders of industry and the economy, promoting some investment decisions for the city.

His own experience connected with reconstruction and repositioning of an important major city and the present-day challenges as a consultant and motivator

Fig. 4 Leipziger Freiheit insert and poster campaign, example of Kurt Masur (LTM 2017)

for decision-makers in the public sector and the industry have led the author to the question: How does one lead a group of municipal companies in cooperation with the stakeholders from the region? Which preconditions and rules produce a value and management concept that is as consistent as possible?

The mission statements of many cities and companies include the guiding principle of actions and work which are geared towards sustainability. Scientific literature, particularly in the field of municipal housing, indeed includes initial approaches for a theoretical foundation of the benefits that refer to the achievement of sustainable goals (Spars and Heinze 2008). Beyond its original goal (in this particular case: appealing residences that are worth the money), municipal housing further contributes to the city's return on investment. These contributions are then described in qualitative terms and found to be 'good' based on an understanding of value-based welfare economics. Qualitative, non-material objectives alone are not sufficient for the development of management systems and processes.

Operationalized criteria to measure the city's return on investment can be found in the scientific literature, e.g., by Professor Ulf Papenfuß (Papenfuß 2013). In practice, the value creation chains surrounding an economic or organizational unit or interacting with other units, will be mapped and accompanied by quantifying objectives. A management culture arises which is geared towards a measurable contribution to the city's return on investment through a general governance code which applies to all members of a group of municipal companies. A monitoring process then secures the constant review of objectives and control of the target-oriented processes. Ideally, the organization evolves into a "learning organization",

Fig. 5 Leipziger Freiheit insert and poster campaign, example of the clinicians team of Prof. Mohr (LTM 2017)

whose individual bodies anticipate the principle of action. As an example from practice, the City of Mannheim chose a corporate governance-based set of rules by adopting the Mannheim Code (Stadt Mannheim 2009).

Fig. 6 Leipziger Freiheit insert and poster campaign, example of the reasonably-priced Wilhelminian-era flats (LTM 2017)

Leipziger Messegesellschaft, the local trade fair company, represents a practical example for the establishment of destination management which is geared towards the city's return on investment. Through a survey entitled "Der ewige Wirtschaftsmotor" ("The Constant Engine of the Economy") which was conducted by the ifo Institute in Munich, the company shows how it influences purchasing power, jobs and tax revenue in the city and the region (Leipziger Messe GmbH 2017). In addition to the original commercial goals of the Leipziger Messe GmbH, the report also provides notes on how to lead cultural institutions, museums and theaters, based on the analysis of associated value creation chains. The author wants to demonstrate how a conscious process can shape the actions of the stakeholders of a destination.

Each destination and region is called upon to find its own path within this context. When choosing a way, decision-makers can secure themselves support, for instance, that of the author.

12 Conclusion

The example of the City of Leipzig demonstrated successful turnaround management with the help of location communication. The distinguished Ursula Lehmann-Grube, wife of the former Mayor of Leipzig and honorary citizen Dr. Hinrich Lehmann-Grube, preserved her diaries from the years 1990 and 1991 as valuable documents from a time of radical change and new beginnings and published them in 2009. She has never been accused of always wanting to have the last word. However, she will have the last word here, concluding the article, with a quote from her book "Als ich von Deutschland nach Deutschland kam" ("When I Came From Germany to Germany") (Lehmann-Grube 2009):

> Jacke und Weber [former Director of the Mayor's Office—author's note] talked one and a half hours about the closed brainstorming session (closed session of Leipziger Messe in Kipsdorf/Erzgebirge) regarding the trade fair. Trade fair grounds are now supposed to be moved! Everyone agreed that the current area (Technical Trade Fair Grounds) is no good: maybe the aboveground structures, but not the things underground and the transport connection. They have already chosen a new area; in the northeast. A massive tour de force, both financially and politically.
>
> Jacke had the idea that maybe Kohl [former German Chancellor—author's note] might like the thought of announcing the commitment of the government to the idea during a Leipzig visit—he'll have to make one soon.

Acknowledgment The article is based on a presentation from the 2016 CASiM Conference entitled "European Cities in Dynamic Competition". I would like to cordially thank Prof. Dr. Pinkwart for inviting me to the conference. As it had been some time since I had last visited the university, I was really impressed with the excellence of academic instruction and what the school offers as well as the good atmosphere on campus. Professor Pinkwart really carried on the torch which Dr. Trippen and Prof. Dr. Meffert lit at the university a good 20 years ago.

References

FREITUM (2010) Friedrich August von Hayek. Der Wettbewerb als Entdeckungsverfahren. FREITUM. http://www.freitum.de/2010/01/friedrich-von-hayek-der-wettbewerb-als.html. Accessed 4 Dec 2016

Heinker H-H (2004) Boomtown Leipzig. Anspruch und Wirklichkeit. Faber & Faber, Leipzig

Kotler P, Haider D, Rein I (1994) Standort-marketing. Wie Städte, Regionen und Länder gezielt Investitionen, Industrien und Tourismus anziehen. Econ-Verl, Düsseldorf

Lehmann-Grube U (2009) Als ich von Deutschland nach Deutschland kam Leipziger Tagebuch 1990-91. Lehmstedt, Leipzig

Leipziger Messe GmbH (2017) Der ewige Wirtschaftsmotor. http://www.leipziger-messe.de/leipzigermessemagazin/DER-EWIGE-WIRTSCHAFTSMOTOR.html. Accessed 10 Apr 2017

Marg V (1997) Neue Messe Leipzig/New Trade Fair Leipzig 1992-1996. Verlag für Architektur, Basel

Marquardt G, Geist-Reithmeier R (2010) Klartext. Ist Leipzig noch zu retten? (DVD). Icestorm, Berlin

Meffert H, Burmann C, Kirchgeorg M, Meffert H (2015) Marketing. Grundlagen marktorientierter Unternehmensführung. Konzepte—Instrumente- Praxisbeispiele, 12th edn. Springer Gabler, Wiesbaden

Papenfuß H (2013) Verantwortungsvolle Steuerung und Leitung öffentlicher Unternehmen. Empirische Analyse und Handlungsempfehlungen zur Public Corporate Governance. Springer Gabler, Wiesbaden

Piekenbrock D (2017) Markt. Gabler Wirtschaftslexikon. http://wirtschaftslexikon.gabler.de/Archiv/4487/markt-v14.html. Accessed 3 Jul 2017

Price Waterhouse GmbH, Institut für Marktforschung GmbH (1993) Angebot. Entwicklung eines Wirtschaftsförderungskonzeptes und eines Wirtschaftsförderungsprogramms für die Stadt Leipzig; Leipzig (unpublished)

Randal JC et al (1995) Leipzigs road to renewal paved with problems; despite aid from Bonn, East German city struggles to make trade-fair project a success. The Washington Post, 30 Jul 1995

Schwelz I, Kull A (1995) Leipzig—eine Stadt will wieder ganz nach oben. Hamburger Abendblatt. 7 Mar 1995

Spars G, Heinze M (2008) Neue Ergebnisse zur Stadtrendite kommunaler Wohnungsunternehmen. Ein Leitfaden für die Praxis. https://www.vhw.de/fileadmin/user_upload/08_publikationen/verbandszeitschrift/2000_2014/PDF_Dokumente/2008/FW_2_2008_Neue_Ergebnisse_zur_Stadtrendite_kommunaler_Wo.pdf. Accessed 10 Apr 2017

Stadt Leipzig (1995) Wirtschaftsförderungskonzept der Stadt Leipzig. Beschlussdrucksache der Ratsversammlung Leipzig. Leipzig (unpublished)

Stadt Mannheim (2009) Mannheimer Corporate Governance Kodex. Leitlinien guter Unternehmensführung. https://www.mannheim.de/sites/default/files/institution/23136/mcgk.pdf. Accessed 18 May 2017

Unification Treaty (1990) http://germanhistorydocs.ghi-dc.org/docpage.cfm?docpage_id=542. Accessed 3 Jul 2017

Christian Albert Jacke studied economics and law at the University of Freiburg, Germany, graduating with a Dipl.-Vw. degree. Since 1985, he has worked as an entrepreneur in various positions; Member of the Executive Board of Bayerische Vereinsbank AG and Vereins- und Westbank AG, responsible for the corporate and real estate clients as well as the public sector. From 1990 to 1997, he served as Deputy Mayor for Economic Affairs of the City of Leipzig (without party affiliation). In this position, he was responsible for the promotion of business development, real estate, the airport, the trade fair, congress and tourism in the City of Leipzig. Christian Albert Jacke is a co-initiator of location communication and a leader of the turnaround in Leipzig. Today, he is a managing partner at his own consulting firm and works as a moderator and strategy consultant at the interface between politics, society and the industry. Another one of his key competencies lies in the real estate industry. Jacke was born in 1960 and lives in Hamburg, Germany, and Arosa, Switzerland. He has two daughters and two sons.

Part III

Success Factors in Global Competition Among Cities

Key Factors for Successful City Marketing: An Example from Münster

Bernadette Spinnen

Abstract

The following paper addresses the most important factors for a successful integrated city marketing strategy. It underlines the importance of goals and objectives and the need for a clear and competitive concept for the desired identity of the city. Further important aspects are strong city advocates and strong leadership, since cooperation between institutions, politics, companies and associations are of key importance to a city marketing organization in these times of a digitalized society.

The key factors and important aspects of integrated city marketing are illustrated with examples from the work at Münster Marketing, where the claim for the city has actually been accomplished. Its success is mainly based on the good communication achieved between the city, the university and the citizens. Furthermore, putting together the claim was done by including the opinions of the citizens, giving them the opportunity to actively participate in the process thereby making the municipality take on the role of a partner rather than an authority.

For the future, there is potential for city marketing organizations to act as intermediaries and troubleshooters between politicians and the citizenry, involving both of them in the creation of city brands and their own future. I hope that the idea of what could be called the civilizing of an agency or organization will be taken into account in the future development of city marketing organizations.

B. Spinnen (✉)
Stadt Münster, Münster Marketing, Münster, Germany
e-mail: Spinnen@stadt-muenster.de

H. Albach et al. (eds.), *European Cities in Dynamic Competition*,
https://doi.org/10.1007/978-3-662-56419-6_7

The following chapter thus identifies the most important factors for the success of an integrated city marketing campaign in nine short chapters, concluded by taking a personal perspective on the sector's future, though it might not be quite complete just yet and also somewhat bold in outlook.

Integrated city marketing is an increasingly important topic in city marketing. Integrated, in this case, means applying corporate marketing theories of goals and objectives, coordination, segmentation and customer orientation to city marketing strategies regarding the citizenry, economy and educational establishments within a city (Hauff et al. 2007). A city cannot just use its innate talents, structure, or folklore for its marketing, it also needs to take into account both the current and future possibilities and potential. Several conclusions can be drawn and clues deduced from the years of experience within the framework of Münster Marketing, Münster's city marketing organization.

1 Clearly State What You Want to Achieve

When municipalities actively choose to properly market their cities, they initially need to clarify exactly what they are aiming for. It is especially important to distinguish between integrated city marketing and city advertising, since those two terms are very distinct from one another. Integrated city marketing aims at visualizing the city's identity through communicating the relevant values and benefits to all of the city's stakeholders in order to make it comprehensible and accessible. City advertising, by contrast, can be one of several instruments for integrated city marketing. In this case, it describes the forms of promotional communication of one or another of the city's facets to separate stakeholder groups.

2 The "Comparative Competitive Advantage" or Leitmotif of the City

The central questions in city marketing are thus: How does our city want to be seen and judged in comparison to our competitors? How is this image to be achieved? And: Is this goal realistic? It is crucial that these fundamental questions be answered honestly and objectively. In Münster, for example, there was a petition to profile Münster as one of the European Capitals of Culture; whereas the local private sector demanded that the city be branded as a prime business location. In both cases, the honest answer to both requests is clear. Even with major efforts and investments, positioning and branding the city in this way in both Germany and Europe is, very likely, unachievable.

The difficulties in choosing a suitable leitmotif for a city are obvious:

First and foremost, the image the city strives for in relation to its target groups must be comprehensively worked out. This means all major stakeholders or "players" within the city need to be convinced of the efficacy of the chosen image and support it. The citizens, as well as the stakeholders from the private sector, and even the political parties and city council must at best unanimously commit to this city leitmotif in order to make it come alive. Integrated city marketing organizations can only succeed if this image or leitmotif is commonly perceived as plausible and appropriate. (Spinnen 2007) However, marketing efforts are often hampered by multiple conflicts within the decision-making process regarding the quintessence of the city brand due to its resulting ambiguity.

Another difficulty arises from the demands placed on the city leitmotif. The image is not supposed to describe the location's strengths; like beauty or historical architecture, or even basic characteristics; like being located near the sea or in the mountains. The leitmotif rather needs to imply a vision of what the city wants to achieve and what it wants to be. Hence, it should be understood as an attainable vision for the future in which the city will change but nevertheless still manage to retain its innate character.

Unfortunately, it is obvious if we consider many of the slogans from German cities that finding an effective leitmotif is hardly ever successful. Some of these examples are "If/When you find us, you'll find us well/you'll like us" (a play on words of "Wenn Sie uns finden, finden Sie uns gut" in the German original for Kaiserslautern), "Jena-Lichtstadt" ("Jena—City of Light"), "Wo der Rhein die Eifel trifft" ("Where the Rhine meets the Eifel"; Andernach), or "Lohne lohnt sich" ("Lohne is worth it").

3 There Is No Way to Force a Willingness

A marketing effort's successes are completely dependent on having a strong city advocate: If a strong top executive does not exist to support and push the enterprise, the city branding is bound to fail. The long-term success of a city marketing campaign cannot develop properly without skilled leadership that captivates and animates people and function-owners. In a pinch, it might be advisable to delay the process and wait for the political leadership to change. There is no way to persuade a mayor to advocate such an undertaking—the city officials need to support it with conviction.

4 The Rising Importance of Integrated City Marketing in Times of Digital Disruption

Nowadays, advertising and marketing are terms that need to be used carefully. People no longer trust advertising and they do not trust the authorities, least of all political ones. Politics and city marketing organizations are under constant pressure from a rapidly individualizing society that garners attention through forming public "shitstorm" movements. The city marketing institutions are denied the previously undisputed prerogative of their particular interpretation of the city's identity.

This also presents us with a chance for city marketing organizations to support the political leaders of the city as well as bolstering them. They should not settle for the communication of pre-determined images of the city. On the contrary, they should establish and support public dialogue. The primary objective would be to enable the citizens to actively participate and be involved in the design of the city's future.

5 Best Practice Example of Münster: How We Translated Our City Claim into Real City Life

For a long time, Münster was a provincial city, a regional center in Westphalia in Western Germany with around 250,000 inhabitants. But, it has also been one of Germany's largest centers of higher education for even longer than that. Astonishingly, the latter had almost no perceivable impact on the daily life of the city or on political dialogue. Scientists and students were not really part of the municipal society, did not participate in various service clubs and were not a primary target group of the local private sector, which mostly targeted the service industry of the middle class. Only when this arrangement was hit by a crisis in the late 1990s and proved to be unsustainable for the future, was an integrated city marketing organization utilized to initiate a change process.

The word "crisis" seems to be a key word with regard to integrated city marketing processes. Those cities that know that their sustainability is at stake are more likely to acknowledge the necessity of utilizing city marketing for change processes and implement it accordingly. A prime example of this is the city of Magdeburg. After German reunification in 1989, the city did not have an appropriate perspective. It was losing inhabitants while at the same time fighting for its status as state capital of Saxony-Anhalt. Through an extensive future-oriented planning process, Magdeburg succeeded in gaining a favorable reputation among Germany's science-orientated cities and linking its economic development closely to its universities.

The emotionalizing campaign "Ottostadt Magdeburg", based on the Emperor Otto the Great, was used to remind the population of the city's great history and gain the confidence to design a process for a future-outlook on a par with the other large German cities. Such processes take a lot of time if they are to be successful in a sustainable way.

In Münster, it took an entire year for the authorities and citizens to debate, discuss and negotiate how the city, which had perceived itself as the "Westphalian writing desk" up to that point, should be positioned, both internally and externally. In the end, the leitmotif of "Science and Living Quality" as a result of the integrated city development and city marketing processes was chosen as a vision for the future. This image represents the change Münster underwent, from the outdated provincial capital to a modern German *Großstadt* which values knowledge and education and strives for a high quality of life. And that is an enormous difference in self-perception!

In the past 15 years since this leitmotif was chosen, the city as a brand has been continuously built up, especially from the inside. This process was not an advertising campaign, but rather somewhat the contrary. Systematically, and with no little amount of tenacity, Münster Marketing aided the evolution of the city into a modern *Großstadt* that offers an extraordinary quality of life and whose most important resource is knowledge. And while realizing this vision, the company stayed true to the principle that marketing is done according to content, and not the other way around. In order to maintain the trust of the citizens' in the process, we initially even refrained from changing the city's corporate design or slogan.

6 Münster: City of Science

Without a doubt, the most challenging struggle in re-branding the city was the improvement of the city's relationship with Münster's nine universities and colleges. Previously, the relationships ranged from poor to non-existent.

In order to improve the relationship between the municipality and the universities, Münster Marketing established a Science Office, the first ever in Germany. Staffed with alumni, the Science Office is an acknowledgment of the universities' value to the city. City planner Klaus Kunzmann called this a "communal affection" of the city towards its universities (Kunzmann 2004). The Science Office is no longer just a mere switchboard. Rather, it translates scientific and academic issues to fit into the city's context, opening doors between partners on both the academic and the municipal side and introducing the academic perspective into Münster's everyday life (Spinnen 2011).

Today, Münster Marketing systematically works with the universities. Work has been done cooperatively on central issues and topics that the university excels in, that are of high social relevance and that fit the city's profile. In order to do just that, the "Alliance for Science" was established; an organizational structure in which academics, economists, representatives of the city's society, as well as the municipality itself work together for the improved visibility of these shared strengths. The alliances between the cluster of excellence "Religion and Politics" with the Peace of Westphalia, the Netzwerk Humanitäre Hilfe (Humanitarian Aid Network) at the Münster University of Applied Sciences or the work done by the Netzwerk Nano Bio Analytik (Nano Bio Analysis Network) are just a few of the success stories (Schmidt 2011).

Furthermore, other interested agents involved in these undertakings are the municipality's Business Promotion Department and all partners concerned with Münster as a congress or convention destination. The ongoing work on the "Science and Savoir-vivre" profile has also impacted the work in the city's Convention Bureau. Nowadays, the focus lies primarily on marketing within the city. Most activities are aimed at the professional classes of the Münster universities and colleges, motivating them to bring congresses to Münster. Marketing Münster is in continuous contact with the academics, takes them on for/organizing on-site inspections, offering training courses for their assistants and letting them look behind the scenes of the congress locations. Most importantly, the Convention Bureau acts as a constant contact prior to, during and after the event. Today, there is even an award for the scientists who organize especially attractive congresses in Münster. And as a result, the number of congresses in Münster is increasing.

Münster Marketing also systematically addresses other target groups within this city of science and has adjusted the tourist marketing accordingly. Examples are the "Elternalarm" ("Parent Alarm") event, to which the parents of Münster students are invited to visit the city, or joint welcoming events with certain faculties for the new Master's students. The company has also partnered with the universities and colleges for alumniprojects—all of which are powerful ambassadors for the city.

7 Participation as a Key Factor for Success

The key term in all of this work is participation. Just as all the concerned individuals who originally got involved in choosing the leitmotif, they still remain partners in all that is done. A network is built up for each topic or issue, within which the stakeholders develop competitive advantages for Münster. They invest their time and commitment and they co-finance some of the activities. The city center development, for example, has been implemented with a strong network of owners from trade, gastronomy and real estate businesses. This alliance invests 200,000 EUR per year in measures to upgrade the city center, which are performed in cooperation with the City Management Department as well as the municipality. Project examples in this case are illumination concepts for the historic buildings, style guidelines for the outdoor furniture of cafés and bars, a sandpit playground for kids during the summer months and the construction of public benches. So what benefits do these alliances bring? Obviously, they co-finance city marketing projects and they generate ideas. But most importantly, they become actively involved in the development of the city in addition to their own separate businesses and they experience that we strive for a better quality of life as a whole in the city center. This leads to a closer connection and a genuine dialogue, with the municipality taking on the role of partner rather than authority. So, when all things are considered, the key term should actually be "trust".

8 Developing a Brand and a Future From the Inside

After 15 years of work, the city development is now facing some different conditions and challenges than before. Münster is a growing city with quite a few conflicts: Foremost is that the growth of the city, however welcome it has been, has led to an imbalance in living spaces, with too little affordable housing and a competition for floor space and resources. This is why a new chapter of our future-outlook process is now starting. This process will be different from the one undertaken 15 years ago;

the city marketing organization will have different tasks and roles than before. It centers on a city development concept (2030) and a concrete implementation plan. A scenario analysis further describes and ultimately determines the city's long-term perspective up to 2050. This analysis will be conducted and scientifically supervised by Professor Backhaus from the Marketingzentrum Münster and supported by the Marketing Advisory Board, which consists of representatives from all significant social sectors. Analyzing these scenarios will prevent short-term requirements, such as the recent increase in refugee numbers, from dominating the strategic orientation of the city. The third aspect of this process is including active citizens as interested agents. The city marketing organization will hold an important role here as well: It will try to create a space for the exploration of the desires, perceptions and demands of the inhabitants within an open project, which will give everyone the chance to try out new and creative ways to co-create and co-design the future of the city.

Even before the beginning of the initial future-outlook process citizens were asked what they are doing for the city's future development, without specifications as to their work, or to their function. So what actions are taken now are not about what the municipality or politicians want, or what measures are desirable to enforce. We are actively and openly listening to and observing what the citizens already do out of their own volition. And this open space, in which the citizens are already agents in the future-outlook process, will be adapted and made sustainable by city marketing.

9 Looking Ahead: City Marketing as an Agency of the Future

In the future, branding a city will get harder and harder as people and citizens become less willing to commit to superordinate communal obligations. City politics and the city marketing organizations will have to constantly counteract a stream of individual opinions, while commonalities will (almost) only exist in the form of protests against (governmental) authorities through social media. Attracting investors will raise the animosity of those who feel concerned or hindered in their personal living environment. Attention drawn towards tourists will lead to constant reminders by the citizens that the city primarily belongs to them. And the list of issues could go on forever. A city in which everyone feels entitled to work for or against governmental decisions and promote any given opinion needs a strong leitmotif, a vision! And this is exactly where I see the city marketing organization's niche: It is perfectly suited to lead a dialogue within society about the city's future, its potential and its opportunities. This is due to the fact that it does not consist of elected members, it is not accountable for political promises and it is not required to dispense feasible solutions. It is rather concerned with the city's future, with the citizen's feelings and perceptions towards the city. It can use a wider variety of modes of communication instead of only political debates, which are known to hardly ever offer any solutions and do not provide any in-depth knowledge. It has the possibility to employ art and culture as communication tools and playfully show the citizens what their city could be like. Potential campaigns or promotions could include city festivals, setting up temporary leisure time facilities for children and families in the city center, temporarily transforming courtyards into picnic areas or communal gardens, or offering public excursions through the lower city river in rubber boots.

Friedrich von Borries, who is a professor of architecture in Hamburg, assigned city marketing organizations the task of acting as an agency for producing wishes as an example, a "Wunschproduktion" (von Borries 2015). This, after all, does not mean that the marketing agencies should generate unrealizable wishes and wants that in turn need to be satisfied by even more consumption. On the contrary; von Borries insists that the organizations' main task is to address the citizens' problems and wishes regarding the future of their city and give them a platform to co-design it. He states that it could be the city marketing organization's task to let the people deal with their problems and wishes, by emotionalizing and creating events.

The headstrong Bazan Brock (Brock 2012) makes a similar demand: A city marketing organization is not supposed to act as a sales agency for any claimed USP's, but as a "civilizing agency" within the urban society. This is a brand-new direction which is worth thinking about.

In a society where processes are hardly controllable anymore, a role allocation as stated above might be of considerable interest to city marketing organizations. I would therefore like to express my hope that we will keep working on and thinking beyond the economic and other relevant problems in order to further develop our city marketing organizations. City marketing can never be finished, it can never be enough; it is about the future. And that is exactly what we should be looking towards!

References

Brock B (2012) Was ist eigentlich Stadtmarketing. Der Blick von ganz außen. Paper presented at Die Stadt, das Stadtmarketing und ich. Stadtmarketing im Spannungsfeld seiner Ansprüche, Hamburg, Nov 2012

Hauff T et al (2007) Marktorientierte Führung für Kommunen. In: Bruhn M (ed) Marktorientierte Führung im wirtschaftlichen und gesellschaftlichen Wandel. Gabler, Wiesbaden, pp 349–384

Kunzmann K (2004) Wissensstädte. Neue Aufgaben für die Stadtpolitik. In: Matthiesen U (ed) Stadtregion und Wissen. Analysen und Plädoyers für eine wissensbasierte Stadtpolitik. VS Verlag für Sozialwissenschaften, Wiesbaden, pp 29–41

Schmidt M (2011) Ein Strategisches Netzwerk für die Wissenschaftsstadt. Münster. In: Lisowski R et al (eds) Wissensbasierte Stadtentwicklung. Universitätsbibliothek Weimar, Weimar, pp 112–117. http://e-pub.uni-weimar.de/opus4/frontdoor/index/index/docId/1452. Accessed 8 Aug 2017

Spinnen B (2007) Kunst für den Standort. In: Kurzhals FG, Langer C (eds) StadtLandMarke. Strategische Markenführung als Erfolgsfaktor im Location-Branding. Murmann, Hamburg, pp 56–61

Spinnen B (2011) Mit Wissen erfolgreich im Standortwettbewerb. In: Lisowski R et al (eds) Wissensbasierte Stadtentwicklung. Universitätsbibliothek Weimar, Weimar, pp 112–117. http://e-pub.uni-weimar.de/opus4/frontdoor/index/index/docId/1452. Accessed 8 Aug 2017

von Borries F (2015) Vom Stadtmarketing zum Urban Curating. Ein kritischer Entwurf. Paper presented at Deutscher Stadtmarketingtag 2015, University of the Arts (HfK), Bremen, Germany, 26–28 Apr 2015

Bernadette Spinnen was born in 1959 near Münster. From 1978 to 1985, she studied German philology and Catholic theology in Münster, Innsbruck (Austria) and Tübingen.

In 1988, Spinnen began work with the Municipality of the City of Münster and assumed—as the youngest chief officer at the time—the management of the municipal cultural office. Under her guidance, this municipal organizational unit evolved into a moderating agency for the free cultural scene, aiming at providing artists with professional working and presentational conditions, as well as visualizing and profiling the cultural potential of the city.

In 2001, Spinnen assumed responsibility for the task of establishing the city marketing organization as an owner-operated municipal enterprise. Münster Marketing is comprised of the divisions City Center Management, Tourism Office, Congress Office, City Information, City and Event Management and Science Office and employs 40 staff members. Together, they successfully work on profiling the city of Münster in a comprehensive and holistic way.

Spinnen rose to become Chairwoman of the Bundesvereinigung City- und Stadtmarketing Deutschland (German National Association of City Marketing) in July 2016, having been Deputy Chairwoman since 2007, thus helping shape the developing identity of city management in Germany significantly. The association has acquired remarkable expertise in its topic areas, hosting two congresses relating to selected and current issues of its field of work and lending said expertise to related disciplines like city development or science.

Spinnen has published several technical contributions in relevant media and is sought after as a national expert on city marketing.

Strategies for Cities in Global Competition: An Essay on Spatial Economics and Management Science

Horst Albach

Abstract

The paper starts with a short history of the economics of cities: one city, location of many cities, competition of cities in a single currency region, global competition of cities. The second section deals with the strategies of cities that compete with each other for growth, attractiveness andwelfare of the citizens. The city of Bonn is used as an example. The limitations of competition strategies are described using the example of Trier. Legal structures of Chicago and Tokyo are analysed for comparison.

1 Introduction

In the year of 2002, a paper was published in the journal Urban Studies entitled "On the concept of territorial competitiveness: sound or misleading?" The author, Professor Roberto Camagni, writes in his abstract:

> In a globalising economy, territories and not just firms increasingly find themselves in competition with each other. In fact, unlike countries, *cities and regions compete in single currency areas,* on the basis of an absolute advantage principle and not a comparative advantage principle. This means that no efficient, automotive mechanism—like currency devaluation or prompt flexibility of wages and prices—exists to grant each territory some role in the international division of labor, whatever its relative performance. The

The paper was contributed to the CASiM Conference 2016 "European Cities in Dynamic Competition" at HHL Leipzig Graduate School of Management, Leipzig, Germany, 6 July 2016.

H. Albach (✉)
HHL Leipzig Graduate School of Management, Leipzig, Germany

Bonn, Germany
e-mail: casim@hhl.de

H. Albach et al. (eds.), *European Cities in Dynamic Competition*,
https://doi.org/10.1007/978-3-662-56419-6_8

> competitiveness of territories thus emerges as a central issue, in order to secure employment stability, benefits from external integration, continuing growth of local well-being and wealth. (Camagni 2002: 2395)

This is exactly what our Symposium is about: competition of European cities in a single currency area.

My paper deals with spatial economics and management science. Spatial economics attempts to find equilibria, management science wants to compute optima. The object of analysis is cities in a world of global competition on imperfect markets.

The paper is divided in three parts. In the first part I will present a short history of thought of spatial economics including location theory and transportation cost theory. The second section applies management science tools to cities. I will apply them to the City of Bonn and add some problems of city management in the City of Trier. In the third part I will compare city management of Chicago and Tokyo with German Cities and suggest structural changes in German cities in order to improve competitiveness.

2 The History of Spatial Economics

I will start with Johann *Heinrich von Thünen* (von Thünen 1930). Thünen rightly stands at the beginning: Paul Samuelson called him the "Founding God". Samuelson says: "Modern geographers claim Thünen. That is their right. But economists like me, who are not all that taken with location theory, hail Thünen as more than a location theorist. His theory is a theory of general equilibrium" (Samuelson 1983: 1482). Be that as it may, I follow *Masahisa Fujita* when he says: "Krugman's core-periphery model is essentially the same as the monocentric spatial structure of von Thünen in which manufactures are exclusively produced in the city and exported to the surrounding agricultural hinterland" (Fujita and Krugman 2004: 151).

The city in Thünen's theory is surrounded by circles of agrarian production characterized by less and less intensity because of rising transportation costs. The most outside circle is wilderness. Consequently, there is just one city.

Transport costs are the dominant factor in the location theory of *Alfred Weber*. In his book "Theory of the Location of Industries" he says: "The transportation factor is basically decisive for the optimal location of firms. Labor costs cause a slight deviation towards optimal labor cost locations. The agglomeration factor causes a second deviation towards an optimal agglomeration location. That is all" (Weber 1929: 35).

Martin Beckmann extended transportation costs to include other costs. He named the extended costs "costs of surpassing distance" (1988, see also Beckmann 1968 and Beckmann and Puu 1985). Changes in information technologies have the same effects as lower transportation costs. *Robert Martin* (1999) speaks of "costs of mastering distance". *Claudia Kolatek* presents an interesting example of the impact of information technology on competition (or cooperation) between cities.

She comes to the conclusion: "Since the diseconomies of agglomeration increase steadily in Tokyo, a significant part of future growth of the Japanese economy will happen in prefectures with an extraordinarily good communication infrastructure. Hokkaido and Fukuoka which are certainly not close to Tokyo have been identified as regions with a very high potential for growth" (Kolatek 1994: 198). The centripetal forces of Tokyo are, however, still very strong. *Morihiko Hiramatsu*, the governor of Oita Prefecture and former high official of the Japanese Ministry of Trade and Industry (MITI) tried to strengthen the centrifugal forces by a new highly attractive type of city. He called it "technopolis".[1] Work places in industry are highly attractive, if there are educational and cultural institutions and recreational areas close by. There is empirical proof that recreational areas close by the city influence strongly the decision of citizens to remain in the city or to move to the city. It is not only the creative citizens that the cities have to attract, it is the enterprises as well. Factors that attract companies are: Lower taxes, good traffic infrastructure, available land property at good prices to build, and non-bureaucratic and quick decisions of the city administration. These criteria of a technopolis are decisive also for firms that seek locations.

The idea of a "technopolis" seems to have cut on in German cities. The city of Gelsenkirchen advertises with the slogan "Economic Location with a Perspective" and with the "City Quarter Count Bismarck". Obviously Gelsenkirchen has a slogan which could be developed into a mission: Gelsenkirchen: the "Innovation City Ruhr" (The Ruhr is a tributary to the Rhine River). The headlines in the brochure (Stadt Gelsenkirchen 2016) are:

1. Location with firm-oriented city administration
2. Location with excellent traffic infrastructure
3. Location with flexible kindergartens, adjusted to the needs of family and work
4. Location with fun places: movies, zoo, art museum, music halls, famous major league soccer club
5. Location between forest and water.

Herbert Giersch extended the one city-model of von Thünen to two and more cities. Giersch was the president of the Kiel Institute of World Economics. He became famous worldwide when he was a member of the German Council of Economic Experts, (called "the five wise men"). In this capacity Giersch rejected the demand policy of Keynes and advised the government to apply supply theory. Herbert Giersch published a seminal paper in the Review of World Economics (Weltwirtschaftliches Archiv) with the title "Aspects of Growth, Structural Change, and Employment" (Giersch 1979). Giersch in his theory of competition of cities said: The cities may cooperate with each other, or they may compete. He analysed the case of competition: The cities compete for the mobile resources, in particular for capital and labor. Creative people are more important in this competition than

[1] Hiramatsu M (1994) Personal conference with the author.

capital. Giersch added to the classical factors of production what he called "the soft factors of competition". One of these soft factors is, e.g., the "economic ethics" of the city administration and of the inhabitants (citizens). The city with the better economic ethics has advantages in her competition with other cities (Giersch 1995). *Fujita and Mori* (2005) cite two papers which show that "attachment to home" is an important soft factor for the choice of cities by individuals. *Karl-Heinz Paqué* regrets that Paul Krugman did not recognize Giersch's paper in the Review of World Economics even though it was written in English. According to Paqué the contribution Giersch made to global competition and growth reads: "It was first of all the simple recognition that world economic growth is not driven by an exogenous technological change, but rather by the knowledge churned out in the innovative (and almost exclusively urban!) centers of the developed industrialized world by deliberate research and development efforts" (Paqué in this volume).

The thesis that cities are "growth centers" is found also in the work of *Jane Jacobs*. However, she starts from a different perspective. She rejects the traditional theory that agriculture is the starting point of economic thinking. Instead the city is the beginning. Demand commences in the city, and agricultural farms supply goods in demand. Agricultural production is constantly improved by technical progress. Firms located in the city supply the agricultural demand for innovations. Jacobs (1961, 1969) calls her theory "The Economy of Cities". In her theory communication between agriculture and city play a significant role. Florida calls Jane Jacobs "the great urbanist" (Florida 2008: 43).[2]

It is *Carl Christian von Weizsäcker* who analyzed the kinds of communication within the city and between cities and farms. Products and services are the contents of communication. Judges, creditors, suppliers of money, attorneys, administrators, and scientists provide the services. They are summarized as "knowledge". The core of von Weizsäcker's theory of competition is knowledge. He distinguished three levels: consumption, production, and innovation (von Weizsäcker 1980, 1981, 2011). Innovation in my view is the level of knowledge. Consumption is the level of demand. Demand is either consumption of *known goods* or demand for *new goods, unknown until now*. I call people with demand for unknown goods "Schumpeter Customers". The second level is characterized by the production of known goods. On this level suppliers compete for the demand of known goods. Competition on this level is stationary. The third level is the level of innovation. New knowledge is produced on this level and results in new goods and services. The demand on this level is dynamic. Von Weizsäcker proves that innovations have to be protected by the state. Otherwise competition on the second level would not function adequately. But not all innovation can be protected (by patents, trademarks, user marks, licenses and publishers protection). Lectures, talks, performance of music cannot easily be protected despite all efforts of royalties collecting societies such as VG WORT and

[2]It is interesting to note that Florida quotes Jacobs frequently in his book, but never mentions Paul Krugman, and that Krugman never refers to Jane Jacobs.

GEMA in Germany. Protection of decisions of organization structures and services of attorneys, judges, and bankers would be very costly—too costly to be efficient.

Herbert Giersch took the existence of more than one city for granted. *Paul Krugman* (1996) asks the question: Given one city what are the conditions for establishing a second city? He argues that the growth of a city leads to higher wages paid by the firms of the city. Eventually they lose their competitiveness. A new city is founded with lower wages and different products. The two cities compete with each other on a market with diversified products. This is imperfect competition. Krugman proves analytically the existence of a dynamic equilibrium of two and three cities. Krugman used numerical simulation to get beyond this small number of cities. In his "race track model" he developed a model with continuous space. And interestingly enough later he proved the results of the simulation analytically.

Krugman does not specify the kinds of products that the firms in the two cities offer on the market. Giersch talked about creative people as production factors. They produce services like those of judges, attorneys, bankers, teachers, scientists, doctors, and barbers. The market for services is an imperfect market for knowledge. *Fujita and Mori* distinguish the creation of knowledge from the transfer of knowledge and refer to an article by *Ottaviano, Tabuchi and Thisse* (2002) that includes R&D as a concrete example of the creation of knowledge.

Rising wages are another reason for inhabitants to move to other cities as a consequence of competition on level III. If wages rise faster than the costs of communication, firms move to other cities, and families willing to move to the city choose another city for their living. Rising wages set "centrifugal forces" in move. The new city does not produce the same products than the old city. Competition between cities is "imperfect competition". *Adam Smith* in his "The Wealth of Nations" analyzed "perfect competition" (Smith 1863). It was a highly interesting but unreal model of the economy.[3] *Edward Chamberlin* (1933) in his book "The Theory of Monopolistic Competition" revolutionized price theory and introduced "imperfect competition" as typical of markets. His theory has become the basis for Krugman's "Spatial Economics". Chamberlin did not distinguish, however, between levels II and III as von Weizsäcker had done.

A very nice picture of such an imperfect competition is the "sunny side egg" of *Bernd Spiegel*. He assumed as a starting point of his model that people are distributed equally over a region. This region is a "region of opinions" (Spiegel 1961). Then Spiegel assumes that a supplier of a certain product enters the region(Fig. 1). Suppose it is a market for cars. The automobile industry lives on progress. The market is a "progressive market", a market of level III. The car attracts buyers. They identify with the car. But not all of the people in the region identify with the car. Many reject the car for various reasons. Potential competitors realize their behavior. They offer a car with different properties which are preferred by these customers.

[3]This is the interpretation of Krugman. Karen Horn (2009: 12) contradicted it.

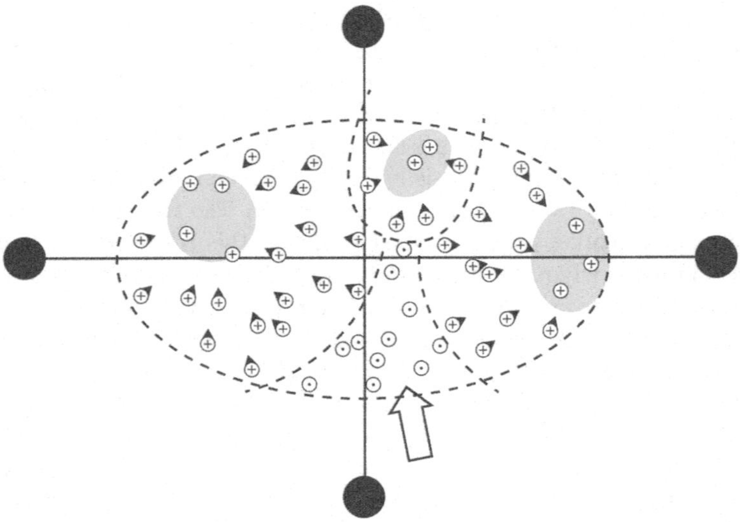

Fig. 1 Bernd Spiegel's region of opinions (modified from Spiegel 1961)

When a third automobile maker recognizes that he might attract buyers who reject the two existing cars because e.g. they eject too much CO_2, he will position his car in a "manifest of latent niche", a car with less exhaust of CO_2.

One of the predecessors of using simulation in the study of cities is *John F. Forrester*. In his book entitled "Urban Dynamics" he developed a simulation model of the city (Forrester 1969) and applied it to Boston.[4] Unfortunately, we have not yet begun to develop a simulation of the city of Leipzig.

In the next chapter I will present the legal and the financial situation of two German cities—Bonn and Trier—and then discuss management science instruments which might help to reform the present situation and improve the competitiveness of the cities in global competition.

3 The Present Situation of German Cities

3.1 The City of Bonn

3.1.1 The Legal Structure of Bonn

Bonn is the former capital of Germany. When Germany was reunited, the capital was moved to Berlin. But in the famous Bonn-Berlin-Contract the German parliament decided to move only 40% of the employees in the ministries to Berlin. 60%

[4]In a presentation of his model at the Berlin Technical University in 1968 Forrester told the audience that he discussed the problems of Boston with the mayor of Boston. He developed the model over the weekend and presented the results the following week to the mayor.

should stay in Bonn. Today, more than 40% of the employees have already been moved to Berlin, and Bonn fights for more money from the federal government as a compensation for the loss of inhabitants.

The legal structure of Bonn does not differ fundamentally from other cities. The city is a parliamentary (or indirect) democracy. The citizens vote for the members of the *City Council*. The city council is the most important decision unit of the city. The candidates are selected by the political parties. Some cities have a group of "free voters"; their candidates also run for membership in the city council.

The council votes for the *Mayor* in a majority decision. His turn is 5 years. He selects the members of the *Administration*. The Bonn administration consists of six divisions:

1. The head of the press (the Mayor)
2. General administration (the City Director)
3. Finances (the Chief Financial Officer)
4. Planning, environment, traffic (a Deputy Mayor)
5. Culture, sports, science (a Deputy Mayor)
6. Families—children, youth, schools, social services, health, law (a Deputy Mayor)

The council is supported by

1. sector representation groups
2. the chief committee
3. other committees (controlling, finances)

These institutions are entitled to decide on certain issues. They may make suggestions to the council.

In the year of 2014 the City of Bonn has issued guidelines for *citizen participation*.

3.1.2 The Financial Structure of Bonn

The city operates with a budget. The city council decides on the budget. The budget has income from various sources that I will mention in more detail in connection with the city of Trier. If total debt exceeds a certain limit, a *Chief Regional Officer* takes control of the city finances. The City of Bonn is rather close to that limit: total debt amounts to 1674 billion EUR or 5.380 EUR per inhabitant. Therefore, the council has decided to embark on a tough savings strategy. In addition the city has raised the property tax B (on the value of houses) by 300 points and the property tax A (on land property with and without buildings) by 150 points.

Income and expenses of the city are available by activities of the city for 2013. Table 1 shows expenses (in total and in per cent of total expenses) and net expenses.

Table 1 shows very clearly the basic problem of city finance in Germany: Social services and safety and order amount to almost one third of total expenses. Net expenses are almost one fourth of total net expenses. The federal government passes

Table 1 The budget of the city of Bonn for 2013 (Stadt Bonn 2014)

No.	Activity	Total expenses (in millions of EUR)	Relative expenses (in per cent)	Net expenses (in millions of EUR)
1	Social services	191.3	16	127.0
2	Safety and order	169.0	14	136.4
3	Children, youth, families	154.7	13	90.7
4	Administration	117.4	10	81.3
5	Supplies and disposal	91.3	7	29.3
6	Regional planning and city development	91.3	7	29.3
7	Culture and science	71.6	6	59.8
8	School activities	69.3	6	55.0
9	Traffic, land and equipment	64.4	5	32.8
10.	Economy and tourism	17.8	1.4	10.3
11.	Sports subsidies	17.1	1.4	16.0
12.	Building and dwelling	10.8	0.9	6.6
13.	Culture and environmental services	8.0	0.7	4.6
14.	Health services	6.2	0.5	5.5
15.	Environmental protection	3.4	0.3	3.1
16.	Foundations	1.0	0.1	1.0
		1084.6	89.3	571.5
17.	General finance	144.8	10.7	465.2
	Sums total	1229.4	100.0	105.3

one law after the other on social benefits, but the cities have to carry the burden, and compensations from the federal budget are inadequate. The German federal government calls these compensation payments "sharp accounting" in my wording: "not enough and tough control".

The German "Social Laws Book" contains the following laws:

1. Asylants Law (Asylbewerbergesetz)
2. Support Law (Betreuungsgesetz)
3. Federal Refugees Law (Bundesvertriebenengesetz)
4. Gender Equity Law (Gleichstellungsgesetz)
5. Youth Support Law (Jugendförderungsgesetz)
6. Youth Safety Law (Jugendschutzgesetz)
7. Children Safety Law (Kinderschutzgesetz)
8. Day Care Facilities Law (Kindertagesstättengesetz)
9. State Children Safety Law (Landeskinderschutzgesetz)
10. Support Safety Law (Unterhaltssicherungsgesetz)
11. Support Advance Payments Law (Unterhaltsvorschussgesetz)
12. Housing Rent Payments Law (Wohngeldgesetz)

and there are more.

I have not found data of the breakdown of total earnings of 610 million EUR. Income taxes have risen from 118.6 million EUR in 2010 to 175.7 million EUR in 2016. Interest payments amount to 49.3 million EUR, and repayments of debt will be 45.3 million EUR during the whole year of 2016.

3.2 The City of Trier

3.2.1 The Legal Structure of Trier

The city council of Trier is the decision-making body of the city. The citizens vote for the 56 members every 5 years. The most recent elections took place in May 2014. Seven political parties are represented in the city council and form "fractions" with several members: Socialists, Christian Democrats, the Green party, Free Electors Group, the Left Party, the Alternative for Germany (Rightwing Party), the Free Democrats. One person represents the Pirates Party.

The council has eight committees. The members are elected by the members of the council. They prepare the decisions of the council or decide themselves. The committees are:

1. Education, Social Activities, Living, Youth, and Labor
2. Tourism, City Marketing, Safety and Order
3. Environment, City Planning, Building, Sports
4. Youth Support
5. Culture
6. Schools
7. City Law
8. Management.

The Lord Mayor is himself responsible for the following activities:

- Media and communication
- City development and statistics
- Migration and integration
- Representation of women
- Equality for genders
- Personnel council
- City's economic improvement
- Finances
- Organization, information technology
- Accounting

The Lord Mayor has three deputees

1. Education, Social Activities, Living, Youth, Labor
2. Culture, Tourism, City Marketing, Safety and Order

3. Environment, Planning, Building, Schools, Sports

It is amazing for many visitors of Trier that there is no separate department for the many remarkable old monuments of the city. Roman buildings include the famous Porta Nigra (one of four portals to the Roman City), the Basilica, the Thermic Baths, the Cathedral with the world-renowned Holy Robe of Christ, the Arch Bishop's Palace of the Middle Ages. They are all under the administration of the federal State of Rhineland–Palatia. Only the city library with its Treasure Room of early medieval books and the original Gutenberg Bible, and the birth place of Karl Marx are under the administration of the city. The following statement in the city's strategy paper "Trier 2025" is very typical of cities with a long history: "By 2020 the Roman Temple District in the Altbach Valley will be dug up partly by archaeologists and will attract about 10,000 tourists annually". (Stadt Trier 2012: 11) But there are obstacles: Presently, the area is occupied by private garden plot holders. They will resist any archaeological digging. And if the digging should eventually be successful, the entrance fees of the expected 10,000 tourists will go to the state's budget and not to the city budget.

3.2.2 The Financial Structure of Trier[5]

The Lord Mayor of Trier said in his budget speech in 2012 that the city can no longer maintain the city streets and keep them clean "because the budget will no longer be accepted by the regional controller" (Jensen 2012: 19). Budget consolidation takes priority over investment in the future. The city according to the mayor hopes that expenses will be covered by income in 2022 but only if there will be solidarity between all levels. Solidarity, however, is nothing but reshuffling of money between the three levels of budgets: city, state, federal government. It does not mean city growth of the city economy as a consequence of a successful strategy for global competition.

The Trier strategic concept says clearly and unmistakably: If Trier was a private company Trier would go bankrupt in 2015. In 2012 the city had dismissed so many employees that it had to postpone approved investments: 50% only of the investments approved by the council could be executed.

Expenses for the personnel of the city administration amount to more than one fourth of total expenses. That seems rather high to me. Even more interesting, however, are the social expenses that amount to one fifth of the budget (Table 2). The budget lists 16 categories of expenses under the heading "Expenses for Social Security": Germany once was a social market economy. Today it is a socialist welfare state.

[5]This part of my paper is based on a talk given at the Fall Meeting of the Order pour le mérite at Trier on September 29, 2012.

Table 2 Budget of the city of Trier for 2012 (Stadt Trier 2013)

Expenses	THSD EUR	Income	THSD EUR
Manageable projects	131.130 (28%)		107.849 (32%)
Infrastructure	37.560	Taxes	71.380
Building management	17.450	Fees	19.209
Youth, families	47.579	Rents	9.989
Economy	3.549	Concessions	7.271
Culture	12.539		
Safety and order	12.453		
Not manageable	(62%)		(68%)
Personell	90.656	Income tax	27.796
Social expenses	66.386	Sales tax	5.201
Solidarity pact	1.563	Fixed income	42.474
Schools, education	20.134	Redistribution	40.688
Interest payments	18.424	Subsidies	26.607
Credit repayments	13.871	Expenses payments	7.954
		Div. income	172
		Credit increase	52.629
	342.164		*342.164*

THSD Thousand

Trier: Expenses for Social Security 2012:

1. Expenses for living subsidies
2. Expenses for education and integration
3. Expenses for children day care
4. Subsidies for private kindergartens
5. Mother-child care
6. Support for situations in need
7. Social group work
8. Subsidies for education activities
9. Social pedagogic help for families
10. 24 hour care
11. Education at home
12. Support for alternative partnerships
13. Help for young persons of age
14. Help for integration
15. Help for applicants of asylum under 18 years of age
16. Social pedagogic help for school children

The city is aware of the fact that the financial situation will continue to be very precarious. Therefore, the city has set up principles for its activities in the coming years:

Trier: Principles for Future Activities

1. Decisions for small activities rather than for big ones, but no strategy for the future.
2. Reduction of expenses for infrastructures and other activities
3. Restoration of infrastructures but no money for new investment
4. Increase of attractiveness for private business
5. Photovoltaic panels on all roofs of city buildings
6. Closing the gap between the poor and the rich
7. Gender mainstreaming and gender budgeting

These principles can of course not be considered to be a strategy for the future.

I leave it up to the reader to decide whether these principles improve trustworthiness of future activities of the city or not.

Trier has formulated a vision for the next 10 years (until 2022). The vision tries to identify the self-understanding of the city. However, it is such a mix of identifications that to me it does not help Trier to become competitive in Trier's global markets. The vision has 12 points—11 too many. They are:

1. Trier is a city with 110,000 inhabitants (presently 104,000).
2. Trier is a virtual European metropolis.
3. Trier is a European center of knowledge.
4. Trier is the capital of culture.
5. Trier is a city of important European tourism.
6. Trier is a competence center for the health economy in the region Trier/Luxembourg.
7. Trier is a social city.
8. Trier is a city of building with social planning principles.
9. Trier is a city for handling refugees.
10. Trier is a city with a "Business Improvement District" in the center of the City.
11. Trier is a city with "creative pilots".
12. Trier is an "early excellence center" of kindergartens.

This list is certainly not a vision and definitely not a mission. The reality of the financial structure of German cities is deplorable.

This list is miles away from a sound and successful strategy for global competition. I will therefore now turn to the application of strategic business management to cities.

4 Management Science Tools for Cities

4.1 Introductory Remarks

Let me start with a story. Forty three years ago I held a 2-week seminar for the higher-level managers of Hoechst, one of the world's top chemical companies in Germany. The seminar was scheduled to start on a Monday. Participants gathered on Sunday evening. They all were rather gloomy. They were afraid their firm might not survive. The OPEC countries had just raised their prices for crude oil drastically. Participants were afraid their company would lose its competitiveness in many fields. I was sure I could not start the seminar teaching cost accounting. I called the Chief Planning Officer and asked him to start the seminar the next morning. He came and talked about the situation. He presented the management tools that he had discussed with the Executive Board of Hoechst. The members of the board had decided on a convincing strategy for survival. The participants of the seminar lost their fear in the course of a heated discussion. You should remember: It was the time period when families and their children could take a walk on the German High Ways (Autobahnen) on weekends because automobiles and trucks were forbidden in order to save gas.

We now ask: Are the tools of strategic planning of firms applicable in global competition of cities?

The theory of the firm is based on five principles:

1. Autonomy
2. Financial equilibrium
3. Efficiency
4. Governance, and
5. Trust

4.1.1 Autonomy

Autonomy is the central principle of firms in a market economy. It is also the most important principle of cities and communities. If a firm loses its autonomy, it goes bankrupt. Communities go bankrupt also, but are saved by the Chief Regional Officer (Regierungspräsident) who takes over the investment and financial decisions. The economic experts (Sachverständigenrat) have analyzed in depth how the autonomy of cities could be improved (Sachverständigenrat 1983). The result is not particularly convincing.

4.1.2 Financial Equilibrium

The financial equilibrium is the precondition for autonomy. Equilibrium is defined as income to be equal or greater than expenses. Income is not only income from activities but also income from raising debt, and expenses include repayment of debt. Income of cities includes city taxes, fees, and returns from city services. Income includes subsidies from the federal budget.

German cities exist in a four-level financial structure: the City, the region (Regierungsbezirk), the state, and the federal government. One could add the German Railroad Corporation, especially in Bonn. This is a very complicated structure that limits the autonomy of the city to compete successfully. In Trier the Roman ruins are under the rule of the state of Rhineland-Palatinate, the university is financed by the state, and the city does not have enough money to clean the city streets. Trier cannot increase its burden of debt because the regional authority would take over financing the city. The federal parliament has—as I have said—passed a "Social Laws Book" but has left the cities with the financial consequences. Communities with less financial trouble have to contribute subsidies to the communities in greater financial trouble. Actually this means that successful cities have to pay a penalty for being efficient to those cities that are managed badly. Most German politicians have obviously forgotten the bankruptcy of the former German Democratic Republic. Interestingly enough, the wealthier cities have to pay 660 million euros annually into a "Consolidation Fund" until 2020. If one applies incentive theory one would expect that the wealthier cities will try to avoid payments into this consolidation fund by spending as much as possible on competitiveness rather than subsidizing less efficient cities and communities.

Cities like Wolfsburg and Leverkusen suffer financially because Volkswagen and Bayer Chemicals now make lower profits and consequently pay lower taxes to their cities.

Income from city taxes in Trier amounts to just 20% of total expenses in Trier, taxes from parts of income taxes and sales taxes amount to 10% and cannot be influenced by the city unless the population of the city grows. Cities like Bonn raise their city taxes (property taxes) despite the protest of the Chamber of Commerce and Industry and despite the fact that it is counterproductive. It deters creative citizens and firms from moving to the city and forces inhabitants to leave the city. Haribo is a striking example: Plants and Capital and Employees have moved to a village in the vicinity of Bonn.

The financial community system in Germany has to be fundamentally changed in order to strengthen the competitiveness of the cities. Some cities try to solve their financial problems by founding Private Public Partnerships (PPP). The City of Schweinfurt runs its museum of nineteenth century art as a PPP: The building was financed by the state of Bavaria, current expenses are mostly financed by the city, and the paintings have been contributed in the form of a family foundation. But PPPs are just a step in the direction of trust in the city administration and of strong emotional bonds to their home city. The Museum Council is the decision body. Its members are the Mayor of Schweinfurt, the representative of the State of Bavaria, the Head of the Museum's Board of Trustees, which represents the donors of the pieces of art, and three independent experts.

Another attempt to improve the financial situation of the cities is close cooperation between the city, the firms, the local university, and the state. The University of Bochum had a very active "Schumpeter President", and it seems that the new president, Professor Axel Schölmerich, has stepped in his footsteps. The city of Bochum has signed a cooperation contract with the university and the state.

The university builds and runs an innovative science center, the state contributes the former Opel (General Motors) administration building, and the city and the university offer young founders of small companies room to settle on the Opel premises (WAZ 2016). Bochum obviously seems to have a mission. Research institutes of the university and founder firms will become a Ruhr Valley, and many citizens call the mission a University City. Bochum has already ten universities, academies and schools of higher education.

4.1.3 Efficiency

Firms in a market economy environs have to be profitable if they want to survive in competition. This means that they have to be productive and efficient in their activities. Adam Smith called this principle the "wealth of nations", in German: Wohlstand für alle. In this sense the cities and the firms in the city have the same objective: improving the wealth of their employees and their citizens.

4.1.4 Governance

The mayor of the city of Bonn is not a "Schumpeter Mayor". His position is that of an administrator, not of a "pioneer". He was voted into his position by just a little over 50%—not a good vote for a mayor who has to compete with other cities in Europe and beyond. He executes what the City Council decides, mostly with just over 50% of the votes. The structure of the Council and its decision processes are not equivalent to those of the board of a corporation. Is this structure adequate for making and maintaining the city competitive? It is obviously not.

There is a strong trend today for citizen participation in various decisions of the city. This may be considered a good sign of the engagement of the inhabitants of the city's affairs. But it is on the other hand a sign of a highly problematic reaction to the dissatisfaction with the representative democracy of our cities (and even of our federal states) (Schäffer 2016). If Botho von Portatius[6] is right with his forecast that the new digital world provides renewed chances for growth of smaller cities, they will have to address the form of city governance under the aspect of competition, trust in a "Schumpeter mayor", and love for the city, or, to quote Fujita and Mori again "attachment to home" in a world of creativity and mobility. Cities have to introduce the rule of "good corporate governance". Appropriately addressed, cities can learn from the discussions in the Federal Commission on Good Corporate Governance which was set up by the federal government of Germany in order to solve conflicts in corporations.

These conflicts were the consequence of a mistaken development in microeconomic theory. Microeconomists assumed that every individual acts in her own interest, maximizes her own profit, and exploits other people even if her behavior violates the interests of other individuals: "homo homini lupus". Indeed, they made irresponsible behavior of egoistic people who misinterpret the objective of maximizing profits or shareholder value as the basis of microeconomics. Instead

[6]Email to the author on 24 June 2016.

of acting in the interest of society, actors use the fact that their partners are less informed than they themselves (asymmetric information) and thus can exploit them in order to increase their own profit. Conflicts between shareholders, members of the board, and executives resulted from this behavior. Good corporate governance opposes moral hazard and asymmetric information.

In the city the members of the city council try to maximize the wealth of their respective political constituency. This frequently (or always?) is not identical with maximizing the wealth of all citizens. Good corporate governance in the city means that the mayor has to reduce conflict and to create trust in his overriding goal to improve the wealth of all the citizens in the city and to attract citizens that help to improve the well-being of the city. The mayor is responsible for a "culture of trust".

4.1.5 Culture of Trust

William Cronon in his 1991 book "Nature's Metropolis: Chicago and the Great West" writes: "Chicago was inevitably destined for greatness" (Cronon 1991: 10). The city became the great metropolis of the American heartland not because of shrewd long-term planning but because of self-reinforcing advantages: The concentration of population and production in Chicago, and the city's role as a transportation hub caused all roads to lead to Chicago (Krugman 1993). Today, however, Chicago seems to blossom because of its "culture of trust". It is a trust of the citizens in the city governance. Some families give money for the welfare of the city. The citizens realize that the mayor of the city is a "Schumpeter Mayor", a creative pioneer. Gerhard Banner voices his opinion that the mayor of the city of Christchurch in New Zealand is such a mayor. He calls this type of city governance "integral leadership". He does not talk about cities in global competition (Banner 2001: 208). The mayor of Christchurch seems to have lost the trust of his citizens after the earthquake and the slow reconstruction of the city.

The Chicago of Germany is Hamburg. Philipp Klais, owner and CEO of the organ manufacturer Joh. Klais Orgelbau, Bonn, gave a talk on the new Elbe Philharmonic Hall arguing that the citizens of Hamburg despite all criticism of the high costs of the building wanted it as a sign of their pride in and love for their city (Klais 2016). And a single donor financed the organ with its roughly 10,000 pipes.[7]

4.2 A Strategy for the City of Bonn

The Elbe Philharmonic Hall is quite obviously in striking contrast to Bonn. The citizens of Bonn eventually gave up trying to replace the old Beethoven Symphony Building with a new more appropriate and future-oriented Symphony Hall.

The reason for the apparent loss of self-confidence and pride of the people in Bonn may be due to the move of the German government from Bonn to Berlin. The city officials including the mayor constantly accuse the Berlin government of violating the Bonn/Berlin Law. They have sound reason for this complaint. Recently,

[7] In my view, this is in striking contrast to the Beethoven Hall in Bonn.

figures were published showing that 61% of the government employees now work in Berlin. The Law of 1994 reads instead: "the majority of the government employees will remain in Bonn" (Baumann and Möhle 2016).

The reason for the lack of confidence in the city may on the other hand lie earlier in history. Bonn in 1961 consisted of three different groups of its population: the old families, the university employees, and the civil servants in the federal ministries. There was little interchange between them, and each group had different interests.

The problems of decision-making in cities given, it may be very difficult indeed to apply the wisdom of corporate management to the city, particularly to Bonn. But I will try. In the following, I will apply four instruments in a strategy for global competition of the city:

1. Mission
2. Competition and Cooperation
3. Risk and Uncertainty
4. Decision

4.2.1 Mission

Let me start with a fact: Conflict among the members of the executive board of companies is reason for the insolvency of the firm. If the CFO quits his job due to strategic conflict in the executive board, the firm will go bankrupt within the next 2 years.[8] Applied to cities: Conflict in the city council leads to wrong actions in the competition with other cities in Europe and on global markets. In other words: Trust of the citizens in their city government is a precondition of success in the city's competition with other cities.

The mission of the city expresses the self-understanding of the city and its citizens. What I have said about Bonn so far shows that there is no self-understanding. The city mayor fights against the drain of employees and ministries who move to Berlin. Wolfgang Clement (2016) advises Bonn not to fight against the inevitable.[9] He seems to favor the mission named "Bonn is a UN City". I have asked several citizens of Bonn: "What is in your opinion the mission of Bonn?" The answers were: Federal City, Beethoven City, Science City, Knowledge City, Suburb of Cologne. On January 30, 2015, a forum "Bonn: City of the Future" strongly demanded an "end with the federal city romance". The Chamber of Commerce and Industry published a report by Professor Dirk Vallée (a city planner) on December 22, 2015 which contains the following "vision": "The city of Bonn and the surrounding communities will establish a sustainable, systematic, and lasting cooperation, thus developing a premium-region in the Metropolitan Region Rhineland" (Vallée 2015: 12), by the way: excluding Cologne. Would anybody believe that such a mission would

[8]This is the result of a study using the data of the Bonn Data Base.

[9]The heading reads: "25 Jahre Umzugsbeschluss. The former Prime Minister of the State of North Rhine-Westphalia Wolfgang Clement says: One should not shut one's eyes in front of the facts. Bonn and Berlin have to find a new level of understanding."

emotionally unite the citizens of Bonn? It should be obvious that a city that does not have a mission cannot set priorities for the management of the city.

In 2016, regional development experts from Bonn, the Rhein Sieg District and the Ahrweiler District presented a report "Wissen hoch 5" in which they underline the importance of the five local universities for the region They see a mission for Bonn in the "science region" (Rheinische Friedrich-Wilhelms-Universität Bonn et al. 2016).

I have been most impressed by the mission "Health City". The university clinics, the many hospitals, cooperation with the clinics in Cologne, the life sciences institutes could be the core of this mission. The Seven Hills (Siebengebirge) on the East bank and the large forest on the West bank of the Rhine (Kottenforst) would be part of this mission. The two big firms in Bonn, Deutsche Telekom and Postbank, fit into this scenario: They do not pollute the atmosphere. It would be counterproductive to close public swimming pools in order to save money. They are essential for the wellbeing and health of the young and the older citizens. The mission "Health City" would mean: Bonn is proud of the many Muslims and their families that visit or live in Bonn and seek treatment in the hospitals and hope for improving their health. Citizens would not complain about the numerous Burkas in the shopping centers in Bonn and Bad Godesberg as they have done and still do. Rather, they would be proud of the visible export of health services to people from many countries.

4.2.2 Competition and Cooperation

The mission defines the type of competition that the city is in. It is obvious that the city cannot compete on many fields. It is amazing that Davos in Switzerland defines its mission as "a resort, a sports, a research, a congress, and a health city". "Research" means a small institute for snow and avalanche research. The city could have added "the Thomas Mann City", "the Ernst Ludwig Kirchner city". Davos obviously does not know what a mission is. On the other side: Davos is a good example for the combination "very strong, change of mission's investments": When the drug for tuberculosis was invented in 1944, the city could maintain its mission "health city", but had to change its investments to dermatology.

A successful city with a clear mission knows its competitors. Usually it is enough to look at the strongest competitor. It is certainly not necessary to define more than three competitors. If the city wanted to compete with more than three cities, it would just squander resources and money. So, who is the strongest competitor of Bonn as the "Health City"? It might be Berlin. But I am not sure. I will just show the competition matrix that the city would have to use in order to test the chances of being successful in its competition with the strongest competitor.

When the city has decided on a mission and identified its strongest competitor, the city might strengthen its competitiveness by seeking a strong partner (with the same mission). In the case of Bonn this would be Cologne. Presently there is cooperation between the clinics of Cologne and Bonn in various fields. Further cooperation agreements would certainly improve the competitiveness of Bonn.

Attractiveness for customers and creative citizens \ Competitor city	City is better	City is inferior
High	City is very competitive	City is in dangerous position: investing necessary
Low	City prepares for change of mission	Mayor should be fired

Fig. 2 Competition matrix

Two factors are of decisive importance for a strategy of survival and success in competition. It is the competitor, but it is also the customers. If the city has a greater market share—attracts more visitors—than the most important competitor, the city will be successful in global competition and thus survive. If the demand of customers increases, the city is on safe grounds. If, however, the demand for the goods and services that the city offers is declining, then survival becomes a big problem. This is, what Fig. 2 shows very clearly.

4.2.3 Risk and Uncertainty

Every mission bears risks. The oil crises of the twentieth century (1973–1974 and 1979–1980) have demonstrated that firms should not only study the sales market and its customers and competitors, but that the supplier market is just as important. Figure 3 shows a risk matrix which represents the risks inherent in the projects that the city wants to invest in in order to fulfill its mission.

Uncertainty is more general than risk. Risks are analyzed with probabilities, uncertainty cannot be handled mathematically. But the analysis of uncertainty is important for cities as much as for firms. "Country risk" is a well-known external factor of uncertainty. One famous one is the risk of Persia. Most firms did not have such a country risk on their agenda. The Deutsche Bank had a "Risk and Uncertainty Form" which included country risk in the then usual form of the World Bank. But the Deutsche Bank had added one question: "rumor and gossip". The director of the Paris branch had filled it out: "There is a strange character here in St. Cloud (a suburb of Paris) named Chomeini. He wants to overthrow the Shah of Persia. I am afraid he will try to do so!" The strategists in Frankfurt took this information seriously. The Deutsche Bank withdrew from Persia, thus minimizing losses in Persia.

The Bayer Corporation operated a chemical plant at Brunsbüttel in northern Germany. Close to the plant was a nuclear power plant. Bayer risk analysts built on the assumption of an accident in the power plant. They forgot completely that an accident might happen in the Bayer plant with consequences to the nuclear plant.

Resources (money, people) \ Projects	Not critical	Doubtful	Critical
Not critical	Realize project		
Doubtful		Further analysis of project necessary	
Critical			Give up project

Fig. 3 Risk matrix

But then an attack of terrorists happened. Fortunately they could be stopped; and then Risk Management of Bayer included the possibility of an attack of the chemical plant in their risk strategy. Considerable expenses for investments for more safety were the consequence of the new risk and uncertainty analysis. Figure 4 shows the tool for coping with uncertainty. The city of Brunsbüttel does not have any risk strategy. The City was obviously considered far enough away from the risk factors.

4.2.4 Decisions

It should be clear that the uncertainties in Fig. 4 are determined by the mission of the city. Figure 4 is just an indication of the type of uncertainty analysis that the city might consider. Ellen Haustein presented the risk management of the City of Rostock at the CASiM Conference "European Cities in Dynamic Competition" in Leipzig in the summer of 2016. Citizens participate in this activity. This is very helpful because citizens may introduce factors of risk and uncertainty which the city administration might otherwise overlook. Unfortunately she did not submit her paper for publication.

In case the mission is clear, the projects for fulfilling the mission to compete are selected and risks and uncertainty are bearable the city has to decide to invest or to reject projects. If Bonn would decide for the mission "Health City", this would require major investments in plant and infrastructure. Fast access to hospitals is important for fighting strokes. Given the Bonn infrastructure, more helicopters might be necessary. If traffic noise is considered to be unacceptably high in the city and has, therefore, to be reduced in the city if the mission is "health city", investment in the highway around the city, a project of heated discussions for many years now, has high priority. Figure 5 is a tool for preparing decisions.

Source of uncertainty \ Degree of exposure to uncertainty		Not critical	Highly critical
External factors	Capital market Taxation Technologies Wages Tourism etc.		
Internal factors	Infrastructure Environmental protection Energy supply Strikes Terrorism		
Factors of competitiveness	Hard factors Soft factors		

Fig. 4 Uncertainty

Uncertainty \ Projects' priority	High	Medium	Low
Small	Invest		
Medium		Analyse further	
Great			Reject or disinvest

Fig. 5 Decision matrix

4.3 A Mission for Trier

4.3.1 Mission

I discussed with a representative of the Chamber of Commerce and Industry of Trier, and also with a top manager of the Trier Employment Agency: What is a mission for Trier? The result was quite clear: Trier is in every domain except for one a "laggard" in the sense of Schumpeter. The officials in Trier talk about catching up. In my view Trier never will. The one and only exception is tourism. Tourism is by far the most successful activity in the city. The mission of Trier is tourism with the heading "Trier—the City of 2000 Years of Living History". This mission would determine projects and investments for improving tourism. Trier is European history—Emperor Constantine, the Medieval Electors, the Archbishop, the Roman Basilica, the Cathedral with the Holy Robe of Christ, the eldest wine cellar in Europe, the Gutenberg Bible, the birthplace of Karl Marx, and nearby Luxembourg with the headquarters of the European Union.

4.3.2 Competitor

Trier is the oldest city of Germany. Trier does not have a competitor. Trier is unique. And Trier would be even better, if the Roman ruins would be turned over to the city from the state. Trier would be more autonomous in its development.

4.3.3 Partner

The partner in the mission "Trier—the City of 2000 Years of Living History" could and should be Rome. Rome would be a wonderful partner—just like Cologne for Bonn. And Luxembourg would no longer be a competitor in shopping centers.

5 Comparative Analysis of Foreign Cities: Chicago and Tokyo

5.1 City Management of Chicago

5.1.1 Introduction

I have quoted William Cronon's book on Chicago already. One may have asked: is it really true that Chicago prospers because of its "culture of trust"? Cronon himself notes that in the early times rural and small town residents of Chicago's hinterland criticized that the city acted as a "magnet for sin" (Cronon 1991: 357). Cronon identifies Chicago as the successful goal of the Turner movement to the frontier: start with the hunters, then traders, pathfinders, pastors, intensive farming, and end with the city and the factory system topped by Chicago's famous Columbian Exhibition of 1893. Chicago was in his view the end product of all the sources of American energy, individualism, and political democracy (Cronon 1991: 31).

I selected Chicago as my example of a well-run city because Dean Donald Jacobs of Northwestern University had told me years ago: "Chicago is one of the best-governed cities in the United States". I had visited Chicago in 1953 when Chicago was still the cattle town of the West, and when Al Capone was still in every citizen's memories.

I was very fortunate when I visited Chicago again in 2016. I had a conversation with Don Haider, a professor of Social Enterprise at Northwestern University. He once ran for Mayor of Chicago (Freemon 1988). I discussed with him five success factors of the City of Chicago:

1. the legal structure of the city
2. the Mayor
3. the financial structure of the city
4. the universities
5. the people of Chicago—melting pot, not ghettos

5.1.2 The Legal Structure of Chicago

a) The Wards

The start of the legal structure of Chicago is the Chicago Fire of 1871. The city was almost completely destroyed. The city decided not to rebuild the coast line. It was turned over to the city as public property. The question was what to do with the lake front. The answer was given by the City Club of Chicago.

The City Club was officially founded in 1903 by private citizens with the purpose "to build a better city for themselves and for posterity". The Club freed the city from corruption which was a major achievement in itself. In 1909 the City Club formulated its goal "to cooperate with public authorities toward constructive results". One of the most important results was the 1909 Chicago plan for an open and free lake front.

It was this club of private individuals dedicated to the best of the city that got the legislation to zoning of the city. After some experimenting the Club decided to divide the city into 50 wards. In 1981 a new Redistricting Ordinance was adopted by the City Council. Each ward had about 60,000 citizens and one leader, called "alderman". The alderman is the mayor of the ward. He is paid a salary for a half-time job. This allows him to do half-time work in his original profession. A second man in the leadership of the ward is the "democratic committee man". His job is an honorary post. The aldermen are elected on a non-partisan basis. The candidates run against each other.

Zoning is extremely important for the success of the city governance. Chicago is a "melting pot" (Haider 2016). Knowingly and willingly the members of the Chicago City Club wanted to avoid a ghetto structure as in New York. Zoning, therefore, maintains the historic diversity of Chicago's electorate (Green and Holli 1987). "The Mayors have faced a tradition of neighborhood solidarity. This geographic parochialism may explain why good government non-partisan members with their city-wide concerns have historically been restricted to a narrow band along the city's lake-shore while the rest of the city residents lived their lives inland in family-oriented communities" (Green 1987: 277).

Zoning is, therefore, an instrument of maintaining the diversity (ethnic, race, religion) of the population, at best in each ward. In 1958 e.g. a re-zoning was discussed with the objective to avoid that the city center would become dominated by African-Americans (Merriner 2003: 70). Of course, diversity cannot be achieved in each ward. Ward 34 has a 100% black population; ward 22 has a Mexican-American 78% population with many illegal aliens; ward 50 is a community of all German-Jews, and ward 41 is dominated by Republicans.

b) The City Council

The aldermen form the City Council. The Mayor of the city presides over the council. The Council does not pass decisions, and the meetings are usually short: They seldom last beyond the lunch hour (Royko 1971: 15).

c) The Committees

The wards form committees for the service of their citizens. The committees of Wards 1 and 2 give you an idea.

Ward 1:

- Buildings
- Budget and Government Operations
- Rules and Municipal Code Revisions, others
- Finance
- Licenses
- Traffic Control and Safety Zoning

Ward 2:

- Energy, Environmental Protection and Public Utilities
- Aviation (the airport is located in Ward 2)
- Budget and Government Operations
- Capital Development
- Historical Landmark Preservation
- Finance
- Human Rights and Consumer Protection
- Intergovernmental Relations
- Licenses
- Ports, Wharves, and Bridges

Ward 1 has seven committees, ward 2 has ten. Only three out of them have the same functions: finance, budget, and licenses. This means that the functions of the wards are remarkably **decentralized**.

d) The City Mayors

A German analysing the legal structure of Chicago might immediately compare it with the legal structure of Berlin. The difference between Berlin as a "State" and Chicago as a "City" does not seem to be essential: The constitution of the United States does not mention cities and communities. Consequently, the city in the US is legally a part of the state.

At first sight the Berlin districts—"Bezirke"—might be considered equivalent to the wards. But on second sight this is not the case. The Bezirke are responsible for their street infrastructure, the wards are not. Fire protection is a Bezirke affair, but not a ward function. When people want to have something to happen in the city, the Mayor does it (Haider 2016), not the alderman.

The Mayor has only three functions. But they are "essentials" (Caraley 1977: 213).

Police
Fire Protection
Streets including Sanitation.

In addition he "does big things" (Caraley 1977: 213), whatever that is. It was Mayor Richard Joseph Daley (1955–1976) who wrote the budget, not the alderman. Daley was indeed the incarnation of power in the city of Chicago.

Paul Green formulates the point very clearly: The combination of **extreme decentralization** and of **unparalleled power** in the hands of the Mayor; in no other American city is the position and dispensation of political power—or, as the Chicagoans call it: the clout—as central to the operation of its government or to the daily lives of its citizens. City management in Chicago meant an understanding of the "overriding issue of power", and Richard J. Daley understood it. He insisted on stability and order in Chicago, and the citizens loved him for it.

Richard J. Daley not only realized that it is important to make the city the best one in the US not just in his field of responsibility: police, fire, streets. He used his power prudently. His city worked. The city had the best traffic system, the cleanest streets, the best lighting system, police and fire alarm systems were the best in the whole country. Chicago had liberal zoning laws and a flexible tax policy which kept the firms in the city. To conclude: Daley was a strong leader, and what was most important: He kept the speed of growth within the border lines that the population could just bear and thus created a degree of stability and order that the citizens could accept. In short: Mayor Daley was the father of the city (Holli 1987).

What have we learned from Chicago so far:

1. Decentralization has very positive effects on citizens and on public service people.
2. Centralized functions that everyone in the city notices and appreciates increase pride and love of the citizens for their city and for their Mayor.
3. Good use of the Mayor in the exercise of his power makes the Mayor a "father of the city".

5.1.3 The Financial Structure of Chicago

Professor Haider in his explanation of the Chicago city governance gave me a surprising answer to my question about financial problems of the city: "there are no financial problems". The city taxes cover the expenses for the three functions that the Mayor has. City taxes are low enough to keep firms and citizens in Chicago.

Under the Kelly administration there was another source of finance: The city tolerated gambling. Vast sums of money became available for city purposes.

The schools are indirectly financed 100% by the state through the school boards.

Mayor Richard J. Daley did not shy away from asking President Nixon for more federal funds for more citizen housing (Sullivan 1993: 172).

Private funds have been available whenever needed although sometimes only after tough discussions. Compared with the fights over the restoration of the Beethoven Music Hall in Bonn there is a significant difference: The members of the Chicago City Club fought constructively with the best for the city in mind: The Chicago Theater was built by the members in 1922 and renewed in the 1980s. The Chicago Art Institute, one of the best museums in the world, was founded in 1866 with private funds, long before the Chicago City Club was founded, but in the same spirit of pride and donorship.

5.1.4 The Universities

There are many universities located in Chicago and its environment, private and public. They play an important role in the successful development of the city, and the Mayors are proud of it. Excellent schools like the University of Chicago with its great number of Nobel Prize winners and Northwestern University with its Kellogg School of Management are widely known and attract students not only from Illinois and from the United States as a whole; they have a global recognition. The best minds apply, and the best students are accepted. They enjoy the Midwest, and after graduation they stay in Chicago, thus contributing to a population of creative and innovative people. This adds to the attractiveness of Chicago. The city has long known what the economists Joseph Stiglitz and Bruce Greenwald have recently analyzed in their book "Creating a Learning Society" (Stiglitz and Greenwald 2014). The best "Learning City" will succeed in global competition for the most creative people. The Mayor of Chicago is aware of the importance of the universities for the city and is proud of them. The most recent attraction of the universities and the city of Chicago is the new building for the School of Management and the Economics Department of Northwestern University. The expenses for this huge building on the lake side have amounted to 325 million dollars all paid by private donors.

5.1.5 The Population

These developments make the people in Chicago self-confident. They do not envy other creative people. They are inspired by them. Wealth accumulated by them is accepted.[10]

Wealth combined with philanthropy is not only accepted, it is welcomed. There is no need for levying "property taxes on the superrich". Consequence for the city: Accumulated wealth increases further, income taxes rise, and so does the willingness for and the pride in investment in public welfare.

[10]This section of my paper draws heavily on Professor Haider's wisdom as an old Chicago citizen and a well-known sociologist.

The population is—and Chicago is evidence of it—not exogenously given. It is an endogenous result of good city management. Why should Professor Haider otherwise strongly recommend reading the book by Richard Florida entitled "Who's your City?" (Florida 2008). Certainly not only because he wanted me to enjoy a new phrasing of a known development which has come under many headings: Schumpeter's innovation theory, the new industrial revolution 4.0, the global digitalization, etc., and now Florida's "Spiky Global World"! The subtitle of Florida's book tells his story—or rather half of it: "how the creative economy is making where to live the most important decision of your life". The other half is the answer "the more smart people and the denser the connectiveness among them, the faster it all goes" (Florida 2008: 96). In Florida's view "smart" means people that add to Maslow's preference pyramid the top two preferences: "constant quest for knowledge and perpetual desire for aesthetics" (Florida 2008: 161).

Interestingly enough, Chicago does not appear in Florida's list of "Best Places". But there is no question but that the people of Chicago have felt their city to be their best place. Frank Sullivan shows a photo of a poster "Expressions of Sympathy for Mayor Richard J. Daley". The text above reads: "I believe that a man should be proud of the city in which he lives and that he should so live that his city will be proud that he lives in it". Originally the text was ascribed to Abraham Lincoln, but the mourning citizens of Chicago expressed their feelings for Daley and of their own by this sentence.

5.2 The City Management of Tokyo

5.2.1 The Legal Structure of Tokyo[11]

a) Introduction

Japan was a highly centralized state until the United States won the Second World War and occupied Japan. Then, the American soldiers forced the Japanese people to accept significant changes.

The structural changes were

- parliamentary democracy (Matsubara 1986)

[11]See e.g.: Foljanty-Jost G, Haufe K, Aoki M (2013) Bürger als Partner. Kooperative Demokratie in japanischen Kommunen. Springer Fachmedien,Wiesbaden or Foljanty-Jost G. (2009) Kommunalreform in Deutschland und Japan. Springer Fachmedien Wiesbaden or Vogt S (2001) Neue Wege der Stadtplanung in Japan. Partizipationsansätze auf der Mikroebene, dargestellt anhand ausgewählter *machizukuri*-Projekte in Tokyo. Iudicum Verl., München or Flüchter W (1978) Stadtplanung in Japan. Institut für Asienkunde, Hamburg.

- firms with strong labor unions (Albach 1994)[12]
- decentralization

Tokyo remained the capital of Japan. But the Tenno, who resides in the garden remote from the people of Tokyo, was no longer a god-like person, but became a human emperor. In her book "Abend-Kranich—Eine Kindheit in Japan" Hisako Matsubara describes the shock she suffered when she listened to the Emperor when he gave his speech of surrender over the radio.

b) The Governor of Tokyo

The capital of Japan, Tokyo,[13] is led by a Mayor. He is elected directly by the people of the Prefecture. The Mayor is the head of the aldermen of the 62 cities, wards, and communities that form the Prefecture of Tokyo. Tokyo had 13.6 million inhabitants in 2016. Administrative headquarters are in Shinjuku, one of the cities. The governor has four deputy governors. The governor is head of the fire department, the water supply, and the infrastructure department. The prefecture is also responsible for the program for the trade of emission rights. According to that law, the prefecture has to reduce emissions by 17% until the year of 2019.

The administration of the Prefecture is organized as follows (Präfektur Tokio 2016; Tokyo Metropolitan Government 2016a):

1. the Headquarters of the Governor
2. the Bureau of General Affairs
3. the Bureau of Finance
4. the Bureau of Taxation
5. the Bureau of Citizens and Culture
6. the Bureau of Sports
7. the Bureau of Urban Development
8. the Bureau of Environment
9. the Bureau of Social Welfare and Public Health, including the Office of Metropolitan Hospital Management
10. the Bureau of Industrial and Labor Affairs, including the Central Wholesale Market
11. the Bureau of Construction
12. the Bureau of Port and Harbor

---

[12]See Albach (1994) on page 336: "Trade unions are not genuine Japanese institutions. They were forced on Japanese firms by the occupation forces after World War II, and modelled after the American trade unions. At first, trade unions were very antagonistic and belligerent. A more cooperative attitude was not achieved until what is called the "management counter-offensive" had proven successful. The last such labor dispute was the miike-strike in 1960". See also Ota K (1989) Die Arbeitskämpfe der Mitsui-Miike-Gewerkschaft. In: Kawanishi H (ed) (1989) Japan im Umbruch. Gewerkschafter berichten über Arbeitskämpfe der Nachkriegsära. Bund-Verl., Cologne, pp 272ff.

[13]To—Big, kyo—City; Kyo-to: the big city, formerly the capital of Japan.

13. the Bureau of Accounting
14. the Bureau of Transportation
15. the Bureau of Waterworks
16. the Bureau of Sewerage, responsible for the Sewerage Network and Sewage Disposal

The prefecture has seven administrative committees. They are

1. the Board of Education
2. the Election Administration Commission
3. the Personnel Commission
4. the Audit and Inspection Commissioners
5. the Public Safety Commission, including the Metropolitan Police Department
6. the Labor Relations Commission
7. the Expropriation Commission

If there is a conflict between the Mayor and one or more aldermen of the wards, the Mayor loses unless the minister of the upper level supports him. But basically the aldermen have great autonomy. The former Mayor of Tokyo Prefecture Yoichi Masuzoe was not re-elected when he tried to exert too much power.[14] Here are some examples:

- The Mayor wanted a big hospital. The alderman of the ward was against it. The Minister of Health in the government of Japan eventually decided in favor of building the hospital. The alderman was not particularly happy.
- The Mayor wanted to renew the streets around Tokyo Station. He wanted to have separate lanes built for bicycles. The alderman was against it. The Mayor lost.
- Next to Tokyo Bay there was a free piece of land. It was surrounded by BMW, Hossa Bus Company and others. The firms wanted a casino built on it. The Mayor wanted a Paralympics Stadium built on it. The Mayor lost.

In his former career Mayor Misuse Yoichi was Minister of Defence and Minister of Health. In these positions he had great power. But as the Mayor of Tokyo he was in a different situation. When he tried to behave like as a minister, he met strong opposition from the aldermen of the wards. In the example of the lanes for bicycles three aldermen were in favour, but one was against it. The Mayor did not have the power to force the fourth alderman to build a connecting lane. Maybe he should have negotiated with all four aldermen in order to arrive at consensus, but this was something he had not learned in his previous jobs.

[14]The Tokyo Shimbun reported on the election of the Governor in 2016. Masuzoe Yoichi, the paper says, left his office due do an expenses scandal. In my discussion with him in October 2016 he strongly rejected the accusation. My personal explanation of his demission is given in the text.

The former Mayor Masuzoe is still of the opinion that 8–10 wards would be enough for the Tokyo Prefecture instead of the present 37: He also advocates a reduction of the number of prefectures because there are many poor prefectures, and they would go bankrupt if there was no redistribution among the prefectures. Maybe he is right but it is quite obvious that his ideas meet strong resistance from the wards.

Tokyo is a rich prefecture. The Mayor receives 8% net sales tax for the prefecture, 20% of this income goes to the federal government, 80% remain in the prefecture. Mayor Masuzoe advocates 90% of the sales tax to remain in the prefecture. That would allow the poorer prefectures to be autonomous (or at least less dependent on redistribution) in their decisions.

The wards levy a property tax on the companies and the private citizens. They have the same problem as the German communities. If property tax is raised above competitive levels, the companies move to other richer wards with lower property tax. Tokyo is rich enough to subsidize 300 companies. This makes moving to Tokyo Prefecture very attractive. This system favors centralization and centripetal movement instead of the overall objective to favour centrifugal processes.

Mayor Masuzoe stressed his opinion that a governmental reform is necessary in Japan. Only a few functions should be in the hands of the government: Defence, Health, Education, and Safety. The rest should be decentralized (according to what in Germany is called Subsidiaritätsprinzip). But he did not tell me how this reform could be accomplished.

c) The Cities, Wards, Towns, Villages

The Prefecture of Tokyo consists of 23 special wards, 26 cities, 5 towns and 8 villages (Tokyo Metropolitan Government 2016b). I will use the word "Ward" for each kind of cities. The Ward has a **mayor** who is elected directly by their constituencies every 4 years. Re-election is possible and without limits of the term. The citizens have the right to recall the election and can insist on re-elections of the mayor, the parliament, and of individual members of the parliament. An interesting aspect of the local autonomy of the wards happened in 1956. The citizens were dissatisfied with the merger of two wards in 1954 and insisted on the separation in 1956—with success (Gemeinde (Japan) 2016).

The **local autonomy** in Japan is a remarkable example of subsidiarity. On the basis of the Japanese constitution the Local Autonomy Act was passed. This law entitles the local governments to more functions than the central government (MIC 2009). The prefectures are responsible for the national and the prefectural roads. In the field of education the prefectures manage the senior high schools and the Elementary and Junior High Schools. They run Public Health Centers and are responsible for the Police. And finally, they supervise passports. The wards have control over the Fire Defence, for the registration of residents and foreigners, for human waste disposal and garbage disposal, they take care of the municipal roads and of urban facilities. They have authority over urban planning and zoning. People in the cities older than 20 years of age have the right to vote, and Japanese nationals over 25 years of age can be voted into prefectural and municipal assemblies and into the office of municipal mayors. The terms are 4 years.

The local autonomy of prefectures and wards includes the **local government finance**. In 2007 the wards had the following revenues:

1. Local taxes 39.3%
2. Other revenue resources 22.8%
3. Local allocation tax 14.2%
4. National treasury disbursements 10.3%
5. Local bonds 8.0%
6. Other general revenue resources 4.0%
7. Local transfer tax 1.1%
8. special local grants 0.3%

The local allocation tax is an intrinsic local revenue source aiming at adjusting imbalances in the revenue sources of local governments and securing revenue so that each local government can provide public services for residents at the national minimum level.

National treasure disbursements are funds from the central government to local governments for specific uses.

The breakdown of the local taxes is as follows:

1. Municipal residents tax 47.7%

   - individuals 33.7%
   - corporations 14.0%

2. Fix asset tax 40.4%
3. City planning tax 5.6%
4. Municipal tobacco tax 3.9%
5. Other taxes 2.4%

The most interesting aspect of the wards is the **Decentralization Reform.** Basically the central government reduced the transfer of money to the wards in order to **improve local authority.** But local authority also means that wards should not depend on transfers of money from the financially strong wards to the weak wards. Therefore, wards were merged to create financially strong and autonomous wards. This is a completely different concept than the mergers of cities in Germany which have the objective to reduce administration costs. In 1999 a "Special Mergers Act" was passed by the Japanese parliament, which reduced the number of wards from 3229 in 1999 to 1777 in 2009. The objective of this law was to promote decentralization, to respond to expansion of residential areas, to streamline municipal administration, and to respond to the aging of society and to the diversifying needs of the citizens.

In 2007 a "Decentralization Reform Promotion Law" was passed. The objective has been to create distinctive and dynamic communities and to enhance the autonomy and independence of local authorities. The wards are regionally cut so that they become "economically and financially independent". The municipal governments have to provide public services closely tied to the community.

In earlier times wards with 100,000 inhabitants were considered optimal. Today the optimal size of a ward is in the view of experts 300,000 inhabitants. The mayor of Kokubunji is of the opinion that decentralization is no longer an important subject of discussion because the population of Tokyo is shrinking. But he admits that other experts still consider decentralization an important issue when decentralization means subsidiarity.

d) The Arakawa ku

Professor Waragai had organized conversations with the Mayor of the Arakawa ku, Taichiro Nishikawa, and the Member of the Arakawa City Assembly, Mr. Shimura.

The Arakawa ward has 213,239 inhabitants who live on an area of 10.20 km^2.

The mayor of Arakawa is appointed for a term of 4 years. Mr. Nishikawa has already served as mayor for the last 12 years. In the fall of October 2016 he was re-elected for another term of 4 years. The citizens have realized that their mayor serves the interests of the citizens, and they trust him. The mayor has indeed just one objective: to "make the citizens happy". The mayor of Arakawa ku selects four vice mayors and presents them to the assembly for approval. Once a month the 23 mayors of the ku's meet to discuss problems of mutual interest. They also discuss the budgets.

The Arakawa assembly has 32 members who meet 80 days per year. Members are proposed by the political parties and elected by the citizens. The LDP has 14 members. They form a partnership with the six Prometo members for a majority in the assembly. The members listen to the citizens and their wishes and try to fulfil them. There are also chambers of commerce and of doctors and a group of people with recycling interests that collect the wishes of the citizens and then present them in the assembly.

The administration of Arakawa consists of 1 mayor, 4 vice mayors, 1 director (personnel), 1 division head, 3 office heads, and 38 department heads. The total number of employees in the administration is 1540 with only 220 with a life-time contract.

e) The Kokubunji shi

My second interview with representatives of the Tokyo wards was also organized by Professor Waragai. The City Policy Director of the Kokubunji shi, Tatsuya Naito (Tatsuya 2015) gave me a very interesting insight into his career in the Kokubunji administration, starting in the Taxation Division in 1979 and presently being the Policy Director (since 2012). His family has lived in Kokubunji for nine generations. 238 years ago the family had to flee from another district of Japan. They took their shrine with them and settled in the Naito area. On the map of Kokubunji one can find Naito 1-chome and Naito 2-chome.

Naito defines a local community as "a space where its residents and citizens live together with a sense of solidarity with their neighbors. The inhabitants have a "fellow feeling as community members". Kokubunji is a "Healthy Cultural City" with 119,875 inhabitants on an area of 11.46 km².

The board of the Kokubunji shi has 24 members. Five different parties are represented in the board. They do not fight each other but strongly discuss with the objective of harmony. One of the major tasks of the board is the local infrastructure; the road construction department has 100 employees out of the total of 666 in the whole administration.

Kokubunji has four projects in cooperation with other wards:

1. merger of the ward libraries
2. development of a bus service for old-age people
3. joint development of big data
4. joint use of public buildings and sports arenas

The Kokubunji shi is still characterized by agriculture. The ward has an Agriculture Promotion Plan. It has a skills improvement project under the urban agriculture management. The administration creates local brands for farming products grown in the ward. Land for industrial development is available.

The local government administration operates on four levels:

1. the Vision with a 10–20 years horizon
2. the Basic Plan with a 5–10 years extension
3. the Implementation Plan for the next 3–5 years
4. the Budget for the next fiscal year

The administration follows several objectives

1. health and welfare of citizens
2. safety and comfort for the citizens
3. protection of lives and property of the citizens
4. promotion of growth of citizens with open minds

The Mayor of Kokubunji meets with the mayors of the other 26 shi's once a month to discuss problems of mutual concern.

6 Conclusion

Cities in Germany and their employees have never before known competition with other cities of the world. They have to learn. So have the inhabitants of their cities. They have to implement the tools for successful global competition that I have presented.

The second lesson I have given is about the role of the mayor. I repeat the citizens of Chicago: "I believe that a man should be proud of the city in which he lives and that he should so live that his city will be proud that he lives in it". The third lesson is decentralization. Cities should be structured into wards small enough to meet the interests of all citizens and to love their wards.

References[15]

Albach H (1994) Culture and technical innovation. A cross-cultural analysis and policy recommendations. De Gruyter, Berlin

Banner G (2001) Reform braucht Führung. In: Middelhoff et al. (eds.) Reinhard Mohn. Bertelsmann, Gütersloh

Baumann A, Möhle H (2016) Region gibt sich kompromisslos. General-Anzeiger (20 June 2016)

Beckmann M (1968) Location theory. Random House, New York

Beckmann M (1988) Information technology and location. In: Orishimo I et al (eds) Information technology. Social and spatial perspectives, Lecture Notes in Economics and Mathematical Systems, vol 315. Springer, Berlin, pp 153–160

Beckmann M, Puu T (1985) Spatial economics. Density, potential and flow. North Holland, Amsterdam

Camagni R (2002) On the concept of territorial competitiveness. Sound or misleading? Urban Stud 39(13):2395–2411

Caraley D (1977) City governments and urban problems. Prentice-Hall, Englewood Cliffs, NJ

Chamberlin E (1933) The theory of monopolistic competition. Harvard University Press, Cambridge, MA

Clement W (2016) Ein "New Deal" für Bonn. General-Anzeiger 20 June 2016, p 3

Cronon W (1991) Nature's metropolis. Chicago and the Great West. Norton, New York

Florida RL (2008) Who's your city? Basic Books, New York

Forrester JW (1969) Urban dynamics. M.I.T Press, Cambridge/London

Fremon DK (1988) Chicago politics. Ward by ward. Indiana University Press, Bloomington, IN

Fujita M, Krugman P (2004) The new economic geography. Past, present and the future. Pap Reg Sci 83(1):139–164

Fujita M, Mori T (2005) Frontiers of the new economic geography. Pap Reg Sci 84(3):377–405

Gemeinde (Japan) (2016) Wikipedia. https://de.wikipedia.org/wiki/Gemeinde_(Japan). Accessed 26 Oct 2016

Giersch H (1979) Aspects of growth, structural change, and employment. A Schumpeterian perspective. Weltwirtschaftliches Archiv (Rev World Econ) 115(4):629–652

Giersch H (1995) Wirtschaftsmoral als Standortfaktor. Fachbuchservice, Jena

Green PM (1987) The Chicago political tradition. A mayoral perspective. In: Green PM, Holli MG (eds) The mayors. Southern Illinois University Press, Carbondale and Edwardsville, IL, pp 274–280

Green PM, Holli MG (1987) The mayors. The Chicago political tradition. Southern Illinois University Press, Carbondale and Edwardsville, IL

Haider D (2016) Personal conversation on October 18

Holli MG (1987) The Daley era: Richard J. to Richard M. In: Green PM, Holli MG (eds) The mayors. Southern Illinois University Press, Carbondale and Edwardsville, IL, pp 217–232

Horn K (2009) Der Realismus des Adam Smith. Frankfurter Allgemeine Zeitung, 16 Jan 2009 (13):12

Jacobs J (1961) The death and life of great American cities. Random House, New York

[15] A bibliography on the topic is available from the author on request.

Jacobs J (1969) The economy of cities. Random House, New York

Jensen K (2012) Haushalt 2012 (Budget speech of the Lord Mayor of Trier), Unpublished Manuscript

Klais P (2016) The Elbe Philharmonic Hall in Hamburg. Address in the Rotary Club Bonn-Süd–Bad Godesberg on 9 June 2016

Kolatek C (1994) Die Wirtschaftswelt am Draht. Informationelle Vernetzung und regionales Wirtschaftspotential am Beispiel Japans. Ed Sigma, Berlin

Krugman P (1993) First nature, second nature, and metropolitan location. J Reg Sci 33:129–144

Krugman P (1996) Self-organizing economy. Blackwell, Cambridge, MA

Martin R (1999) The new "geographical turn" in economics. Some critical reflections. Camb J Econ 23(1):65–91

Matsubara H (1986) Abend-Kranich. Eine Kindheit in Japan. Bastei-Lübbe, Bergisch-Gladbach

Merriner JL (2003) The City Club of Chicago. A centennial history. The City Club, Chicago, IL

MIC (2009) Ministry of Internal Affairs and Communications. Local autonomy in Japan. Current situation and future shape. http://www.clair.or.jp/j/forum/other_data/pdf/20100216_soumu_e.pdf. Accessed 26 Oct 2016

Ottaviano G et al (2002) Agglomeration and trade revisited. Int Econ Rev 43(2):409–435

Präfektur Tokio (2016) Wikipedia. https://de.wikipedia.org/wiki/Pr%C%A4fektur_Tokio. Accessed 26 Oct 2016

Rheinische Friedrich-Wilhelms-Universität Bonn et al (2016) Wissenschaftsregion [Bonn]. Mehr als die Summe ihrer Teile. Insert of General-Anzeiger 9. November 2016. http://www.wissenschaftsregion-bonn.de/fileadmin/redaktion/01_Wissenschaftsregion/05_Wissen_hoch_fuenf_Reihe_Generalanzeiger/0501-Erste-Ausgabe/01-Wissen-hoch-fuenf-09-2016.pdf. Accessed 15 July 2017

Royko M (1971) Boss. Richard J. Daley of Chicago. New York

Sachverständigenrat (1983) Sachverständigenrat zur Beurteilung der gesamtwirtschaftlichen Entwicklung. Ein Schritt voran. Jahresgutachten 1983/84. Kohlhammer, Stuttgart 1983:399–406

Samuelson P (1983) Thünen at two hundred. J Econ Lit 11:1468–1488

Schäffer A (2016) Die Brexit-Entscheidung hat der CSU nicht die Freude an der direkten Demokratie vergällt. Frankfurter Allgemeine Zeitung, 09 July 2016:10

Smith A (1863) An inquiry into the nature and causes of the wealth of nations. Book K, Chapter VII. Ad and Ch Black, Edinburgh

Spiegel B (1961) Die Struktur der Meinungsverteilung im sozialen Feld. Das psychologische Marktmodell. Enzyklopaedie der Psychologie in Einzeldarstellungen 6. Huber, Bern – Stuttgart

Stadt Bonn (2014) Haushaltsplan 2013/2014 https://opendata.bonn.de/dataset/haushaltsplan-20132014. Accessed 15 July 2017

Stadt Gelsenkirchen, Der Oberbürgermeister (2016) Wirtschaftsstandort mit Perspektive. Mit uns wird's was. https://www.gelsenkirchen.de/de/wirtschaft/zukunftsprojekte/graf_bismarck/_doc/expose_grafbismarck_web.pdf. Accessed 15 July 2017

Stadt Trier (2012) Entwurf Strategisches Konzept "Zukunft Trier 2025". https://www.trier-mitgestalten.de/sites/default/files/zukunft2025_0.pdf. Accessed 07 Aug 2017

Stadt Trier (2013) Haushalt der Stadt Trier. http://www.trier.de/rathaus-buerger-in/stadtverwaltung/haushalt-finanzen/. Accessed 08 Aug 2013

Stiglitz JE, Greenwald BC (2014) Creating a learning society. A new approach to growth, development, and social progress. Columbia University Press, New York

Sullivan F (1993) Legend. The only inside story about Mayor Richard J. Daley. Random House, Chicago, IL

Tatsuya N (2015) Local government administration and personnel management. Case study on Kokubunji City. Address presented to the Ho Chi Minh National Academy of Politics, September 11 (manuscript)

Tokyo Metropolitan Government (2016a) Wikipedia. https://de.wikipedia.org/wiki/Tokyo_Metropolitan_Government. Accessed 26 Oct 2016

Tokyo Metropolitan Government (2016b) The structure of the Tokyo Metropolitan Government. http://www.metro.tokyo.jp/ENGLISH/ABOUT/STRUCTURE/index.htm. Accessed 26 Oct 2016

Vallée D (2015) Abschlussbericht. Gutachten zu Fragen einer "vertieften Kooperation zwischen den Gebietskörperschaften Bundesstadt Bonn, RheinSieg-Kreis sowie den Städten und Gemeinden des RheinSieg-Kreises". https://www.ihk-bonn.de/fileadmin/dokumente/Downloads/Presse/Prof._Vallee_-_Bericht_Kooperation_Bonn_RSK_IHKBonn_final.pdf. Accessed 17 July 2017

von Thünen JH (1930) Der isolierte Staat in Beziehung auf Landwirtschaft und Nationalökonomie, Vol. 1 1826, Vol. 2 1842, Vol. 3 1863. Fischer, Jena

von Weizsäcker CC (1980) Barriers to entry. A theoretical treatment. In: Lecture Notes in Economics and Mathematical Systems 185. Springer, Heidelberg

von Weizsäcker CC (1981) Rechte und Verhältnisse in der modernen Wirtschaftslehre. Kyklos 34(3):345–376

von Weizsäcker CC (2011) Wettbewerb auf den drei Ebenen wirtschaftlicher Aktivität. In: Bechtold S et al (eds) Recht, Ordnung und Wettbewerb. Honoring Wernhard Möschel on his 70th birthday. Nomos, Baden-Baden, pp 865–869

WAZ (2016) Ruhr Universität baut auf Mark 51/7.WAZ Westdeutsche Allgemeine, 23 September 2016, Section Bochum

Weber A (1929) Theory of the location of industries. University of Chicago Press, Chicago

Horst Albach was born in 1931 in Essen, Germany. After a year of study at Bowdoin College in Brunswick, Maine, U.S., he continued his studies of management and economics at Cologne University, Germany, where he received his doctoral degree in business economics in 1958. He taught at Darmstadt Technical University (1958–1960) and Kiel University (1960–1961), Germany, and Graz University (1960), Austria. He accepted an offer to become Full Professor of Business Economics at Bonn University in 1961, co-founded the private Coblence School of Management in 1984, and taught there on leave of absence from Bonn until 1987 when he became Professor of Industrial Economics at the Free University Berlin. After the unification of Germany, he became a Professor of Management Science at the Humboldt University of Berlin. Professor Albach holds honorary degrees from the Swedish School of Management in Stockholm, the Finnish School of Business in Helsinki, the universities of Kiel, Bielefeld, Cottbus, Graz, Alcalá de Henares, Waseda, Bowdoin College in Brunswick, ME, and the Russian Academy of Sciences. He is a member of the German Order Pour le mérite for Sciences and Arts and was its Chancellor from 2004 to 2009. From 2012 to 2016 Professor Albach was a member of the Executive Board of the Center for Advanced Studies in Management (CASiM) at HHL Leipzig Graduate School of Management, Leipzig, Germany. In 2016, HHL Leipzig Graduate School of Management conferred the title of Honorary Senator to Prof. Dr. Dr. h.c. mult. Horst Albach.

Part IV

Complementarity Between Region and City

The Significance of the Region for Urban Growth: The Example of Bonn and the Rhein-Sieg District

Hermann Tengler

Abstract

Urban growth is driven by structural change in the economy. While the manufacturing sector is moving away from the cities, the fast-growing company-oriented and knowledge-based services are drawn into the urban centers. There they find the most favorable conditions, allowing them to develop in an above average way.

The suburban area is becoming increasingly significant to urban growth. In addition to its traditional relief function regarding residential and business areas, it is the spatial division of labor that emerged in the sectoral structural change, which supports urban growth. The highly competitive industry located in the suburban area represents the most important consumer of services concentrated in the cities. To stand its ground within the global competition of innovation, industry must be able to revert to application-oriented knowledge. For this purpose, an increasing number of training, research and technology transfer services were established outside of the major cities over the last few years. They are tailored to the specific needs of the regional economy and benefit the development of the entire region.

The City of Bonn and the Rhein-Sieg District can serve as a model for the cross-pollination of the city and its surrounding area. After losing its status as Germany's governmental seat, the region has so far successfully mastered the structural change through cooperation. At the same time, the first signs indicating a gradual shift of the growth from the city towards the region can be detected

H. Tengler (✉)
Department of Business Development and Strategic Regional Development of the Rhein-Sieg District, Siegburg, Germany
e-mail: hermann.tengler@rhein-sieg-kreis.de

H. Albach et al. (eds.), *European Cities in Dynamic Competition*,
https://doi.org/10.1007/978-3-662-56419-6_9

from the development of the two local authorities as well as the recent migration movement in the large cities.

1 Growth of Cities: Causes and Perspectives

Urbanization is increasing worldwide. We are experiencing the first *urban* century; for the first time in history, more people live in cities than in the country. Whereas the proportion of people residing within a city was 29% in 1950, urbanization will increase according to prognoses by the United Nations to 57% by 2025 and 70% by 2050 (United Nations 2008).

Population growth typically goes hand in hand with economic development. The process of urbanization is a reflection of the location preferences of private households and companies alike. In this context, the structural change of the economy plays into the hands of increasing urbanization. Originally, industrialization mainly initiated the development and growth of cities. Now, however, services mold the economic structure and the job offer, particularly in the metropolises.

The structural change, which was forecast by Fourastié as early as 1954 in the three-sector hypothesis, from agriculture through production to services (Fourastié 1954) has proven to be true. Differing from what Fourastié described, it is not the household-oriented services but those rendered for companies which are mainly responsible for the rise of the tertiary sector (Tengler and Hennicke 1987). The sub-group of so-called *knowledge-intensive* services, which includes information and communication services, research and development, corporate consulting, legal and tax consulting, auditing, advertising and market research, shows the strongest growth of these company-oriented services. The common feature of these services is highly qualified staff. The proportion of employees holding a college degree is at least 20% above the average of the industrial economies of the EU and USA (Deutsches Institut für Wirtschaftsforschung e.V. 2016).

The significance of knowledge as a production factor is growing steadily in this world characterized by globalization, competition, increasing division of labor and complexity. According to Florida's "Theory of the Creative Class" (Florida 2003), knowledge workers and the innovations generated by them are the deciding factor for economic growth. The companies of the knowledge economy find the most favorable conditions in large cities. The geographical proximity of companies from the same industry (localization economies) or various industries (urbanization economies) reduces transaction costs, increases productivity and creates competitive advantages based on knowledge spillover, exchange and transformation (Porter 1999). Moreover, knowledge-intensive services are neither emitting nor space intensive, making them compatible with cities in a special way, when compared to production and logistics, for instance.

For Germany, the strong growth of knowledge-oriented services, their affinity for large cities and the location benefits which they have in large cities, have been empirically proven. According to a study by Geppert and Gornig examining cities which are administered as a district in their own right and have a minimum of 500,000 inhabitants;

- the number of employees working in knowledge-oriented services in Germany increased by 15.4% between 1999 and 2009 while overall employment only increased by 0.1% and the number of jobs in the industry even decreased by 8.5%,
- large cities are the preferred location of knowledge-intensive services; while their proportion in overall employment in Germany was 10.8%, they provided for 18.9% of the jobs in large cities;
- the knowledge-intensive services in the large cities are met by particularly beneficial growth conditions; at 23%, their increase in employment in the cities was substantially above their average national growth of 15.4% (Geppert and Gornig 2010: 7).

Large cities are highly attractive not only to companies from the knowledge economy but also to that especially mobile group of young people willing to obtain or already holding a qualification. Large cities have always been major university locations. A growing number of young people are seeking higher education and therefore moving into the cities. The fact that they prefer the city when starting their career at the completion of their training can mainly be attributed to the availability of a broad and attractive job market. As a pull factor, these highly differentiated, metropolitan labor markets are gaining more and more significance. On the one hand, this is due to a change in the labor markets themselves. In the face of unstable and ever shorter employment relationships, the city offers the best option for people searching for a new job. Another factor is the change in women's employment behavior. The compatibility of family and work is often easier to achieve in a large city, with its infrastructure, than in rural areas.

However, cities are not just better suited to the new working world. Thanks to their abundance of leisure and cultural institutions, their image changed for the better as well. Those moving into the city these days are among the winners, or at least not among the losers in society (Brühl et al. 2006: 10). Living in a large city is associated by many well-educated young people with the promise of quality of life. For many millennial, searching for self-fulfillment in an environment adequate to their life style and age represents just as big a motive for choosing to live in a large city as the jobs on offer (Scharmanski 2015).

The preferred locations of knowledge-intensive service providers and the knowledge workers tend to be moving towards the city and mutually stimulate each other. The best growth prospects for the future are expected to occur in cities which offer a broad spectrum of creative minds and knowledge-intensive services. In relevant rankings, for instance those by the Cologne Institute for Economic Research (Bahrke and Kempermann 2015) and Prognos AG (Prognos AG 2016); Munich, Darmstadt, Heidelberg and Erlangen have reached the top positions. They are cities which stand out with their high innovative power for the knowledge-oriented economy, thanks to a high density of research institutions and human capital.

2 The Development of Major Cities in Germany: Suburbanization and Reurbanization

The development of the population and employment in Germany was characterized by very different phases over the last 20 years (Figs. 1 and 2).

The overall number of inhabitants steadily increased in reunified Germany until 2002. This was followed by a period of decline which lasted until 2010. Since 2011, the population has again been increasing due to high migration gains from other countries.[1]

The population development in the 15 largest cities in Germany[2] at times deviates greatly from this overall trend. In contrast to the rest of Germany, the largest cities

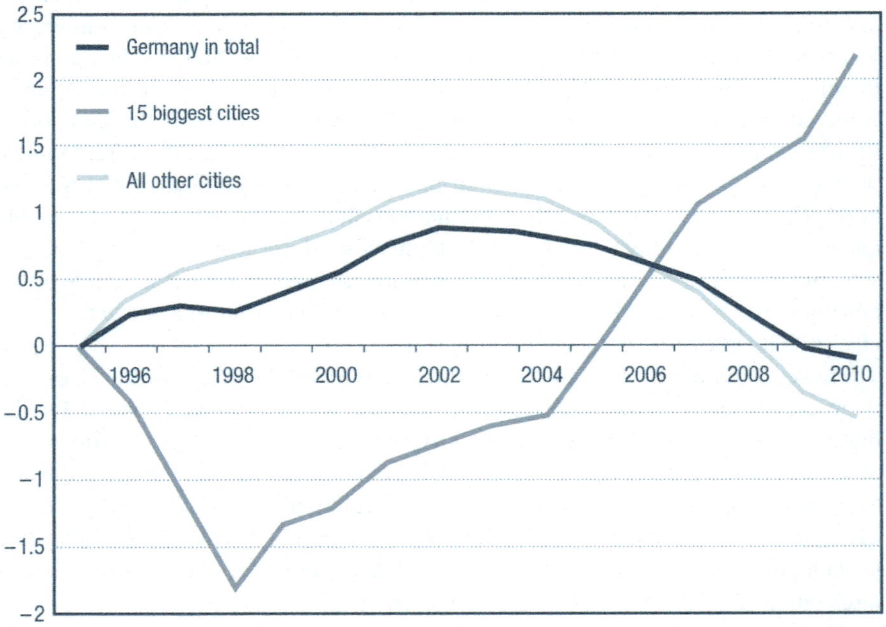

Fig. 1 Population development in Germany and the 15 largest cities from 1995 to 2010

[1]Following the 2011 census, Germany's number of inhabitants, which, until then, had been continually based on the 1987 census, had to be corrected downwards by 1.4 million. Therefore, a reliable comparison of the years 2010 and 2011 is not possible.

[2]The 15 largest cities in Germany range between more than 3.5 million inhabitants in the capital Berlin to 491,000 inhabitants in Duisburg. In total, they have 14.1 million inhabitants, which equals a proportion of 17.2% of Germany's total population of 81.8 million inhabitants.

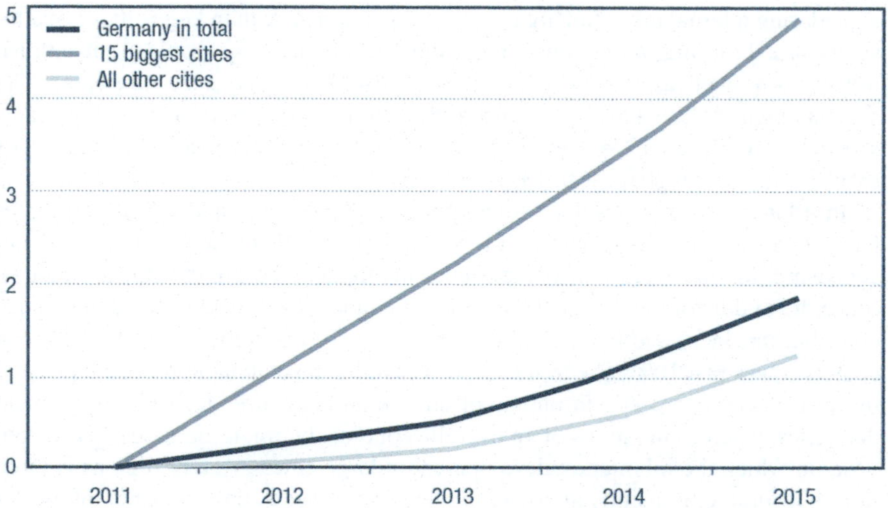

Fig. 2 Population development in Germany and the 15 largest cities from 2011 to 2015

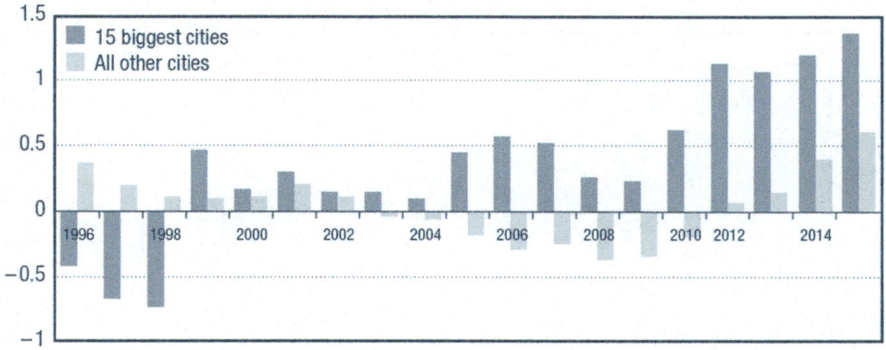

Fig. 3 Annual changes in the population development in the 15 largest cities and the rest of Germany from 1995 to 2015 (excl. 2011)

had to face population losses due to migration to the surrounding areas over a longer period in the 1990s. This "high phase of suburbanization" (Osterhage and Kaup 2012: S. 125) ended in 1998/1999 with a clear reversal of the trend benefitting large cities (Fig. 3).

Since then, not a single year has passed in which the large cities have not developed better than the rest of the country. Even during the long period of the declining number of inhabitants in Germany between 2003 and 2010, the largest cities saw increases each year. In the last few years, reurbanization has become even more dynamic.

The attractiveness of large cities which continued for years and increased even more does not apply to all population groups. Milbert and Sturm prove that, solely considering internal migration figures, the population growth in large cities is exclusively based on migration gains among the 18 to under 25-year-olds (educational migrants) as well as the 25 to under 30-year-olds (career entry migrants). The German metropolises have experienced migration gains from educational migrants starting as early as 1974 and from career entry migrants since the mid-1990s (Milbert and Sturm 2016: 130, 137).

In a landscape that has determined professional training and job opportunities have long been the main causes of population growth in large cities, it is not surprising that these cities also experience the highest job growth (Figs. 4 and 5). Since the middle of the 1990s, the number of employees subject to social insurance contributions increased by 15% in the 15 largest German cities; outside the urban centers it was just 10%. The trend shows a parallel development in large cities and the rest of Germany; i.e., in phases of an overall economic decline, employment decreases, whereas in phases of an overall economic boom, it increases.[3] However, years in which the job market development in large cities or other regions is more or less favorable frequently alternate. In the last few years, the pace of employment growth increased more strongly in large cities just like it did for population. Thus,

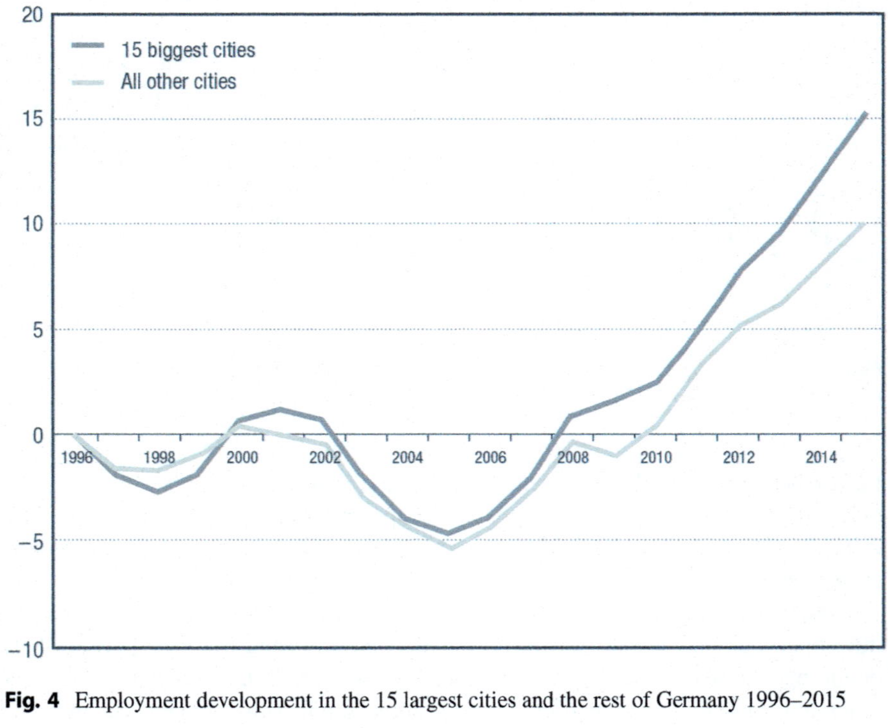

Fig. 4 Employment development in the 15 largest cities and the rest of Germany 1996–2015

[3]The last exception occurred in 2009. Apparently, large cities suffered less from the economic and financial crisis at the time than the rural areas.

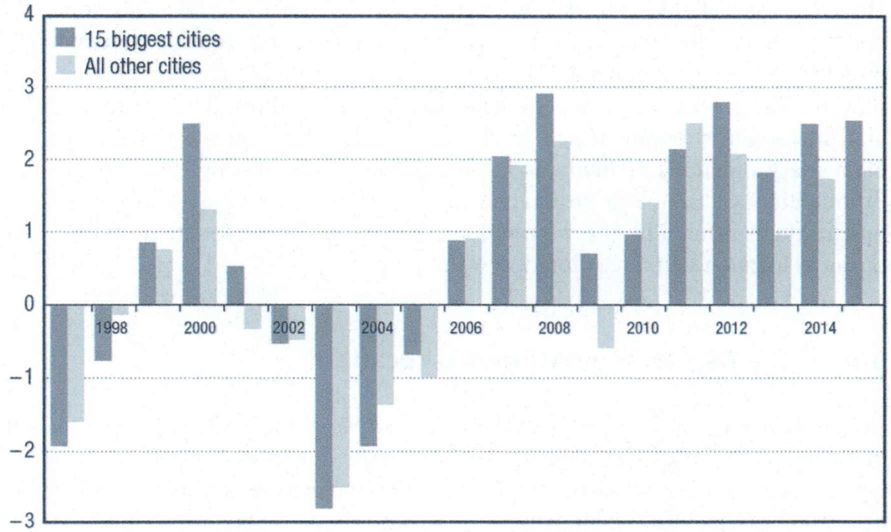

Fig. 5 Annual changes of the employment development in the 15 largest cities and the rest of Germany 1996–2015

there is reason to presume that the progressing concentration of jobs in large cities—in 2015, the 15 largest cities provided 21.3% of all jobs in Germany— is closely connected to the structural change and/or tertiarization of the economy and the preference of the service sector for urban centers.

3 The Significance of the Region for Urban Growth

Suburbanization seems to be a thing of the past as large cities are booming. Caused by the growth of the mainly knowledge-intensive services concentrated here, young people willing to obtain or already holding a qualification, who also have a strong affinity for urban life, are drawn into the cities. The concurrence of supply and demand for human resources in the cities results in cumulative growth processes.

The city—a permanently autonomously growing island? There is reason for doubt. Germany, with its polycentric structure, has always been characterized by alternating phases of urbanization and suburbanization. If the growth of the city is carried by the 18 to under 30-year-olds, as shown, the question arises how this development will be affected if the absolute number and relative proportion of this age group decreases significantly for demographic reasons (Jessen and Mayer 2010: 29–30). Moreover, the social charges from ecological damage and bottlenecks regarding real estate and infrastructure capacities, which increase progressively as the concentration of people grows, cause agglomeration disadvantages. One certainly does not have to go so far as to assume that the ongoing process of urbanization already carries a "tendency for self-destruction" (Fürst et al. 1976: 45).

However, one should ask if the large, highly-compacted cities can solve the approaching challenges on their own. Consequently, the view is automatically directed to the surrounding suburban areas and the role which they play and can play for the growth and competitiveness of the cities. From the vast relationship and interaction structure which exists between the city and the region, only the elementary functions of *living* and *doing business* will be singled out for further examination so as not to go beyond the scope of this article. Additionally, the opportunities offered by the metropolitan area in the global competition regarding business location will be explored as well.

3.1 The Region as a Residential Location

In parallel to the dynamic population growth in large cities, the suburban areas in Germany had to face slight overall decreases in the number of inhabitants over the last 10 years. At the same time, it not only maintained its strong position in the age group of the 30 to under 50-year-olds, but was even able to expand it further. For decades, the migration behavior of these cohorts has been influenced by moves from large cities into the neighboring districts. Young families with children or households in the process of starting a family who buy or build a home surrounded by nature, are typical representatives of this age group (Milbert and Sturm 2016: 132ff.).

Following the strong growth of cities, the desire of young families with children regarding the amount of space and type of residence can no longer be fulfilled in large cities. A tense housing situation with high real estate prices[4] and a limited offer of large apartments, but also deficits in the residential environment by burdens such as noise and pollution, cause many families to leave the city for the surrounding region (Hirschle and Schürt 2008: 216). This could be one reason why suburbanization migration has again increased strongly among the 30 to under 50-year-olds in the last few years (Milbert and Sturm 2016: 133).

At an average of 9.5 km, the migration distance was relatively short (Wagner and Mulder 2015: 121). This is another indicator for the fact that, as a general rule, the desire to change housing and not to change jobs is the main motive behind the move.

The—often well-educated—30 to under 50-year-olds form a large and important group for the regional job market. In the course of the demographic change, which will be characterized by a shortage of human resources and specialists, the importance of qualified employees will increase for the prosperity potential of a region. In the future, people with higher qualifications will often be able to choose

[4]As a result of the regionally diverging population development, real estate prices in Germany have also developed in different ways in the various regions. While on national average a single or two-family detached home cost 197,000 EUR in 2014, the price in large cities administered as a district in their own right was 383,000 EUR—almost twice as much (BBSR 2016: 92).

between several job offers. The attractiveness of the residential location and the associated quality of life will play an important role in their decision-making.

While in the past, commercial property policy influenced the economic development of a region, it now increasingly depends on the housing offers as well. Large cities, which are less and less able to satisfy the housing demand of qualified specialists and their families, have to rely on cooperating with their regional neighbors. The land use policies of these municipalities must consider the spill-over effects to be expected from the urban centers. It is a win-win situation for both sides: The city secures for existing and future companies the urgently needed offer of qualified employees while the surrounding municipalities gain families with children as an important foundation for society and their own future economic sustainability.

3.2 The Region as a Business Location

In highly developed economies, the structural change is characterized by strong tertiarization. Whereas the number of jobs in manufacturing is decreasing, employment in the service industry is increasing. At first glance, the secondary sector loses significance benefiting the tertiary as a consequence. More than 70% of all employees in Germany work in the service sector.

The growth of the tertiary sector is based more on increased corporate demand than on an increase in household demands. Thus, the winners of the sectoral structural change are business-related services. Their growth dynamics are closely related to the changes in manufacturing, framework conditions for production and production methods (Hamm 2012: 633f.):

- manufacturing will be increasingly complemented by services such as customer service, logistics and marketing, which are used to promote production and sales;
- the framework conditions for production are becoming more complex because of legislation, environmental constraints or internationalization issues, which increases the demand for consulting services;
- technological progress requires more research and development, information and communication technology, planning and supervision.

The increase in demand for services leads to a rise in the proportion of tertiary activities at the expense of manufacturing activities in industrial companies.[5] On the other hand, the industry is procuring more and more services from external sources. As per calculations by Eickelpasch, outsourcing associated with manufacturing will create 3.5 million jobs in Germany in the field of business-related services.

[5] In the knowledge-intensive industry, 60% of the staff conduct tertiary activities; and even in the non-knowledge-intensive industry, tertiary activities predominate with a proportion of 54% (Cordes and Gehrke 2015).

This is equal to a proportion of 20% of total employment; in the knowledge-intensive services of consulting, scientific and technological services, advertising and marketing the figure is as high as 28% (Eickelpasch 2015: 74f.).

The widely cited structural change from manufacturing towards services is not so much the result of a declining significance of production than increasing division of labor between both sectors. Industry and services mutually stimulate each other. The close geographical proximity seems to play an important role in this context. An analysis of the intersectoral economic interdependencies in the Rhineland found that industrial companies procure 55% of the services which they require within a radius of 50 km and that more than 50% of the service providers' customers come from the region (Hamm 2012: 636ff.). Earlier research conducted by the Institut für Mittelstandsforschung (Institute for SME Research) in the chamber of commerce and industry districts of Bonn and Duisburg/Wesel/Kleve (Institut für Mittelstandsforschung 1986: 79f.; Schanz and Tengler 1986: 75f.) came to similar conclusions.

The geographical connection of industry and services is not just a factor which is beneficial to the economic success of companies but also that of a region. If the industrial foundation of a region is weak, the demand for business-related services will suffer as well. It has been shown for the Bonn area that, due to its previous status as the governmental seat of Germany, the thin concentration of industry is accompanied by low settlement effects on business-related services with potential for growth and the lack of industry therefore proving to be a growth brake for the region (Institut für Mittelstandsforschung 1986: 65f., 214).

In the course of the sectoral structural change, a new form of labor division has in fact occurred in the area. The division of labor between the center and the surrounding area is mainly characterized by a spatial separation of planning and operative activities. While industrial planning functions and higher-quality services are concentrated in the urban centers, functions, such as production and logistics, have migrated to the surrounding area. Two thirds of all industrial jobs in the federal state of North Rhine-Westphalia are located within those districts these days. Industrial employment in cities administered as a district in their own right decreased by 7% over the last 10 years; in the districts, it increased by 4%. Conversely, rapidly growing business-related services such as the information and communication sector are increasingly concentrated in the larger cities; the districts only provide for one fourth of all jobs.

From the pattern of spatial division of labor one should not conclude that the rural area generally lags behind in the fields of value creation, innovation and competitiveness. Rather, the opposite tends to be the case in the industry. Simon, who coined the term "hidden champions" (Simon 1996), points to the fact that a great part of the small and medium-sized world market leaders in Germany are based outside the large cities (Simon 2013: 66). He views this decentralization as one of the reasons for the high international competitiveness of the German economy.

To support the companies of the region within the technology and innovation competition, an increasing number of application-oriented research and academic institutions, such as universities of applied sciences, were settled outside the large cities over the last few years (Kujath 2012: 230ff, 2016: 197). Through the training of specialists, application-oriented research and technology transfer, these scientific institutions are becoming important engines of regional economic development. Ideally, institutions such as technology parks, business incubators and industry initiatives, which lead to a consolidation and expansion not only of the existing technology fields but also of the industrial foundation, develop in the surrounding area—often initiated by encouraging local or regional economic promotion.

Despite the progress in information and communication technology, physical proximity between the industry and the service sector is and remains a competitive advantage for both sides. There is complementary interdependency between the industry and the service sector; none of the two can exist independently. The continuing withdrawal of industrial production from large cities assigns important structural tasks to the region. Only the surrounding area has the available space to accommodate any industry that leaves the city. This complies with the companies' wishes regarding the location of their business. In most cases, relocation is not based on the great appeal of the new location, but rather on problems at the old one. A lack of space for potential expansion, residential areas moving closer together, urban development measures and strict environmental constraints are the main causes why a site within the city can no longer be sustained (Tengler 1989: 192).

On the other hand, the companies look for migration distances that are as short as possible, as it is important for them to retain their staff. However, if they cannot find a new location within the region, the search will focus on other criteria and might be expanded beyond district, state and national borders.

Against this background, commercial space policies which are solely geared towards the demand of the individual municipalities do not reach far enough. Only if commercial space is planned beyond municipal limits and is coordinated by the center and the surrounding area, will it be possible to retain companies and their jobs in the region. Both the city and the rural areas will benefit from this approach.

3.3 The Region as an International Location: The Concept of the Metropolitan Area

In connection with the development of information technology, globalization has led to a new transnational system of cities, the so-called *global cities*. Global cities are major metropolises which are characterized not so much by their political-cultural function, but rather by their economic governance. As the location of important financial market institutions, headquarters of multinational corporations and important business-related services, they are vital impulse generators and spatial anchoring points of global financial and economic activities (Sassen 1996).

Based on the size and competitiveness of the German economy, German cities are underrepresented in the ranks of global cities. Frankfurt as an outstanding financial center with a major international airport is unquestionably included in the list; Berlin, Hamburg and Munich to a lesser extent as well. One reason is certainly the small size of the German cities in international comparison. Berlin, which is by far the largest city in Germany, with its 3.5 million inhabitants is ranked 59th in the world; Hamburg (1.8 million) is in 138th place, Munich (1.5 million) holds 195th place.

For many large cities in Germany, the advancement of global cities not only marks a loss of significance, it also threatens their competitiveness. Large cities are the hardest hit by international competition. If they do not want to become the losers of globalization, they have to stand their ground internationally in the competition for the best minds, companies and jobs.

To counter the imminent loss of competitiveness, Germany and Europe developed the concept of the metropolitan region. Metropolitan regions were first defined in Germany in 1995 by the Ministerial Conference on Spatial Planning. According to the definition, metropolitan regions are spatial and functional locations whose outstanding features radiate beyond their borders. As a motive of societal, economic, social and cultural development, they are meant to maintain Germany's and Europe's achievement potential (Bundesministerium für Raumordnung, Bauwesen und Städtebau 1995: 27).

The aim of the metropolitan region is to generate visibility and increase the appeal that is necessary for achieving international competitiveness by extending the scale from the city to the region. Under globalization conditions, cities can no longer achieve success from an island position but only as part of an alliance (Kanter 1996: 439). If core cities cooperate with the suburban and rural areas, not only a larger, but also a more diverse and better equipped area will develop. The economic, knowledge-based and cultural benefits of the city are complemented by the typical advantages of the rural area such as space for land-intensive production as well as residential, leisure and recreational quality (Ahrend and Glocker 2016: 625).

The surrounding area can also contribute to complementing and enhancing specific competencies which the city may already have, for instance, through a certain scientific cluster.[6] Thanks to the regional connection of companies, suppliers, research institutions, universities and service providers along the value creation chain, growth poles can be created, increasing the visibility of the metropolitan region and making it more appealing to companies and the labor force (Reinhardt 2016: 641).

So far, 11 metropolitan regions have been established in Germany. Whether the economic goals associated with them will be achieved remains yet to be seen. However, the acceptance of this relatively new type of space is very high. It is carried by the widely-shared view that development can only be driven by interdependencies and cooperation between cities, their suburbs and surrounding rural areas, which ultimately benefits all spatial units involved (Kawka and Staats 2016: 536).

[6]For the term "cluster" cf. Porter (2000).

4 The Example of Bonn and the Rhein-Sieg District

Below, the structure of relationships between the city and surrounding area will be examined more closely using the specific example of the City of Bonn and the Rhein-Sieg District. The City of Bonn and the Rhein-Sieg District are particularly suited as a prototype for several reasons:

- Size and geographical location: The City of Bonn is almost completely surrounded by the Rhein-Sieg District, almost like a necklace. With about 320,000 inhabitants, Bonn is one of the major cities in Germany (19th place) and represents the regional center for vast areas of the district. The Rhein-Sieg, for its part, is the second largest district in Germany with approximately 600,000 inhabitants and an area of 1150 km^2, representing both the suburban as well as the rural type of space. The fact that the relationship between the city and the surrounding area can be examined using statistical data from just two local authorities is a practical benefit for this analysis.
- Economic structure: As the former governmental seat of the Federal Republic of Germany and the site of a major university, Bonn has an extensive service-oriented infrastructure that is also shaped by science. The industry structure of the Rhein-Sieg District is similar to that of the average district within Germany. Therefore, both local authorities represent the typical sectoral division of labor between the large city and the surrounding area very well.
- Long-standing cooperation experience: The decision to move the parliament and the government from Bonn to Berlin, which was made by the Bundestag, the German federal parliament, in 1991, had serious potential for throwing the entire Bonn region into a deep crisis. However, it also triggered the close cooperation between Bonn and the Rhein-Sieg District so that the example of these two local authorities has already produced empirical values outlining the cooperation between a specific city and its surrounding area.

4.1 Challenges of the "Double" Structural Change

Bonn was named the temporary federal governmental seat on November 3, 1949 following an official decision made by the Bundestag, which influenced the economic and structural development of the city and the surrounding Rhein-Sieg District in a sustainable manner. By the end of 1980s, public service had by far developed into the largest employer in Bonn because of the settlement and expansion of federal bodies and other institutions associated with the governmental seat (embassies, organizations, media). With a proportion of 42% of all employees, it was represented over twice as strongly in Bonn compared to other major cities (20%) and the national average (18%).

It goes without saying that the decision, which was made by the German Bundestag on June 20, 1991, to transfer the parliament and parts of the government to Berlin during the reunification of Germany marked a massive watershed for the Bonn region as one third of all people employed in federal administrative institutions lived in the Rhein-Sieg District. While a division of labor between Berlin and Bonn was planned so that Bonn would remain an administrative center of the Federal Republic of Germany even after the move, a loss of about 22,600 jobs in the ministries, embassies, organizations and media had to be expected (RWI 1991).

From a quantitative point of view alone, a reduction in the workforce on such a scale marked a substantial cut for the region. The qualitative aspect was no less significant: Following the high economic value of the jobs which were moving away in regards to purchasing power and consumer demand for the regional economy, it was expected that every job lost would lead to another 1.3 positions cut from the economy, namely in the crafts, trade and service. Without quantitative and qualitative compensation for the jobs moving to Berlin, the Bonn area was facing the loss of up to 52,000 jobs.

As a consequence of the decision to move the governmental seat, the Bonn region had to undergo a fundamental change in its economic structure. Public service and administration jobs would fall away; so, in order to avoid a downward spiral, this loss had to be compensated for by the creation and settlement of new jobs. After the dismantling of the public sector, it was mainly the private sector which came into consideration. In addition to the normal ubiquitous structural change from manufacturing to services, the Bonn region also faced a second, much more severe challenge of handling the structural change from the public to the private sector. The magnitude of this task marked the birth of the close cooperation between the City of Bonn and the Rhein-Sieg District.

4.2 Structural-Political Measures and the Development Since the Decision to Move the Governmental Seat

The structural-political measures which were taken in the Bonn region as a reaction to the decision to move the governmental seat and the development of the region since will be examined below. In contrast to the general perception which naturally focuses on the "fate" of the City of Bonn after losing the status of capital, the role of the Rhein-Sieg District in particular will be determined as the result of a more-in depth examination.

4.2.1 Population and Residential Market

The fear that the Bonn region would experience population losses after the governmental seat was moved to Berlin did in no way come true. Only between 1992 and 1995, and then again between 1998 and 2000 when the ministries moved to Berlin, did Bonn experience short periods of population decrease. Afterwards, since the new Millennium, the number of inhabitants has continuously and dynamically increased. In contrast to the overall development in Germany, whose population decreased each year between 2003 and 2010, Bonn did not ever experience another year in which the number of inhabitants declined. The population development in the Rhein-Sieg District is even more impressive. The number of inhabitants strongly increased throughout the entire 1990s. Only in the early 2000s, did the growth rates start to flatten out; in 2008, there was even a slight decrease. Since 2012, the growth has again been continuously increasing (Figs. 6 and 7).

The ratio between the city and the district shows that the 1990s can be characterized as a phase of suburbanization, just like Germany as a whole, and the period from 2005 as a phase of reurbanization. Starting in 2005, the City of Bonn had a higher population growth than the Rhein-Sieg District every year. In 2015, this again changed in favor of the district (Fig. 8).

Most of the population growth in Bonn is fed by migration gains, likewise in all the Rhein-Sieg District. While Bonn is one of only very few cities these days which has a birth surplus, the natural population development in the Rhein-Sieg District has been negative since 2005 which is more than compensated for by migration gains. The main source of the migration gains in the Rhein-Sieg District is the City of Bonn, and the trend is rising. These gains mainly come from the age groups of the 30 to under 50-year-olds and the under 18-year-olds. So, it is mainly families and their children who move from Bonn to the Rhein-Sieg District to fulfill their housing needs.

The close interdependency between Bonn and the Rhein-Sieg District becomes even more obvious when looking at the movement of commuters. Of the 233,700

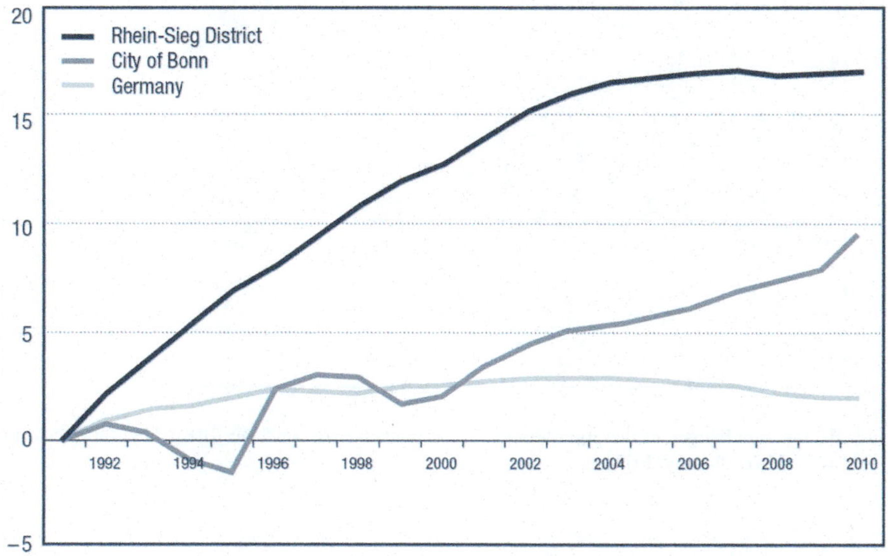

Fig. 6 Population development in Bonn, the Rhein-Sieg District and Germany from 1991 to 2010

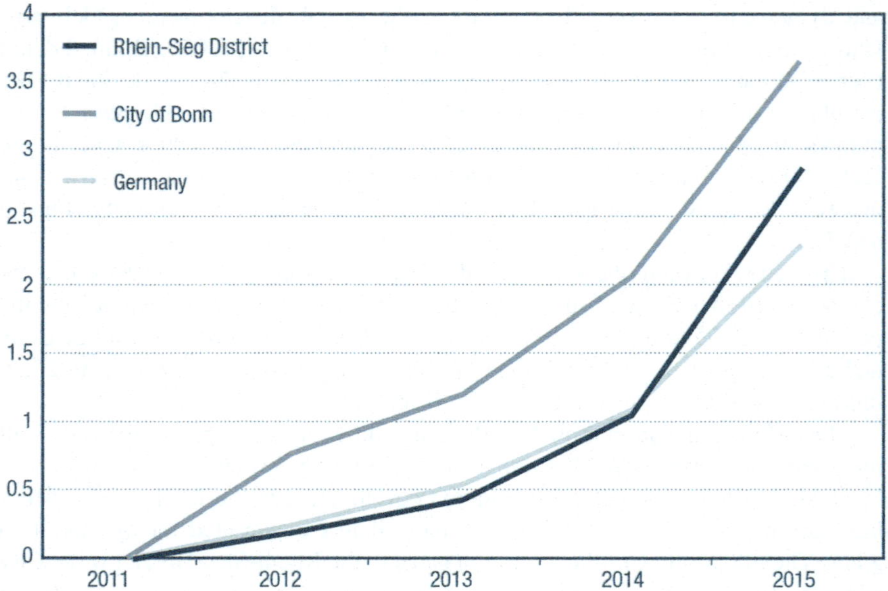

Fig. 7 Population development in Bonn, the Rhein-Sieg District and Germany from 2011 to 2015

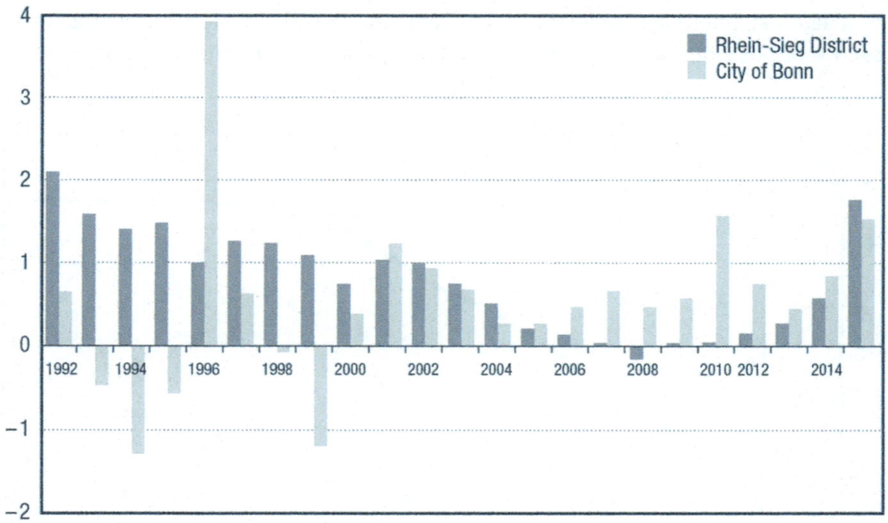

Fig. 8 Annual changes in the population development in Bonn and the Rhein-Sieg District from 1991 to 2015 (excluding 2011)

jobs in Bonn, 126,500 are filled by commuting employees (54%) of which 59,500 (25%) come from the Rhein-Sieg District. There are 0.75 jobs for every inhabitant of Bonn. The city therefore has one of the highest employment densities among the large cities in Germany, benefitting from its highly tertiary economic structure and good employment development (cf. Sect. 4.2.2). Due to this compaction the city is less and less able to offer residential space to incoming employees fulfilling their requirements and at acceptable prices. The economic development of the city is becoming increasingly dependent on the appeal of the surrounding Rhein-Sieg District as a residential location. Institut Empirica has forecast that the spilling over of housing demand from Bonn to the Rhein-Sieg District will continue to increase (Empirica AG 2016).

4.2.2 The Economy and Labor Market

Economic growth and the development of new jobs are generally the main reasons for a population influx. This connection is unambiguous for the Bonn region: despite a loss of more than 15,000 jobs on balance to Berlin as the new governmental seat, employment in Bonn and the Rhein-Sieg District has increased by 72,000 (29%), which is significantly higher than the national average (7%), since the decision to move the governmental seat. The increase in Bonn constituted 35,000 jobs (26%), in the Rhein-Sieg District 37,000 jobs (32%).

In the 1990s until the actual move of the governmental seat in 1999/2000, the Bonn area was even able to buck the overall trend of negative labor market development. The dominance of the public sector, which was connected to the capital status, had, to some extent, made the region independent from the national economy. Only since the move to Berlin and the subsequent reduction of jobs in the public sector is employment carried by the private sector like in other regions, with the consequence of the labor market development following the same trend as the national economy. The fact that the reduction of employment during regressive phases is not as drastic and the job growth during economic upturns is higher than the national average can be considered as a success of structural politics in the Bonn region (Fig. 9).

Apart from a few exceptions—for instance in 2000 and 2001 when the City of Bonn had to deal with the ministries being moved to Berlin—employment has run parallel in the city and the district. However, the amplitudes are much higher in the Rhein-Sieg District than Bonn, which applies to both peaks and valleys. The reason for this circumstance is the fact that Bonn has remained a federal city and the second center of national politics, therefore still has a large number of

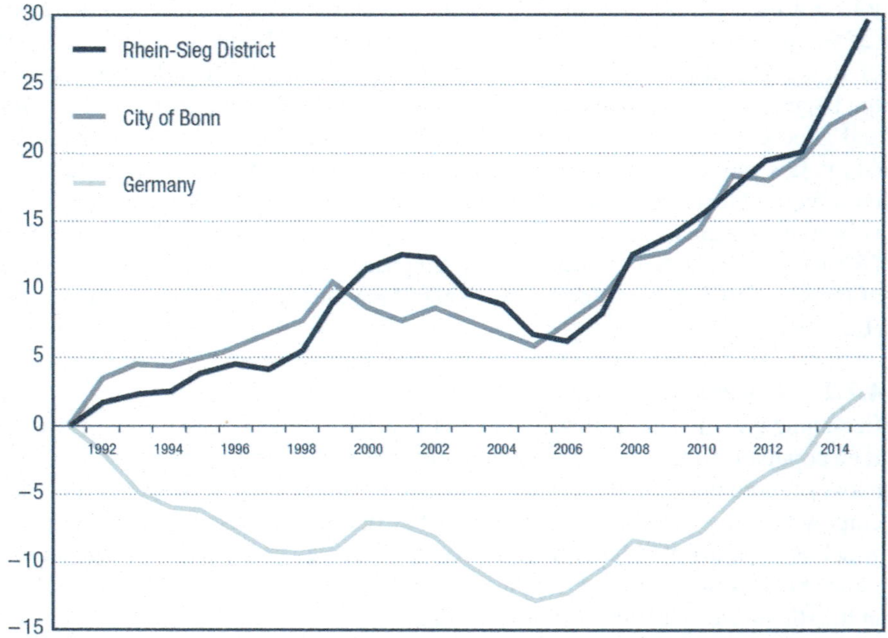

Fig. 9 Employment development in Bonn, the Rhein-Sieg District and Germany from 1991 to 2015

public service institutions and subsequently shows below-average responsiveness to economic developments (Fig. 10).

Despite all parallelism, the economic structure and the development of individual sectors in Bonn and the Rhein-District show significant differences as well:

- Although less than 20% of employees were working in manufacturing 25 years ago, the number of jobs in this field decreased by another 46%, therefore much more strongly than in the Rhein-Sieg District (29%). To this day, employment in manufacturing in the Rhein-Sieg District (27.3%) is more than three times as high as in Bonn (8.4%)
- While originally at the same level, the trade, hospitality and transport sector decreased by 7% in Bonn and increased by 52% in the Rhein-Sieg District.
- The service sector in Bonn was already pre-eminent in 1991 and it increased by another 57% to an employment proportion of 76.4% despite the move of the governmental seat. The growth was carried by private services, the proportion of public services was reduced to 11.3%. Employment in the service sector more than doubled in the Rhein-Sieg District but it still only makes up less than half of overall employment (Table 1).

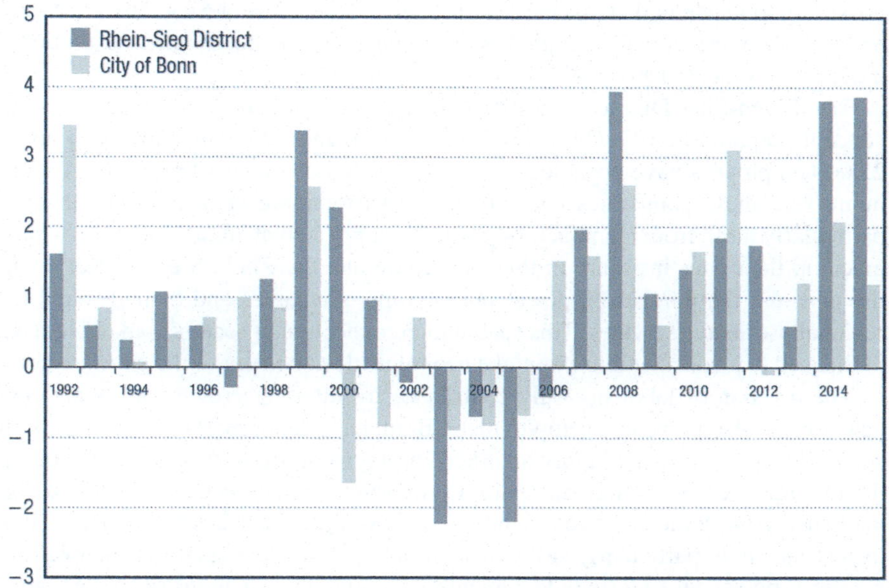

Fig. 10 Annual changes in the population development in Bonn and the Rhein-Sieg District from 1991 to 2015

Table 1 Number of employees subject to social insurance contributions from 1991 to 2015 by economic branches

	Bonn				**Rhein-Sieg District**			
	1991		2015		1991		2015	
Economic branch	Total	%	Total	%	Total	%	Total	%
Agriculture, forestry, fishery	460	0.3	99	0.1	1674	1.5	1008	0.7
Manufacturing	25, 991	19.4	14, 058	8.4	55, 502	48.7	39, 639	27.3
Trade, hospitality, transportation	26, 815	20.0	24, 977	15.1	23, 944	21.0	36, 493	25.2
Other services	80, 933	60.3	126, 657	76.4	32, 830	28.8	67, 945	46.8
Total	134, 199	100.0	165, 791	100.0	113, 950	100.0	145, 085	100.0

While the industrial structure and growth of the City of Bonn is entirely focused on the service sector, the Rhein-Sieg District is much more diverse in its economic structure and development. Consequently, the district serves as an important addition and backup to the city. The Rheinisch-Westfälisches Institut für Wirtschaftsforschung (RWI) in Essen had already emphasized the important task of the district in a report immediately after the decision to move the governmental seat: As a large part of the property in Bonn which was given up by the government would be unacceptable as commercial property because of its central location and close proximity to residential areas, the potential space in the Rhein-Sieg District should be used to compensate for the job losses arising from the government institutions' moving away (RWI 1991: 24f).

The Rhein-Sieg District committed to the task with its industrial real estate concept prepared in 1991/92. Since then, more than 1700 companies with about 25,000 employees have occupied the newly created commercial property. A large number of these companies come from the surrounding area, many of them—particularly those from manufacturing which require a great amount of space—have given up their sites in Bonn. In this way, Bonn and the Rhein-Sieg District retain the jobs and the purchasing power but also the companies and their demand for regionally-oriented services. This spatial interconnection of sectors is likely to have influenced to a considerable extent the economic development of the entire region.

The division of labor not only contributes to initiating growth and generating new jobs. It also prevents unemployment. Bonn has a labor market which has been shaped by specialists and highly qualified employment. Bonn ranks seventh among the 69 largest cities in Germany with a proportion of employees subject to social insurance contributions of 25% (Bahrke and Kempermann 2015). In return, this means that it is particularly difficult to find a job for less qualified people and auxiliary personnel, who would typically be employed in industrial companies. Considering the low mobility of these workers, a deindustrialization of the region would massively increase unemployment. To some degree, this effect is already noticeable in Bonn: going against the national trend, the unemployment rate in Bonn has slightly increased continuously since 2011 and at 7.3% is now higher than the national average (6.4%). Without the Rhein-Sieg District, which has a significantly lower unemployment rate (5.5), as a backup, unemployment in the city and the region would be much higher.

4.2.3 Education, Science and Research

The Institut für Mittelstandsforschung (Institute for SME Research) had forecast a severe lack of skilled workers for the Bonn region, and its industry particularly, as early as the mid-1980s (Institut für Mittelstandsforschung 1986: 174ff). One of the main reasons was probably the special "socialization" of the Bonn region. Back then when it seemed to be the region of the permanent governmental seat of the Federal Republic of Germany, the public sector was dominant and influenced the structure of the population so much that a job in the industry was outside most people's professional orientation. The University of Bonn, which has a strong focus on humanities, was unable to offer a solution for the lack of skilled workers in the region which consisted mainly of small and medium-sized businesses.

The lack of skilled workers and the recognition that qualified young junior staff would become more significant in dealing with the structural change after the loss of the capital status but also less available due to the demographic development has had a lasting effect on structural policies in the Rhein-Sieg District. The district used a great part of the subsidies which the federal government provided to the Bonn region, and therefore to the Rhein-Sieg District as well, as compensation for the loss of government functions for the establishment, settlement and expansion of application-oriented universities. While the Rhein-Sieg District was a no man's land regarding its academic landscape in the early 1990s, it now has three high-performing university-level institutions, which are important for the region and offer more than 10,000 places: the public Hochschule Bonn-Rhein-Sieg, University of Applied Sciences (H-BRS); private IUBH School of Business and Management Bad Honnef Bonn; and the private Alanus University of Arts and Social Sciences. Consequently, the Rhein-Sieg District is one the districts in Germany with the best and most diverse academic offer.

The universities are in many ways valuable engines of regional economic development. With their educational offer, they help fight the lack of skilled labor, they provide access to their knowledge in science and research, they are a source of innovative start-ups and they enrich the cultural diversity as well as the public image of the region. Some of these effects have been quantified for the largest and most important university in the Rhein-Sieg District, the Hochschule Bonn-Rhein-Sieg, University of Applied Sciences (H-BRS). Whereas 40% of its students come from the region, 60% of its graduates accept a position in the region, so the school "imports" qualified workers into the region (ExperConsult 2010). Moreover, the university has already produced more than 100 successful start-up businesses.

The new universities in the Rhein-Sieg District reflect the widely noticeable spatial division of labor between more leading-edge and fundamental research in the centers and more application-oriented science in the surrounding area through their geographical distribution between Bonn and the Rhein-Sieg District. The networking practiced in numerous joint projects in education, research, innovation and entrepreneurship proves to be an increasingly important location factor for the economic sustainability in the entire region.

4.3 Conclusion

The City of Bonn and the Rhein-Sieg District show high growth dynamics—both together and on their own. With their science and research institutions and their highly qualified human resources, they are well-prepared for the challenges of the knowledge society. The cooperation in structural and location policies which arose during the crisis of the governmental seat moving to Berlin has generated added value for the entire region. This exemplary experience should be built upon.

The division of functions between living and working, which corresponds with the classic pattern of the relationship between the city and the surrounding area, as well as the concentration of the service sector in the city and manufacturing in the country are still visible in the relationship between Bonn and the Rhein-Sieg District. However, this description is no longer completely accurate. It neglects the fact that the Rhein-Sieg District has gained a substantial amount of urban quality, not only through the mere growth of its cities, but also through functional enrichment in the fields of science and research as well as transport infrastructure—the central high-speed train stop for the region was created in the district town of Siegburg. The district these day is now more than just the suburban area surrounding Bonn as a regional center.

All data shows: The good development which the Bonn region has experienced in the last 25 years is carried on two strong shoulders. Bonn and the Rhein-Sieg District mutually stimulate each other; they both contribute to evening out each other's deficits and they both have structural and location advantages with which they complement each other.

These synergy effects will also be of great importance when dealing with future problems. The Bonn/Berlin decision which continues to be questioned, the demographic development, globalization with its recurring crises, all represent challenges which might quickly overburden an individual municipality. However, territorial entities which complement their own appeal with their neighbor's, therefore bundling potential, will be successful and competitive.

"The region is tomorrow's city." Much of the core of this statement has already become a reality in the relationship between the City of Bonn and the Rhein-Sieg District. The Bonn/Rhein-Sieg region could serve as a model for other relationships between cities and the surrounding area in Germany.

5 Outlook

This article has shown that regions with their potential regarding housing, commercial property, retention of the demand for business-related and knowledge-oriented services, knowledge application and interdependency fulfill important tasks which support urban growth. However, there are the first indicators that urban growth will reach its peak soon and might not continue to the same extent. In 2014, for instance, more German nationals moved out of the 15 largest cities than into them for the first time since 2002 (Federal Statistics Office of Germany 2016).

It is certainly too soon to tell if this marks the end of urbanization and the beginning of a new phase of reurbanization. There is some evidence that living and working in major centers will be less and less compatible due to compaction, lack of space and the development of prices. As employees are more mobile than companies they will be the first ones to revert to the surrounding area. Commuter traffic and congestion, which already have reached or exceeded the limit of tolerance for many employees and companies, also regarding costs, will continue to increase.

Eventually, this could trigger a suburbanization of jobs as well. The winners would be medium-sized cities with good infrastructure. A spatial development which moves towards a decentralized concentration would counter the overburdening of the major cities and the highly compact agglomerations while boosting a model for nationally and internationally competitive metropolitan regions.

References

Ahrend R, Glocker D (2016) Stadt-Land-Partnerschaften. In: Bundesinstitut für Bau-, Stadt- und Raumforschung (ed) Metropolregionen. Kooperation und Wettbewerb in Deutschland und Europa. Informationen zur Raumentwicklung 5.2016. Bonn, BBSR, pp 625–630

Bahrke M, Kempermann H (2015) Städteranking 2015. Deutsche Großstädte im Vergleich. Institut der deutschen Wirtschaft, Köln

BBSR (2016) Bundesinstitut für Bau-, Stadt- und Raumforschung (ed) Wohnungs- und Immobilienmärkte in Deutschland 2016. Analysen Bau.Stadt.Raum 12, Bonn, BBSR

Brühl H et al (2006) Wohnen in der Innenstadt – eine Renaissance? Difu-Beiträge zur Stadtforschung 41. Deutsches Institut für Urbanistik, Berlin

Bundesministerium für Raumordnung, Bauwesen und Städtebau (1995) Raumordnungspolitischer Handlungsrahmen. Beschluß der 24. Ministerkonferenz für Raumordnung in Düsseldorf am 8. März 1995. Bonn, Bundesministerium für Raumordnung, Bauwesen und Städtebau

Cordes A, Gehrke B (2015) Industrielle Entwicklung und funktionale Verschiebung in Europa. Eine empirische Analyse ausgeübter Tätigkeiten. Vierteljahreshefte zur Wirtschaftsforschung 84(1):79–101

Deutsches Institut für Wirtschaftsforschung e.V (2016) DIW Glossar. https://www.diw.de/de/diw_01.c.412453.de/presse/diw_glossar/wissensintensive_dienstleistungen.html. Accessed 10 Oct 2016

Eickelpasch A (2015) Outsourcing und Offshoring in der deutschen Industrie. Vierteljahrshefte zur Wirtschaftsforschung 84(1):55–77

Empirica AG (2016) Regionale Wohnraumbedarfsanalyse für den Rhein-Sieg-Kreis. Empirica, Bonn

ExperConsult (2010) Regionalwirtschaftliche Bedeutung der Hochschule Bonn-Rhein-Sieg und zukünftige Einbindung in die strategische Entwicklung der Region. ExperConsult, Dortmund

Federal Statistics Office of Germany (2016) Federal Statistics Database. https://www.destatis.de/EN/FactsFigures/SocietyState/Population/Population.html. Accessed 12 Aug 2016

Florida R (2003) The rise of the creative class. Basic Books, New York

Fourastié J (1954) Die große Hoffnung des zwanzigsten Jahrhunderts. Bund-Verlag, Köln-Deut

Fürst D et al (1976) Regionale Wirtschaftspolitik. Werner-Verlag, Düsseldorf

Geppert K, Gornig M (2010) Mehr Jobs, mehr Menschen. Die Anziehungskraft der großen Städte wächst. DIW Wochenbericht (19):2–10

Hamm R (2012) Verbund von Industrie und Dienstleistungen wird enger. Wirtschaftsdienst 92(9):632–639

Hirschle M, Schürt A (2008) Suburbanisierung... und kein Ende in Sicht? Intraregionale Wanderungen und Wohnungsmärkte. Informationen zur Raumentwicklung 3/4.2008:211–227

Institut für Mittelstandsforschung (ed) (1986) Die Wirtschaftsregion Bonn. Strukturprobleme und Entwicklungschancen. C.E. Poeschel, Stuttgart

Jessen J, Mayer H (2010) Reurbanisierung und Flächenrecycling. Portland und Stuttgart. Informationen zur Raumentwicklung 1(2010):29–30

Kanter RM (1996) Weltklasse. Im globalen Wettbewerb lokal triumphieren. Ueberreuter, Wien

Kawka R, Staats J-U (2016) Metropolregionen und Bundesraumordnung. In: Bundesinstitut für Bau-, Stadt- und Raumforschung (ed) Metropolregionen. Kooperation und Wettbewerb in Deutschland und Europa. Informationen zur Raumentwicklung 5.2016. Bonn, BBSR, pp 535–541

Kujath HJ (2012) Reurbanisierung des Wissens. Zur Herausbildung von Metropolregionen unter dem Einfluss der Wissensökonomie. In: Brake K, Herfert G (eds) Reurbanisierung. Materialität und Diskurs in Deutschland. Springer, Wiesbaden, pp 216–238

Kujath HJ (2016) Die ländlichen Regionen in der Wissensgesellschaft und im globalen Weltmarkt. Informationen zur Raumentwicklung 2(2016):189–200

Milbert A, Sturm G (2016) Binnenwanderungen in Deutschland zwischen 1975 und 2013. In: Milbert A, Sturm G (eds) Landflucht? Gesellschaft in Bewegung. Informationen zur Raumentwicklung 2.2016, pp 121–144

Osterhage F, Kaup S (2012) Reurbanisierung als neue Phase der Stadtentwicklung? Eine Analyse der Bevölkerungs- und Beschäftigtenentwicklung in Deutschland 1999 bis 2009. In: Pohlan J et al (eds) Jahrbuch StadtRegion 2011/2012. Verlag Barbara Budrich, Leverkusen, pp 125–141

Porter ME (1999) Unternehmen können von regionaler Vernetzung profitieren. Harv Bus Manage 23(3):51–63

Porter ME (2000) Location, competition, and economic development. Local clusters in a global economy. Econ Dev Q 14(1):15–34

Prognos AG (ed) (2016) Prognos Zukunftsatlas 2016. Das Ranking für Deutschlands Regionen. Prognos, Berlin

Reinhardt ER (2016) Spitzencluster. Regional vernetzt, international erfolgreich. In: Bundesinstitut für Bau-, Stadt- und Raumforschung (ed) Metropolregionen. Kooperation und Wettbewerb in Deutschland und Europa. Informationen zur Raumentwicklung 5.2016. BBSR, Bonn, pp 639–642

RWI (1991) Rheinisch-Westfälisches Institut für Wirtschaftsforschung (ed) Regionalpolitische Flankierung des Bonner Raumes bei Verlagerung des Parlamentssitzes nach Berlin – unter Berücksichtigung auch der Empfehlung des Deutschen Bundestages zur Verlagerung von Regierungsfunktionen nach Berlin. Endbericht, Gutachten im Auftrag des Bundesministers für Wirtschaft. RWI, Essen

Sassen S (1996) Metropolen des Weltmarkts. Die neue Rolle der Global Cities. Campus Verlag, Frankfurt am Main/New York

Schanz HJ, Tengler H (1986) Der niederrheinische Wirtschaftsraum. Standortpotential und Perspektiven. Schriften zur Mittelstandsforschung 14 (N.F.). C.E. Poeschel, Stuttgart

Scharmanski A (ed.) (2015) Triumph der Städte. Schwarmverhalten und Migration als Motoren der Reurbanisierung Quantum Focus 16. https://www.quantum.ag/fileadmin/user_upload/QU-FOCUS_NO16_MAIL.pdf. Accessed 12 Oct 2016

Simon H (1996) Die heimlichen Gewinner (Hidden champions). Die Erfolgsstrategien unbekannter Weltmarktführer. Campus Verlag, New York

Simon H (2013) Weltwissen im Dorf. Manager Magazin 8:66

Tengler H (1989) Die Shift-Analyse als Instrument der Regionalforschung. Schriften zur Mittelstandsforschung 28 (N.F.). C. E. Poeschel, Stuttgart

Tengler H, Hennicke M (1987) Dienstleistungsmärkte in der Bundesrepublik Deutschland. Schriften zur Mittelstandsforschung 19 (N.F.). C. E. Poeschel, Stuttgart

United Nations (ed) (2008) World urbanization prospects. The 2007 revision. Population Database. United Nations, New York

Wagner M, Mulder CH (2015) Spatial mobility, family dynamics, and housing transitions. Kölner Zeitschrift für Soziologie und Sozialpsychologie 67(Suppl):111–135

Hermann Tengler born in 1956, studied economics at the University of Bonn from 1981 to 1988 before working as a research associate and project manager at the Institut für Mittelstandsforschung (Institute for SME Research) in Bonn. His scientific work focused on questions of regional economic development and the sectoral structural change of the economy. The expert has prepared structure and location assessments as well as development concepts for numerous cities and regions. After obtaining his doctorate (dissertation: "Die Shift-Analyse als Instrument der Regionalforschung"/"The Shift Analysis as an Instrument of Regional Research"), he moved to the Rhein-Sieg District in 1989. Being responsible for the promotion of the economy, he played a key role in shaping the successful structural change of the Bonn/Rhein-Sieg region after the decision to move the governmental seat to Berlin was made. His work focuses on the expansion of education, science and research, regional labor market politics, commercial property concepts, start-up promotion, regional marketing and the promotion of regional tourism. Today, Dr. Tengler heads the Department of Economic Promotion and Strategic District Development in the Rhein-Sieg District. In addition to the promotion of the economy, he is also responsible for regional transportation and land politics.

The Digital City: Using the Example of "Mönchengladbach on eBay"

Gerrit Heinemann and Stefan Wenzel

Abstract

The digital revolution inevitably alters brick and mortar retailers. In particular, retail cities face enormous challenges. If they want to survive as a retail location, they have to improve their image and work on their appeal for digitally oriented customers. These cities need to digitalize their infrastructure. Local retailers must go online. Retail has to be reinvented to create new kinds of digital experiences. It needs to integrate digital commerce into the offline world. This process can be supported by most city councils. They should create more centrality for the city centers, especially in small and medium-sized towns. A city has to find its unique identity. It can build up attraction points for the city center as shopping location. This was the aim of the project "MG Retail.2020", using Mönchengladbach as a pilot city. The study produced a joint master plan for local retailers, the municipal policy and also the real estate industry. Core result was the concept of "Mönchengladbach on eBay" as a regional marketplace. This platform serves as a model for other cities. It has already received nationwide and international attention. The "Digital City" initiative launched by the German Retail Federation (HDE) and eBay is another outcome of the project.

1 "Online Versus Offline": Baseline Scenario

The triumphant advance of online retailing continues unabated. Measured by total sales in the non-food retail sector, the share of online commerce has already reached

G. Heinemann (✉)
eWeb Research Center, Niederrhein University of Applied Sciences, Mönchengladbach, Germany
e-mail: professor@gerritheinemann.de

S. Wenzel
eBay Germany, Kleinmachnow, Germany

H. Albach et al. (eds.), *European Cities in Dynamic Competition*,
https://doi.org/10.1007/978-3-662-56419-6_10

the 20% mark in 2016 (HDE 2016). Including all everyday necessities, this figure is likely to apply to the entire retail sector as early as 2020. The development of traditional retail in terms of "online versus offline" varies greatly depending on the commodity group. For example, the food retailing sector lags behind any online development and is virtually idle in Germany. In non-food and particularly in the area of toys, media/books, consumer electronics and clothing, bricks and mortar retail is strongly affected by the online versus offline trend. In these segments, there have already been downsizing measures, format reductions and branch closures (GfK 2015). Overall, this has already given significant rise to a potential threat for inner cities. This is currently evidenced by the increasing vacancy rate of retail properties, which often reaches 40% in small and medium-sized cities. It is expected that at least 45,000 stores—i.e. every tenth shop—will face closure in the next 5 years (IfH Köln 2015).

1.1 Development and Prospects of Online Retail

Online retailing already accounts for about 10% of the total retail volume in Europe. The figure for non-food is nearly twice as high and is expected to rise up to 40% in the developed economies and up to 30% in today's emerging markets by 2025 (Heinemann 2017; Deutsche Post DHL 2014). The numbers for Germany are right in line with the average. Online commerce will continue to become increasingly important by 2025, not only in the industrialized nations, but will largely shape the retail world in developing and emerging countries as well, and even to a much greater extent than previously anticipated. This is one of the key results of the "Global E-Tailing 2025" study, which was initiated by Deutsche Post DHL, with the participation of a number of international experts from retail, logistics and research (Deutsche Post DHL 2014). In Germany, customers are increasingly making purchases with a click of the mouse. According to estimates by the German Retail Federation (HDE) and the German E-Commerce and Distance Selling Trade Association (bevh), the online retail share was between 11% and 12% in 2016, and therefore growing five times faster than retail as a whole (HDE 2016; BEVH 2016). However, the published sales figures still vary enormously as before. At least the projected growth rates by HDE and bevh are identical for the first time, though, suggesting better quality with regard to the collection of the data and figures (see Fig. 1).

In this respect, the "online versus offline" substitution effect will steadily continue in the coming years and take a major toll on bricks and mortar retail (Brandeins 2015). Measured by total sales in the non-food retail sector, which mainly represents the inner-city retail business, the share of online commerce already reached the 20% mark in 2016 (HDE 2016). Including all everyday necessities, this figure is likely to apply to the entire retail sector as soon as 2020. This was the finding of a study conducted by IFH Köln (Die Welt 2015). Although media, books and toys have long had the highest online shares, every commodity group can now be regarded as internet-compatible (FAZ 2014). In particular, high-volume commodity groups

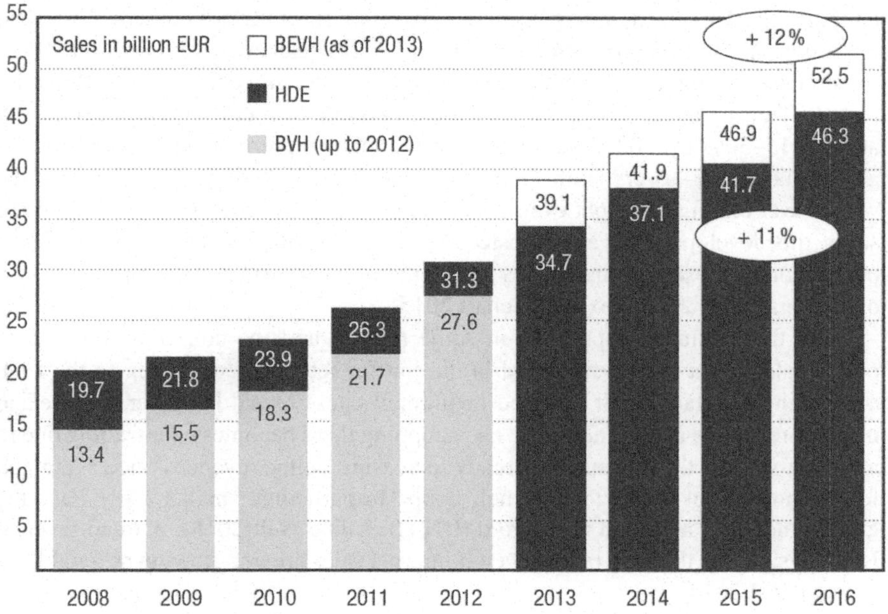

Fig. 1 Online retail market development in Germany (bevh 2016; HDE 2016)

such as furniture, DIY/hardware and home improvement products and especially food have confirmed high growth potential which will increase over the next few years and will boost online retailing as well (bevh 2016).

1.2 Impact on Bricks and Mortar Retail

Consumer interest in online shopping is steadily rising and online retailing will continue to take sales away from the traditional retail sector in the coming years (Süddeutsche Zeitung 2014). Many retailers—especially weaker ones—will probably close their physical stores or need to reinvent themselves very quickly. According to a recent survey by the Center for Research in Retailing (Institut für Handelsforschung Köln/IFH) every third consumer has already reduced the number of trips to the city center, making more online purchases instead (Die Welt 2015). According to the German Retail Federation (HDE), more than 60% of "normal" retailers complain about declining numbers of customers to their stores (Süddeutsche Zeitung 2014). The study "Stadt, Land, Handel 2020" ("Urban, Rural, Retail 2020") conducted by the IFH comes to the conclusion that almost every tenth bricks and mortar store will face closure by 2020. Accordingly, all regions are affected by the store closures, but structurally weak areas and cities are hit harder than others. Therefore bricks and mortar retailers in metropolises like Hamburg and Berlin can expect to see the least negative impact. The same applies to Baden-Württemberg, Central and Southern Bavaria, Southern Hesse and the southern Lower Rhine region (IfH 2015; Textilwirtschaft 2015; Die Welt 2015). In contrast, the biggest cuts are expected for the German federal states of Saxony-Anhalt, Thuringia and Saxony, where bricks and mortar retail sales will decline by at least 15–30% by 2020. Nationwide in Germany, approximately 45,000 bricks and mortar stores—every tenth shop—will face closure over the next 5 years. In the worst case, that figure might even reach 78,000 store shutdowns. According to the study, this development is also boosted by the fact that the expected decrease in the population in these regions creates more supply gaps, which are then covered by online retail (IfH 2015; Textilwirtschaft 2015).

Both the declining population in some regions and the continuing growth in online sales put a downward spiral in motion for retailers. According to the IFH, a shrinking population will bring a drop in retail sales as well. However, if more and more stores in the inner cities close and shopping there becomes unappealing due to a lack of variety, this boosts the already increasing online revenues once again and forces more shopkeepers to shut their doors. In particular, smaller cities have the greatest need for action in this regard (IfH 2015; Die Welt 2015). A trend reversal is not in sight for the time being, even if internet sales are not growing as quickly as before (FAZ 2014).

Nevertheless, GfK anticipates that retail spaces will remain relatively stable. Given the current development, this is not comprehensible and rather suggests a lack of solutions in the bricks and mortar retail sector. A corresponding study indicates that the next few years will see sustained but modest growth in retail space, averaging about 0.1% annually. In this study, however, the development also varies greatly depending on the location and forecasts even higher increases in retail space for strong, established retail locations. Consequently, the polarization of the space structure will continue. In addition to the top seven locations, this also pertains to medium-sized cities with high purchasing power and high centrality or to high-profile and car-friendly specialized retail areas. Those facing the greatest loss will be the economically underdeveloped cities in the Ruhr region, disadvantaged small towns in Eastern Germany, peripheral and low-density rural areas as well as secondary locations in all city categories where the erosion of bricks and mortar retail had already started prior to the internet era (GfK 2015).

1.3 Impact on Cities and Municipalities

The growing tendency of German citizens to buy online predominantly affects bricks and mortarretailers with non-food product ranges, i.e. inner city retailers, since retail food sales mainly take place in the peripheral areas. The spatial effects of online retailing are classified as a "new topic" and therefore, they have only been systematically examined on a sporadic basis (WFMG 2015b). Nevertheless, there are numerous empirical findings on commodity group-specific spatial orientation of consumers that consider the online and distance selling share, both on the side of specialized consultants as well as other research and consulting stakeholders, which can be spatially and temporally differentiated (IfH Köln 2014). The same applies to the spatially differentiated offer structures observed in the cities. Similarly, data on the relationship between online shops and bricks and mortar availability is continuously being collected and evaluated on the retail side. The provision of such data is extremely important for the quality of the results. However, one of the challenges here is the classification of the causality of the development of online retailing and spatial findings as well as other influencing factors. However, a distinction between other influences on the structure and function of the centers is essential for making specific and targeted recommendations for actions. Figure 2 shows the general interdependency. The technological development has already undoubtedly changed consumer and shopping behavior to a great extent. In particular, the main driver for the shift in consumer behavior is the rapid development of new and powerful information and communication technologies and, above all, the penetration of high-speed and mobile internet connectivity. At the same time, fewer market entry barriers create a new, internationally competitive landscape. Consequently, the bricks and mortar retail sector is facing fundamental challenges that will lead to an elemental change in the types of business models that are conventional in the retailing sector. These developments especially apply to bricks and mortar retailing, which on the one hand is strongly affected, but on the other hand, has now also taken on a pioneering role in this sector.

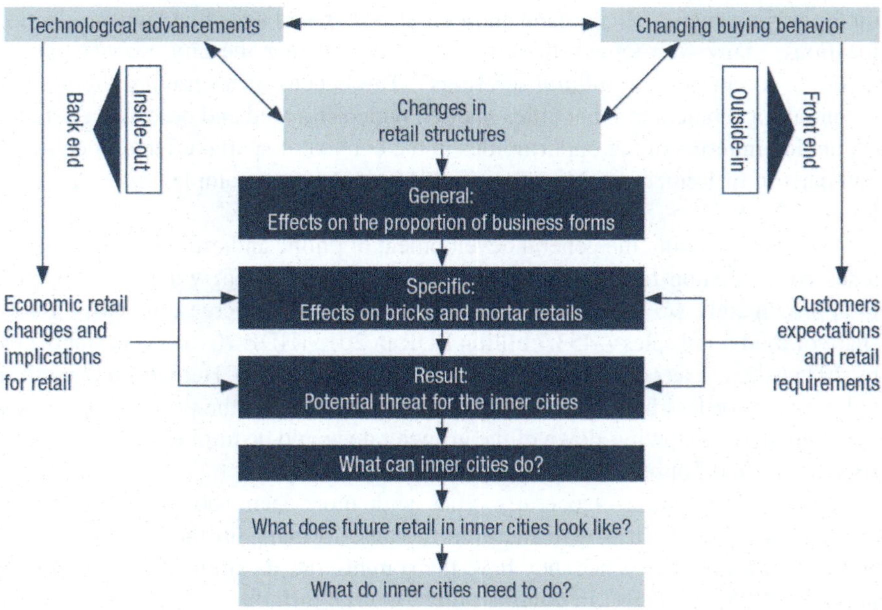

Fig. 2 Interdependency of the effects of online retail on inner cities (based on eWeb Research Center 2016)

Therefore, of central importance—although it is not the subject of this paper—is to apply a dual approach and assess and expand both the theories of buyer behavior in relation to the new opportunities and framework conditions as well as examine the changes in the types of business models and evaluate institutional trade theory in this regard. The result will be a modified, possibly even new buyer behavior model and at the same time a further development of the theory of the dynamics of business forms and the "wheel of retailing". This revolves continuously, and it is not without reason that it has always been said that "retail is change" (Ahlert et al. 2009). The (re)action of retail businesses with bricks and mortar stores is also changing. (Former) pure players such as Zalando and JakoO have local stores; showrooming business models, which offer exclusively online purchases within the shop, provide a new, economically feasible way for furniture dealers, for example, to do business in inner city locations. Customizing, e.g. for sporting goods and fashion retailing, is developing at a dynamic pace and offers ambivalent approaches for forecasting the spatial implications for medium-sized cities.

The impact on bricks and mortar non-food retailers, and thus on the inner cities, is indeed obvious, but will manifest itself very differently depending on the commodity group and store location. In the top city locations, particularly in the metropolitan cores, retail chains and real estate developers continue to scout for new locations, the development of rent and property values will be above average in the coming years. For example, Harald Meilicke, Chairman of the Advisory Board of Breuninger, says that "bricks and mortar retailers will focus even more strongly on the urban centers" (Beckmann and Föhrer 2014), and adds that "when selecting locations, many well-known brands also check whether the city attracts tourists or has a good range of cultural offerings". The benefit of leveraging the tourism potential for retailers in inner cities is often underestimated and deserves a detailed evaluation in terms of the opportunities in the context of spatial effects, such as the comparison of Leipzig by Monheim in 2014 shows, for example (Beckmann and Föhrer 2014).

As a starting point, the general development of online and offline retail has to be assessed. In the non-food segment, interactive distance selling, which is attributable to approximately 4/5 of online commerce, is expected to increase its current 10% share of total retail sales—453.7 billion EUR in 2015 (HDE 2016)—to around 25% by 2025 (+250% as compared to +300% in the past 8 years). Here, distance selling will be more or less handled completely online and despite the progressive growth in recent years, a slowing-down of the growth rate would be implied in this scenario (Beckmann and Föhrer 2014).

The regional centers—generally cities with more than 100,000 residents and above-average centrality—will therefore be able to maintain their retail share of currently around 38%, since they have the sought-after locations that all providers jump at (WFMG 2015b). In contrast, there will be turmoil in small and medium-sized cities, which accounted for approximately 48.5% of traditional retail in 2015, and about 24% of the retail space sales will dwindle by 2015 (see Fig. 3). In cities that are farther away from the surrounding areas, where the offerings in the main shopping areas are already streamlined, it is becoming increasingly difficult to

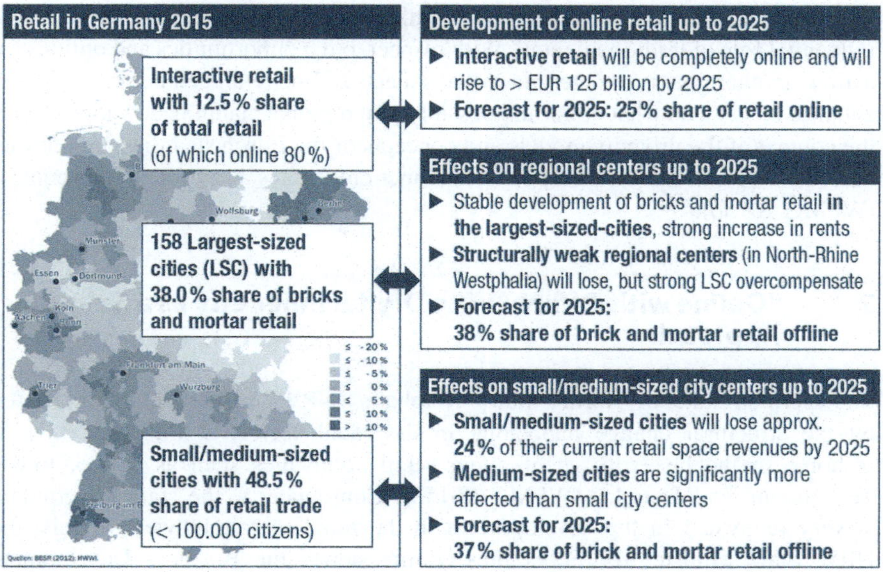

Fig. 3 Impact of online retail on inner cities (based on eWeb Research Center 2016)

attract customers. Small towns are already struggling with high vacancy rates. In Tönisvorst, a town with a population of 30,000 situated just outside of Krefeld, 50 shopkeepers taped black foil over their windows back in 2013 to draw attention to competition from the internet (Rheinische Post 2013). Similar actions have taken place in other cities as well. Major companies that were previously present in the pedestrian zone shopping areas in medium-sized towns have already eliminated cities with fewer than 100,000 inhabitants from their expansion strategy (Beckmann and Föhrer 2014).

Customers are increasingly switching from going to the inner city to going online. This is currently evidenced by the increasing vacancy rate of retail properties. Unfortunately, there are hardly any reliable figures on vacancy rates in Germany. CIMA, a consulting and management firm, published the average vacancy rates for 113 small and medium-sized cities in 2009, and the figures then ranged between 10.5% and 11.5% (CIMA 2009). These figures have likely at least doubled since then and are now at more than 20%. The results of a survey of 62 cities conducted by the Hanover Chamber of Industry and Commerce (IHK Hannover) in 2010 found that almost half of the municipalities had vacancy rates of more than 20%, and today, that figure is probably closer to 40% (IHK Hannover 2010). The crucial questions concern what retailing in the inner cities will look like in the future and what the best measures are that cities and municipalities can and should take with regard to this development. Moreover, the link with processes in initiatives such as "Weißbuch Innenstadt" ("Downtown White Paper") and "Innovationen in Innenstädten" ("Innovations in Inner Cities") plays an important role. The aim is to identify which functions correspond with the "frequency-relevant" core of the influential role of traditional retail. With respect to the opportunities and options for action, another goal is to determine what aspects offline retail can flank, substitute, enhance or add, and what urban and possibly also regional planning developments in the context of the urbanity models and concepts of the European cities are relevant here. The topic of the "digitization of the inner city" plays a key role in this context (WFMG 2015b).

2 "Online with Offline": The Digital Inner City as a Solution Approach

The German state of North Rhine-Westphalia (NRW) is particularly impacted by the structural change happening in the retail sector, at the same time it is home to the head offices of major retail companies such as Metro, Rewe, Tengelmann and Douglas (WFMG 2015b). Consequently, the state government is very interested in the developments in the retail sector. In view of this, the NRW State Minister for Economics commissioned the Business Development Corporation Mönchengladbach (WFMG) and the eWeb Research Center at the Niederrhein University of Applied Sciences to jointly work on a project examining the "Impact of Online Commerce on Cities and Municipalities in North Rhine-Westphalia and Perspectives for Action for Bricks and Mortar Retailing in the Inner Cities". The research project, titled "MG.Retail2020", primarily aims to develop actionable solution approaches for the sustainable development of inner cities in order to combat the migration of consumers, for the purpose of deriving meaningful recommendations for action for the cities, the state, relevant organizations and the retailers. As a first step, a qualitative focus group study was conducted with customers and retailers to research and identify the reasons for the shift in consumer behavior, with the goal of developing appropriate guidelines. This was followed by an extensive quantitative survey to develop experimental measures to be used in practice by the pilot city, Mönchengladbach. Finally, concrete recommendations for actions for the bricks and mortar retail sector, which could be transferred to comparable cities and towns, were derived on the basis of scientifically sound surveys. These serve to secure the competitiveness and innovation of retailers in the inner cities and provide guidance for urban development with regard to the sustainable development of inner cities as well as the creation and preservation of jobs. A key recommendation for action arising from MG.Retail2020 was the pilot project "MG on eBay".

Already before the project start it was obvious that it is essential for bricks and mortar retailers to be present on the internet. This can be done via their own website, own online store or via online marketplaces. In connection with regional marketplace models, the topic of local commerce is also being increasingly discussed (Locafox 2014). This approach is still quite new and represents a further development of the e-commerce concept. The aim is to not only sell goods on online shops or marketplaces, but to link local stores to the internet and vice versa. Local commerce thus represents the dovetailing of online trading and sales in local stores. This can be in the form of "digital shop windows" or apps offering promotional discounts, or even regional marketplaces. Any solutions in this direction will encourage consumers to continue to patronize local retail stores, but without having to sacrifice the advantages of the internet as a source of information (Locafox 2014). Accordingly, on one hand, local retailers should participate in the booming online trade by joining forces and competing together against online competitors, but on the other hand, local marketplaces also want to offer customers an alternative to online pure players.

2.1 MG.Retail2020 Project as Jump Start

The objective of the "Impact of Online Commerce on Cities and Municipalities in North Rhine-Westphalia and Perspectives for Action for Stationary Retailing in the Inner Cities" project was to develop concepts and strategic recommendations for bricks and mortar retailers that will help them deal with the irreversible development of the digitization of retail. These measures could comprise both purely on-site offers, such as special services and events, as well as a combination of online and offline retail offers. Accordingly, part of the focus was on multi-channel considerations, online options for bricks and mortar retailers, and potential digital services. In this regard, the different requirements of bricks and mortar retail stores needed to be considered, for example owner-managed shops versus chain stores, business forms, and shopping centers. Here, the goal was to develop implementable concepts that the inner cities can adapt in alignment with the changing framework conditions in the retail and service sectors.

The pilot city was to be Mönchengladbach, a city with a population of approximately 260,000 people that was founded in 1975 as a result of the merger of the two independent city districts Mönchengladbach and Rheydt and the municipality of Wickrath. Due to the merger, two inner city areas still exist: The larger one is the Mönchengladbach city center, while Rheydt is the smaller district. Therefore, the analysis and survey also differentiated between these two "micro-locations". The intent was to develop recommendations for action and guidelines for inner cities as part of the development project for the entire pilot city (Mönchengladbach). This could then be directly transferable to other regions. The aim of the project was to derive actionable recommendations for the city, the state, for associations and retailers that would enable sustainable development of the inner cities in order to counteract the migration of consumers. The recommendations should be specifically geared to ensure the survival of the local retail stores in Mönchengladbach and other NRW cities and to efficiently respond to the increasing threat of online retailing.

In January 2014, an initial orientation session for the research and development project took place. During this period, a kick-off meeting was organized internally and the first appointment was made with the eWeb Research Center and the Business Development Corporation Mönchengladbach ~~Economy~~ (WFMG). The team unanimously chose "MG.Retail2020" as the project name and logo. "MG" is an abbreviation for Mönchengladbach, the dot symbolizes internet affinity, and the year "2020" represents the target date for implementing the measures in the guidelines. The project organization comprised a steering committee, which, in addition to the project leads, also included the management of WFMG and directors of the eWeb Research Center at the Niederrhein University of Applied Sciences, as well as an advisory council. The advisory council was made up of the steering committee and representatives from the Mönchengladbach retail sector, the Rheydt~~er~~ City Management Association, the Mönchengladbach City Management Association, and chain stores (e.g. the owner of the Engbers Group), along with e-commerce experts (including the CEO of Shopmacher e-commerce GmbH) and shopping center operators (executive board of mfi Mönchengladbach Arkaden). The public project launch and official kick-off took place on February 20, 2014. At that time, the joint meeting with the advisory council and a subsequent press conference was held at the WFMG premises, during which all of the project partners and participants were introduced. The project planning and schedule provided for four phases in which guidelines for inner cities and specific recommendations for action were to be systematically developed with the involvement of all concerned and the relevant stakeholders. The special component of this development project was a combination of scientifically sound, theory-based data collection and immediately implementable actions.

Phase 1: Conceptualization of the Research and Study Design and First Round of Expert Discussions In the first project phase, which lasted 2 months, the research and study design was conceptualized and the first interviews with the experts took place. In addition, the first retailer surveys were conducted, which surveyed the retailers' reactions to the perceived threat of online retail. The following five response patterns were most frequently mentioned by the retailers:

- **Give up/do nothing**: Trying to compete with online retailing is considered to be pointless and infeasible. Ignorance or giving up are the most common outcomes of this assumption.
- **Save on costs:** In order to keep pace with the price pressure from the internet, personnel expenses and costs for store displays and designs should be minimized.
- **Go online:** An online presence (website, online store, social media activity, etc.) guides customers from the internet to the store or even opens up new sales channels on the internet.
- **Multi-channel elements:** Use and efficiently combine several sales channels to ensure that customers have a shopping experience that is as pleasant and convenient as possible.
- **Emphasize the advantages of** local **stores:** Identify the weaknesses of online commerce and use them to emphasize the advantages of traditional retail. Friendly and capable expert advice, haptic (tactile) feedback and the shopping experience are significant examples of these strengths and benefits.

Phase 2: Qualitative Survey The second project phase, lasting 5 months, was dedicated to conducting the qualitative component of the study. The main content was a focus group study with retailers and customers from Mönchengladbach. During this phase, four groups of customers were formed, with each group consisting of two consumers from Mönchengladbach and two from Rheydt. In addition, three groups of retailers were formed. Between six and eight people were represented on each team. Customers were recruited in both Mönchengladbach's city center area and in Rheydt, in accordance with a predefined quota. The selection took into account criteria such as age differences, percentage of online and offline purchases, knowledge and familiarity with the inner city areas, occupations categorized by full or part time employment, as well as the proportion of school-aged students, higher education students and retired persons. The retailer focus groups included sole proprietors from both Mönchengladbach and Rheydt as well as chain store retailers. The WFMG assisted with the recruitment process, while the eWeb Research Center was responsible for the organization, design, implementation and evaluation of the focus groups. The customer perspectives elicited during this phase were especially insightful, and also provided the initial hypothesis for the quantitative survey. According to the survey, bricks and mortar retailers are more strongly affected by the development of online commerce with regard to the purchase of necessities, than with regard to the experience shopping, which, in the opinion of the retailers, generally happens in the inner city.

Phase 3: Quantitative Survey with Concurrent Measures Implemented by Retailers as a Real-World Test The 8-month-long third phase of the project constituted the core of the project. The aim was to conduct a main quantitative study based on the results of the qualitative survey. Moreover, the project called for facilitated workshops to be held on various topics, both with retailers and with consumers, which enabled the development of experimental actions. The quantitative data was collected from the participants from January 27 to February 21, 2015, using a hybrid survey which combined an online survey with a traditional telephone interview. To obtain a representative composition of the sample, quotas were specified for the characteristics of gender, age, household income, and place of residence. Half of the participants came lived in Mönchengladbach, the other half from the surrounding areas. Thus, they represented both the Mönchengladbach and Rheydt districts that were the subjects of the project. Another criterion was that the participants must have previously shopped online at least once. A total of 1002 people participated in the survey. To enable an accurate interpretation of the results, the participants were divided into groups based on their shopping frequency. Accordingly, the survey was used to determine the appeal of shopping in the inner city areas of both Mönchengladbach and Rheydt. The results also identified the degree of importance of inner city attributes during a typical shopping trip in the two inner city areas.

The differentiation of the participants yielded a classification according to inner city shoppers and internet shoppers, and for both categories, a further subdivision into frequent, regular and infrequent shoppers as well. Within the inner city shopper category, infrequent shoppers, with a share of 46.1%, comprise the largest cohort. This is characterized by the fact that the majority of them come from the surrounding areas and live in 1 to 2-person households. At maximum, they shop in the inner city once every 2–3 months. The second largest group within the inner city shopper category is made up of regular visitors (41.5%), who go to the inner city for shopping at least once a month. These shoppers are predominantly male and live in Mönchengladbach. With a figure of 12.4%, frequent shoppers, who shop in the inner city at least once a week or even daily, comprise the smallest cohort. This group mainly comprises males living in Mönchengladbach and has the largest proportion of retired people.

In the category of Internet shoppers, regular shoppers represent the largest group, with a share of 52.5%. These shoppers, who shopped online at least six—and even up to 30—times in the past 12 months, mainly come from the surrounding areas and include the highest proportion of 18–29 year olds. Frequent internet shoppers go online to shop at least 31 times a year, and the majority of them reside in the surrounding areas. This category has the largest share of 30–39 year olds. The majority of regular and frequent internet shoppers have a university degree. This group also includes a relatively high proportion of smartphone owners (70%). The group of infrequent internet shoppers comprises 31% of the internet shopper category and only buys online 1 to 5 times a year. Participants in this category have the highest proportion of 40–69 year olds, live mainly in 1- to 2-person households in Mönchengladbach, and are also characterized by a relatively low level of education.

Phase 4: Development of Guidelines for the Inner City The fourth phase of the project, which lasted 3 months, concentrated on the development of guidelines for the inner cities. The evaluation of the analyses, however, showed that retailers vary in their degree of willingness to deal with the issue of digitization. Some retailers have an attitude towards their business that obviously does not contribute to the success of their actions. They see their store more as a form of self-expression and not as a means of revenue. Other retailers, in contrast, reveal effective displacement mechanisms. They attribute the reason for the migration of customers to the internet, to politics, or to the city administration, and do not feel impelled to take any action themselves. But the problem with these "internet-objectors" is that online retail openly discloses their obvious existing weaknesses. It subsequently acts as a catalyst that will lead to a streamlining of competition. Appropriate and effective supportive actions, however, can only be derived for retailers who operate professionally in bricks and mortar retail and who also have prospects for their existence as a retailer. Accordingly, identical actions cannot be derived for all retailers alike. In view of this, the retailers were divided into four groups based on their ability to make the digital transformation—regardless of their business form or size:

Group 1: Retailers who do not have an internet presence in any form and also do not have any willingness to engage with the internet

Group 2: Retailers who have not yet been digitally present in any form, but are willing to engage with the internet

Group 3: Retailers who already have an initial digital presence and want to further expand it and also meet the prerequisites (e.g. electronic inventory management system)

Group 4: Retailers who are already present on the internet in various ways, fulfill the criteria for the taking initial multi-channel approaches, and want to expand further

The guidelines are differentiated and tailored to the different needs and requirements of the groups. They provide concrete recommendations for all project participants for counteracting the consumer migration and contain specific actions with practical solution approaches for retailers in Mönchengladbach. At the same time, the recommendations are designed and structured in a way that makes them transferable to other municipalities (WFMG 2015b).

2.2 Analysis of Results and Guidelines from MG.Retail2020

With respect to the attractiveness of the inner city as a shopping location, the results for Mönchengladbach and Rheydt were similar. When asked the question "How attractive do you think the inner city is for shopping?", participants could select a rating between 5 (for "very attractive") and 1 (for "very unattractive"). The average rating was 3.03 for Mönchengladbach and 2.97 for Rheydt. The ratings concerning practicality and recommending the inner city for shopping were also right around 3. In this regard, no significant differences were found in the rating between necessity shoppers and pleasure shoppers in the inner city and online.

In terms of the importance of inner city attributes during a typical shopping trip in local retail stores, the participants could rate this aspect on a scale from 1 for "not important at all" to 5 for "very important". Figure 4 shows a comparison of all of the degree-of-importance values, differentiated by participants from Mönchengladbach and customers from the surrounding areas. It is worth noting that the participants rated attributes such as opening hours, product selection, brand selection, access to the inner city, and a pleasant atmosphere as being the most important. In contrast, children's play areas and public restrooms were assessed as being less important. The most significant differences were found with regard to the attributes of cleanliness, product selection, brand selection, available parking spaces, and pleasant atmosphere. Consequently, if the aim is to attract customers from the surrounding areas, these attributes should be given particular consideration. These can partially be influenced by the retailers, but also by the municipalities.

The primary result of the quantitative analysis was that the consumers do not differentiate between experience shopping and necessity shopping when it comes to assessing online and inner city shopping. However, all of the groups rated online shopping as more attractive than shopping in the Mönchengladbach inner city area. This result disproves the central initial hypothesis that was obtained from the

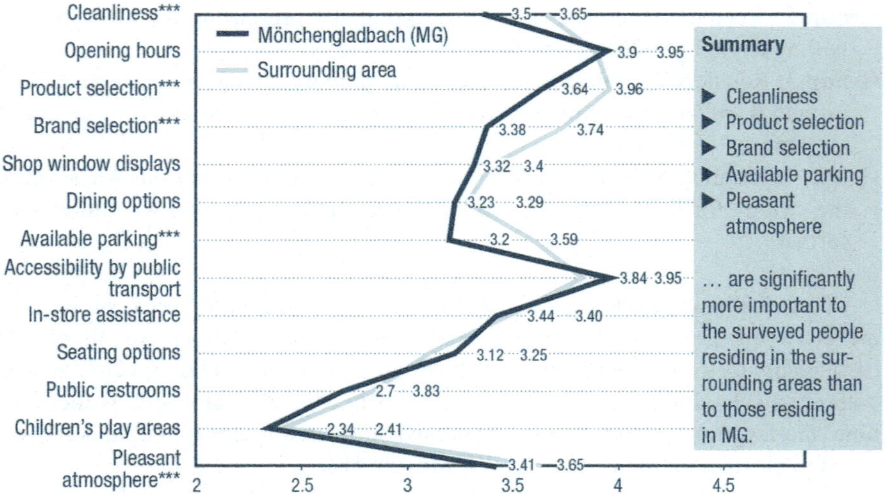

*** Significant differences in importance ratings depending on if residence in MG or surrounding areas, significance level .000 (Differences between variables are deemed highly significant (***) if the probability that they would happen randomly does not exceed a threshold of 0.1 %.)

Fig. 4 Importance of inner city attributes (WFMG 2015b)

qualitative study, according to which the potential threat of online commerce would be differentiated in terms of experience shopping and necessity shopping. With regard to the attributes of an inner city, it is evidently a matter of seemingly trivial things, but ones which reflect basic needs. Quite simply, customers find seating, affordable dining options and restrooms to be particularly important. With regard to cleanliness, product selection, brand selection, parking situation and atmosphere, however, the results showed significant differences between the project participants from Mönchengladbach and the participants from the surrounding areas. These attributes are obviously more important to the respondents from the surrounding areas and accordingly also assessed as less important by the Mönchengladbach residents. They gave the number of Sunday shopping days and the opening hours in Mönchengladbach a lower rating than the participants living in Mönchengladbach did. This also serves to explain why the majority of the intensive online shoppers come from the surrounding areas, because they have to invest more time in getting to the Mönchengladbach shopping area and therefore have higher expectations of the inner city. "Inner city adversaries" from Mönchengladbach accordingly rate the accessibility by bus and train as worse than the "inner city fans" who enjoy shopping there. In contrast, these "inner city fans" gave a lower rating to the atmosphere in the inner city than the "inner city adversaries". In general, there is a desire for more digital communication. In particular, the intensive Internet users primarily get their information about products online and want more digital communication from the stores and businesses in the inner city. But the "inner city adversaries" in Mönchengladbach also expressed the desire for more online information about products and offers from local stationary stores. They also want more online shops from local retailers. The key results of the quantitative analysis were:

- The attractiveness of online retail/the inner city is perceived equally by all consumers, regardless of the type of shopping (pleasure shopping versus shopping for basic necessities).
- All groups feel that online shopping is more appealing than shopping in the MG inner city.
- Infrequent MG inner city shoppers want more online information about in-store offers and web shops of inner city stores.
- Frequent online shoppers want inner city stores to do more digital communications.
- Frequent online shoppers give lower ratings to the selection of brands, range of products, opening hours and the short-term parking situation as well as the accessibility by public transit.
- Infrequent MG inner city shoppers give lower ratings to accessibility by public transit, and frequent inner city shoppers give lower ratings to the atmosphere in MG.
- Importance ratings differentiated by MG and the surrounding areas—significant differences: cleanliness, product selection, brand selection, available parking, and pleasant atmosphere are significantly more important to the surveyed participants residing in the surrounding areas of MG than to those residing in MG.
- Participants residing in the surrounding areas of MG gave lower ratings to Sunday shopping days and opening hours.

The results emphasize the important fact that ordering online is much more attractive to all customers than shopping in the inner city. Even those who still prefer to shop in the inner cities want more digital communication from the city and want to have more information about the retailer available online. It therefore follows that an exclusively analog and stationary-based retail structure will no longer be competitive in the future. By contrast, local retailers can also leverage their advantages if they use the Internet as a way to acquire new customers, provide customer care, and ultimately to close sales as well. Therefore, the guidelines should also especially strive to identify and address those retailers that have a clear idea of why customers come to them and which benefits they offer them. Such retailers are already familiar with the online topic, know their customers personally, and understand how to maintain customer loyalty. An action plan was developed for these retailers, which comprised the following seven steps:

Step 1: Digitization awareness. The interested party must first be informed and taught about the topic. At this point, it makes sense to provide relevant seminars and information by the associations, the Chamber of Industry and Commerce (IHK) or private providers. This should be done quickly and should necessarily include "digital awareness" training for the dealer as well.

Step 2: First "online steps". In the second step, the retailer should start taking the first "online steps" and gain initial experience. This includes publishing general information online, such as opening hours, a product range overview, or directions. The insertion of these information, together with the web site in overview plans can also be helpful. The aim of this measure is to ensure that customers can find information about the retailer online and contact the retailer if necessary.

Step 3: Lay the necessary foundations. The basis for selling via the Internet is a functioning inventory management system. Well-organized inventory management can speed up business processes and make them more efficient. Also, in preparation for potential online sales, automatic adjustment of the inventory on linked systems is essential. Many retailers still do not meet this elementary requirement yet. The necessary objective is to be able to provide reliable information on the availability of goods at a given location in real time. Very affordable entry-level solutions are already available for this purpose.

Step 4: Presence on an established marketplace. Linkage of the individual local retailers to an established platform and/or online marketplace which has a large number of online customer contacts. Preferably, the retailer will get involved in online retailing via this platform, which is available for both the necessary customers and the necessary infrastructure. This approach can be used to initially "train" the retailer both with regard to the presentation of merchandise as well as online sales. The retailer can become familiar with and "practice" shipping, returns processing and working with an inventory management system. In this step, retailers can already provide their customers with an additional benefit by offering a "pick up in store" option.

Step 5: Full-fledged online shop. By implementing a full-fledged shop solution that can complement the ongoing marketplace activities, the local retailer can become a true online retailer. The conditions for the retailer should be as simple as possible. However, an inventory management system is essential here as well, in order to be able to offer the entire product range online.

Step 6: Local cooperation. If a large number of retailers have reached step 5 and thus the Internet customers can find a relevant assortment of products offered by retailers in their city, the retailers can work together to develop joint logistics solutions in the city. If the products are in stock in the branch stores anyway, same day delivery is probably possible. Such a cooperation is easiest to realize in a shopping center.

Step 7: Multi-channel linking: A retailer with full-fledged online shop can take the next step and establish a link to its local store. Appropriate multi-channel solutions can be offered for this purpose. These allow the retailer to offer more customer value and benefit by providing an availability indicator and the option to reserve and pick up the products. At the same time, of course, the measures to ensure the local findability of a retailer have to be maintained and updated.

In order to find an acceptable solution for the local retailer to offer its local inventory to a wider consumer base, various online marketplaces were analyzed as part of the recommendations for action. The marketplaces were compared from both a customer and retailer standpoint. The study focused on the familiarity, usability, added value, reliability and trustworthiness of each platform. The selected marketplaces had to be transaction-based and be appropriately suitable and relevant.

2.3 Marketplace Linkage for Local Retailers

Therefore, relevant online marketplaces were selected and evaluated as part of MG.Retail2020, for the purpose of identifying a suitable partner for local retail and to give specific recommendations for action to retailers in Mönchengladbach. In a first step, a long list of more than 100 marketplaces was created based on extensive research and using the criteria of media presence, market relevance, search volume and trends. After pure city portals and non-transaction-based platforms were filtered out, the result was a shortlist of five online marketplaces: eBay, Atalanda, SugarTrends, HierBeiDir and Unitcity. Simply Local and Locafox were not included in this comparison, since for these platforms, the retailer needs to have its own online sales channel.

However, local marketplaces are not necessarily a new trend in German e-commerce. Several similar pilot projects have already been initiated by local players in the past, although none of the previous approaches—such as the Hamburg@Work project with Hamburg's trendy "Schanze" district in 2011—have met with great success yet. All new portals start from scratch and therefore first have to establish and expand their reach, which is extremely difficult for local marketplace models. The established eBay platform, for example, offers a wide-reaching online brand (Neuhandeln 2015).

An expert panel ~~comprised~~ of representatives from economics and research under the direction of the eWeb Research Center ultimately evaluated seven relevant online marketplaces using a set of criteria, with ten criteria being equally considered from both a retailer and customer perspective. The individual ratings were aggregated into a final ranking using a scoring model from the eWeb Research Center and then into a final recommendation for action. The marketplaces that were evaluated are briefly described below in order to provide an overview of which marketplace is best suited for retailers in a municipality. The results are summarized in Fig. 5.

As the figure shows, eBay emerged as the clear winner from the benchmarking process. However, for the recommendations for action, the marketplaces were critically analyzed once again within the scope of MG.Retail2020, particularly with regard to the aspect of planning reliability for retailers. The results found that with the exception of eBay, all of the marketplaces at the time of the evaluation were constituted by young companies with a narrow reach and are thus still "trial balloons". However, traditional retail no longer has time for open-ended tests. All of the project participants therefore unanimously recommended eBay as the preferred partner for local retail in Mönchengladbach and beyond.

The analysis of the various marketplaces illustrated the advantages of a cooperation with eBay from different perspectives. Retailers can particularly benefit

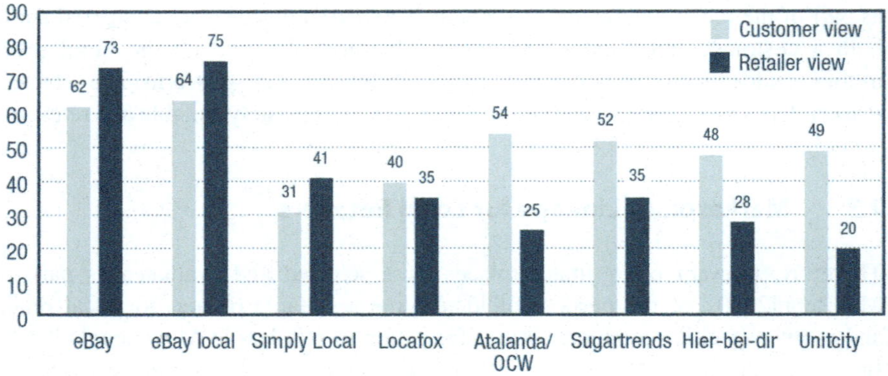

Fig. 5 Overview of total scores, differentiated by retailer and customer perspective (WFMG 2015b)

from eBay's high recognition and large customer base. The technical prerequisites (for example, the technical maturity of the interfaces to inventory management systems) were also rated as very good. Planning reliability played an important role for retailers as well, because the online marketplace will continue to exist for many years to come. In addition, another key point is that eBay—unlike its competitors—does not sell its own products and therefore is never in competition with its partners. From a customer perspective, eBay scores points due to its large range of products, high degree of reliability and trustworthiness, and convenient user experience, which also counts when it comes to mobile optimization, for example. It was therefore decided to propose the "Mönchengladbach on eBay" project to eBay as a pilot project (WFMG 2015b).

2.4 "Mönchengladbach on eBay" as Recommendation for Action

As an Internet pioneer, eBay implemented the now omnipresent concept of peer-to-peer transactions in 1995, and made the online auction as a new selling, trading and pricing format accessible to a broad audience. In Germany, eBay has been online since 1999 and is available via its mobile apps in 190 countries. With more than 165 million active buyers and an annual gross merchandise sales volume of USD83 billion worldwide, eBay is now considered to be one of the most important e-commerce companies. eBay generates around 56% of its sales outside the USA. In Germany, far more than 100,000 sellers reach over 17 million active buyers on eBay. Since its launch, eBay has evolved from the auction house into a dynamic global online marketplace and is therefore an essential sales channel for commercial retailers as well as major brands (Zoll and Marks 2016). On eBay, about 87% of all products are offered at a fixed price, mostly from commercial retailers, with a resultant range of a total of one billion listings at any time.

The idea of a cooperation with the local retailers in Mönchengladbach was also quickly met with a positive response from eBay, since it was a good fit with the seller side of the corporate strategy. After all, small and medium-sized enterprises (SME) are the main drivers of the unique product range and depth on eBay and generate a large share of sales on the online marketplace. Also, the fact that many stakeholders from the region were actively involved in the cooperation under the joint umbrella of MG.Retail2020 was a distinct advantage from the perspective of eBay. In particular, in addition to the willingness and necessary know-how, the Business Development Corporation Mönchengladbach (WFMG) also had the necessary resources to jointly tackle a regional project. Furthermore, the WFMG had direct contact with the Mönchengladbach retailers. Moreover, there was a strong consensus among the potential partners about the objectives of the project right from the very start.

The envisaged cooperation between eBay, the Business Development Corporation Mönchengladbach GmbH (WFMG) and the eWeb Research Center at the Niederrhein University of Applied Sciences was intended to support local retailers in making their product range accessible both online and via mobile channels. Other project partners included the German Retail Federation (HDE), the Chamber of Industry and Commerce (IHK), the Mönchengladbach City Management Association, the Rheydt City Management Association, and the Marketing Gesellschaft Mönchengladbach mbH company.

In October 2015, the pilot project was launched with more than 50 retailers and five chain stores as well as over 200,000 products with local availability. Titled "Mönchengladbach on eBay," the project gave local retailers a unique opportunity to not only greatly benefit from the booming online commerce, but also to be able to offer their customers real added value over the long term as compared to other market participants. Right from the start, the cooperation was designed as a pilot project to be run for a limited period of about 10 months. During the planned duration of the project, from October 2015 to the summer of 2016, the aim was to collect information and knowledge about customer and retailer benefits. The issue of whether and in what form the marketplace can then be continued or expanded to other cities, was deliberately left open from the beginning of the project. In terms of sustainability and with a view to possible continuation, efforts were made to establish certain core responsibilities locally at the same time. In particular, these include the acquisition of retailers, organizing opportunities to exchange and share insights, experience and information with participating retailers, as well as local consumer marketing. In addition, eBay provided the technical component of the online marketplace, initiated an advisory service for the retailers just starting in online retailing, covered the costs for a 12-month basic shop subscription, and created a separate homepage with a local visual reference at the URL www.mg-bei-ebay.de. To facilitate their entry into online commerce, the retailers participating in the pilot project received a startup package. The package comprised the eBay advisory service and if needed, tool support from Inventorum, which offered an iPad point of sale system featuring eBay integration.

Since autumn 2015, consumers have been able to access offers from Mönchengladbach retailers via the "Mönchengladbach on eBay" homepage, order items online, then pick them up at their local retailer. Customers can also conveniently have most of the products delivered to their home instead. Interested retailers from Mönchengladbach are presented on the platform and their products are marketed on the "Mönchengladbach on eBay" site to customers on eBay. This way, local retailers have access to an online and mobile sales channel and in addition to consumers in Mönchengladbach, can also potentially reach all active eBay customers in Germany.

3 Results and Success Factors of "MG on eBay"

For the majority of the retailers participating in the online marketplace "MG on eBay", this was their first engagement with e-commerce. However, many of the participating retailers were able to record a significant growth in sales after a short time. In the first 12 months after the project launch, at the end of 2016, the 79 retailers participating at the time sold each 2250 items on the online marketplace on average, realizing total sales of more than 6.7 million EUR. In mid-2016, 9 months after the start of the project, sales were already at 3.2 million EUR, with 87,000 items (eBay 2017). The retailers delivered their items not only within Germany, but also to 84 different countries, including Sweden, Italy, France and Austria, as well to far more distant markets, such as Guadeloupe and New Zealand. Including seasonal effects, total sales of four to five million EUR are projected for the year as a whole. On average, the active retailers have about 450 items listed for sale and earned sales revenues of approximately 90,000 EUR annually on "MG on eBay". Annual sales of well into six figures could even be forecasted for the top 3 "newcomers". And the participants' experience is also positive: "Our first experiences with the project are very positive. We were able to generate more traffic and have sold a lot more items than we would have without the platform. Some of them even to Sweden," said one retailer (Zoll and Marks 2016).

Consequently, in the "MG on eBay" project, the majority of sales were made with customers outside of Mönchengladbach (WFMG 2015b). This development is not really surprising because customers do not only search the internet locally, but globally. The trending topic of local commerce as a way to rescue the inner cities is thus often overestimated. When local retailers want to use the internet to sell to customers in their region, they are generally appealing to a minority. The pilot project in Mönchengladbach was neither aligned in this direction~~, either~~. Rather, it focused on showing bricks and mortar retailers how they can benefit from the booming e-commerce market and make up for the declining sales in their stores. The decisive goal is to save the local retailers—and that is only possible if they are achieving a healthy turnover. Whether such sales are generated on the Internet by customers from the region or other areas is of secondary importance. However, not all retailers manage to profit from additional online sales. Just over half of the local retailers have a "digital allergy" and also balk at the effort to list products on an online marketplace. Many marketplace models—such as Online City Wuppertal, for example—take the approach that only regional retailers can present their products there. Such models are quickly doomed to failure, however, because if only a few retailers from one region sell products on a portal, customers are not presented with a broad product range and thus lose the incentive to visit the portal. Without this incentive, customers quickly stay away, and without significant reach, retailers shy away from investing in the extra expense and effort needed to achieve additional online sales, which in turn continues to makes the offer unattractive to customers (Neuhandeln 2016). It is very unlikely that customers will stumble upon a regional online portal unless there is advertising. This risk is thus a vicious circle: no customers without familiar brands, and no retailers without customers. In view of this, three success factors are critical, namely brand, product range, and effort: So first and foremost, it is about making customers curious and eager about the product range, making the products desirable. In reality, however, retailers on local marketplaces often offer the same products that online retailers also sell, and usually for a higher price.

Based on an initial interim result of the "MG on eBay" project, key factors can be derived that were instrumental to the success that "Mönchengladbach on eBay" experienced so far (Zoll and Marks 2016).

Accept the change: On the retailer side, the key to successful participation in "Mönchengladbach on eBay" is to accept the fact that "online" is an irreversible trend. This also necessitates the willingness to be present on all channels. As one participating retailer said, "The market is changing and consumer behavior is changing. You have to either join in or perish" (eBay 2016).

Profit from agility: Small retailers can be faster and more flexible than large retail chains. After making the decision, many of the smaller retailers were able to list a large share of their product range on eBay within a few days or weeks, while retail chains usually need much longer due to all the process modifications involved. "With this project, the Mönchengladbach retailers now have the chance to step in at the peak of a trend that is unstoppable," said Andree Haack, Manager of the Business Start-up and Support Department at the Chamber of Industry and Commerce for the Central Lower Rhine region (Zoll and Marks 2016).

Use the reach of online marketplaces: Once a retailer has listed its online offerings on "Mönchengladbach on eBay," it also reaches users in Berlin, London and New York. Only the packaging and shipping of products involve more effort, but the additional sales potential is significant. Several of the participating retailers have sold items into more than 80 countries, among them Guadeloupe and New Zealand.

Go with established partners: The effort and expense that retailers incur when digitizing their product range should be compensated as soon as possible by sales revenues. Sales can be generated more quickly in the short term on an established online marketplace with few barriers to entry. "Our presence on eBay let us tap into a broader customer base. Of course, we also benefit from the eBay name and the reach that the online presence affords us. We have thus created a shop display window that we did not have before" (eBay 2016).

Gain efficiency advantages with an inventory management system: The most important service feature of a local online marketplace is providing information about the availability of local goods (KPMG 2015). In the local retail trade in Mönchengladbach, however, there is a certain lag in terms of using inventory management systems to manage and integrate the online and offline product range. Most of the participating retailers work exclusively with the eBay seller tools, and thus there is no automatic synchronization with the in-store stock. From the perspective of the project partners, the implementation of an inventory management system should therefore be a next step for the retailers in the pilot project, in order to avoid duplicate sales and gain efficiency advantages.

Trust in local contacts: The retailers' trust in the local project partners is critical to success. That was the only way that more than 50 retailers could be acquired at the start of the project in such a short time. In particular for the "newcomers," personal dialogue during workshops, store visits and phone calls were conducive in this regard. As one participating retailer said: "We have been with the pilot project since the start and did not have an online shop before. 'Mönchengladbach on eBay' is therefore our first step into the online world" (Zoll and Marks 2016).

Establish a "local overseer": For the "Mönchengladbach on eBay" project, WFMG provided resources right from the onset. A specially designated employee was assigned to the project full-time, and was responsible for tasks such as retailer acquisition and dialogue, planning local top offers, and coordinating local PR and marketing activities. Other colleagues from WFMG also provided support as needed. "We are pleased that Mönchengladbach is the first city in Germany to start a local cooperation project of this type with eBay," said Dr. Ulrich Schückhaus, Managing Director of WFMG (WFMG 2015a).

Go online with the full product range: A mere presence on "Mönchengladbach on eBay" is not a source of revenue that goes beyond the "ROPO effect" (Research Online, Purchase Offline). The approach to first list a few items and then gradually increase the amount did not prove promising within the scope of the project. Sales success was generally not achieved until at least 50 to 100 items were listed. The goal should be to present the full product range online.

Maintain close dialogue with the retailers: Everyone involved in the project noted that the direct and institutionalized channels of communication between retailers, WFMG and eBay were very productive to the project. The retailers and project partners continuously communicated and exchanged experiences and knowledge via regular roundtable meetings, e-mail newsletters and personal contact. The successful cooperation is also reflected in the many media stories in which participating retailers expressed themselves. One retailer stated: "So far we are very satisfied with the progress. This is also due to eBay, which provided support right from the start of the pilot project. In this regard, we can explicitly commend eBay and the Business Development Corporation Mönchengladbach" (eBay 2016).

Based on the positive experiences, the decision to continue the project was made in mid-2016. Not all of the features will be continued—such as the offer of the week—but the basic core project will remain intact. In addition, new retailers have come on board since then, including furniture dealer Schaffrath in July 2016. The successful "Mönchengladbach on eBay" pilot project was the inspiration for the "The Digital Inner City" initiative, which was jointly launched by the German Retail Federation (HDE) and eBay. Any city could apply and submit project documents to demonstrate that it is serious about the topic of digitization of its inner city retail. A jury of experts evaluated the applications and chose the city of Diepholz as the winner (HDE and eBay 2016).

References

Ahlert D et al (2009) Handelsmanagement in der Textilwirtschaft. Einzelhandel und Wertschöpfungspartnerschaften. Deutscher Fachverlag, Frankfurt a. M.

Beckmann RM, Föhrer M (2014) Experimenteller Wohnungs- und Städtebau (ExWoSt) Mögliche räumliche Auswirkungen von "Online-Shopping" auf Innenstädte, Stadtteil- und Ortszentren. Unpublished project proposal for the BBSR – Bundesinstitut für Bau-, Stadt- und Raumforschung (German Federal Institute for Research on Building, Urban Affairs and Spatial Development), Dortmund

bevh (2016) Online-Handel wuchs 2015 um 12 Prozent. BEVH-Studie "Interaktiver Handel". http://www.internetworld.de/e-commerce/zahlen-studien/online-handel-wuchs-2015-um-12-prozent-1078072.html. Accessed 23 Feb 2016

Brandeins (2015) Wehrt Euch! Oder ist es dafür zu spät? Streitgespräch zwischen Jochen Krisch und Gerrit Heinemann. Brandeins (4):62–67

CIMA (2009) Leerstandsproblematik in Klein- und Mittelstädten. CIMA Beratung + Management GmbH (internal presentation)

Deutsche Post DHL (2014) Global E-Tailing 2025. E-Commerce und Logistik weltweit auf Wachstumskurs, Studie von Deutsche Post DHL. http://www.dpdhl.com/de/presse/pressemitteilungen/2014/global_e-tailing_2025.html. Accessed 02 Feb 2017

Die Welt (2015) Deutschland droht das große Ladensterben. Die Welt, 04 Sept 2015. http://www.welt.de/print/die_welt/wirtschaft/article146060584/Deutschland-droht-das-grosse-Ladensterben.html. Accessed 23 Feb 2017

eBay (2016) Quotes from participating retailers. Minutes of the interviews/discussions available on request from the author

eBay (2017) Lokal und digital. Chancen und Potenziale für den Einzelhandel. Impulse presentation at a HDE/eBay discussion forum in Berlin, 29 Mar 2017 (unpublished)

eWeb Research Center (2016) Die Online-Zahlen 2015 (Internal study on the sales of online retailers in Germany). eWeb Research Center at Niederrhein University of Applied Sciences, Mönchengladbach

FAZ (2014) Zukunft des Online-Handels liegt in den Nischen. Frankfurter Allgemeine Zeitung, 10 Nov 2014, no. 261:22

GfK (2015) Wandert die Verkaufsfläche vom PoS ins Netz? GfK-Prognose zum Verkaufsflächenbedarf der Warengruppen bis 2015. GfK GeoMarketing GmbH, Bruchsal. http://www.gfk-geomarketing.de/fileadmin/gfkgeomarketing/de/beratung/20151006_GfK_WP_Verkaufsflaechenprognose_fin.pdf. Accessed 15 Aug 2017

HDE (2016) E-Commerce-Umsätze. Entwicklung der E-Commerce-Umsätze in Milliarden Euro in den vergangenen Jahren. http://www.einzelhandel.de/index.php/presse/zahlenfaktengrafiken/item/110185-e-commerce-umsaetze. Accessed 22 Mar 2017

HDE, eBay (2016) Diepholz gewinnt Städte-Wettbewerb "Die digitale Innenstadt" von HDE und eBay (press release of 06 July 2016). http://presse.ebay.de/pressrelease/diepholz-gewinnt-stpercentC3percentA4dte-wettbewerb-percentE2percent80percent9Edie-digitale-innenstadtpercentE2percent80percent9C-von-hde-und-ebay. Accessed 18 Aug 2016

Heinemann G (2017) Der neue Online-Handel. Geschäftsmodell und Kanalexzellenz im Digital Commerce, 8th edn. Springer Gabler, Wiesbaden

IfH Köln (2014) Handelsszenario 2020. Zwischen Online und Offline, Discount und Mehrwert. Jahrgang 2014. IfH-Köln Retail Consultants, Cologne

IfH Köln (2015) Stadt, Land, Handel 2020. IfH Köln Retail Consultants, Cologne

IHK Hannover (2010) Ladenleerstand in der IHK Region Hannover. Daten, Fakten und Gegenmaßnahmen. Hanover, IHK Hannover (unpublished study)

KPMG (2015) Consumer Barometer. Trends und Treiber im Sektor Consumer Markets. Thema Lokale Onlinemarktplätze (4)

Locafox (2014) Local commerce. https://www.locafox.de/blog/glossar/local-commerce/. Accessed 18 Aug 2016

Neuhandeln (2015) Local Commerce. Wann Einzelhändler eine Chance haben. Neuhandeln, 20 Oct 2015. http://neuhandeln.de/local-commerce-wann-einzelhaendler-eine-chance-haben/. Accessed 18 Aug 2016

Neuhandeln (2016) eBay-Pilotprojekt zeigt: Local Commerce wird überschätzt. Neuhandeln, 4 Feb 2016. http://neuhandeln.de/ebay-pilotprojekt-zeigt-local-commerce-wird-ueberschaetzt/. Accessed 18 Aug 2016

Rheinische Post (2013) Tote Innenstadt. Händler protestieren. Rheinische Post, 5 July 2013. http://www.rp-online.de/nrw/staedte/willich/tote-innenstadt-haendler-protestieren-aid-1.3514203. Accessed 27 June 2016

Süddeutsche Zeitung (2014) Der Online-Handel bedroht die Innenstädte. Süddeutsche.de 17.02.2014. http://www.sueddeutsche.de/news/wirtschaft/verbraucher-der-online-handel-bedroht-die-innenstaedte-dpa.urn-newsml-dpa-com-20090101-140217-99-02325. Accessed 20 Feb 2017

Textilwirtschaft (2015) Jedem zehnten Laden droht das Aus. Textilwirtschaft, 11 Aug 2015. http://www.textilwirtschaft.de/business/Jedem-zehnten-Laden-droht-das-Aus_98482.html. Accessed 23 July 2016

WFMG (2015a) Wirtschaftsförderung Mönchengladbach. Projekt MG.Retail2020. Auswirkungen des Online-Handels auf den stationären Handel in Städten und Gemeinden in NRW und Handlungsempfehlungen für den innerstädtischen stationären Einzelhandel am Beispiel von Rheydt und Mönchengladbach. http://www.wfmg.de/news-lesen/auswirkungen-des-online-handels-auf-den-stationaeren-handel-in-staedten-und-gemeinden-in-nrw-und-handlungs-empfehlungen-fuer-den.html. Accessed 18 Aug 2016

WFMG (2015b) Wirtschaftsförderung Mönchengladbach. Maßnahmenprogramm und Guidelines im Rahmen von MG.Retail2020.Auswirkungen des Online-Handels auf Städte und Gemeinden in NRW und Handlungsperspektiven für den innerstädtischen stationären Einzelhandel. http://mgretail2020.de/fileadmin/user_upload/documents/mgretail2020_Massnahmenprogramm.pdf. Accessed 18 Aug 2017

Zoll S, Marks S (2016) Mönchengladbach bei eBay. Wie Online-Marktplätze dem Handel helfen, den digitalen Wandel zu meistern. In: Heinemann G et al (eds) Digitale Transformation oder digitale Disruption? Vom Point-of-Sale zum Point-of-Decision im Digital Commerce. Springer Gabler, Wiesbaden

Gerrit Heinemann is Director of the eWeb Research Center and Professor of Retail and Trade at Niederrhein University of Applied Sciences in Mönchengladbach, Germany. Prior to this, he occupied different top management positions in the retail sector and was working as a top management consultant, specialized in retailing for international clients. He is a frequent lecturer at international conferences and author of numerous articles in professional press and academic publications. He works as a senior advisor for retail companies and is author of several science books on retail and trade, multi-channel retailing and eCommerce. As member of the supervisory board of some start-ups as well as leading online retailing companies he is also involved in all the actual key issues affecting the e-commerce sector.

Stefan Wenzel was Vice President eBay Germany until May 2017. In this role, he was responsible for the Marketplaces business of eBay in Germany. Stefan Wenzel had been working for eBay Inc. since August 2014. Before holding the role of Vice President eBay Germany, he was Senior Director eBay Fashion in Germany and Managing Director of brands4friends, an eBay company. Prior to joining eBay, he held several positions at the OTTO Group where he was instrumental in advancing OTTO's positioning as a pure e-commerce player in the Dutch market. Further stages of his career included the establishment of e-commerce at Mexx Fashion and McLaren Formula 1.

Born in 1972, Stefan Wenzel holds a degree in educational sciences from Helmut Schmidt University, Hamburg.

Part V

Cost Efficiency in City Management

A Mechanism Design Approach to Planning Problems in Intermodal Transport Logistics of Large City Sea Ports and Megahubs

Dominik Kress, Sebastian Meiswinkel, Jenny Nossack, and Erwin Pesch

Abstract

Globalization and digitalization have lead to new challenges and perspectives in intermodal transport logistics of large city sea ports and megahubs. In particular, due to an enormous increase of the container throughput over the last decades and the automatization of megahubs, new planning problems in this field must consistently be addressed by smart software solutions. In this research article, we sketch some challenges that arise at megahubs and outline how mechanism design, as a popular tool that combines ideas from game theory and computer science, can be an approach to tackle logistics problems that involve multiple selfish players.

1 Introduction

The creation and widespread use of neologisms like Economy 4.0, Industry 4.0, or Logistics 4.0, emphasizes the fact that digitalization has released fields to a new era. Immediate communication via internet, big data analysis, new technologies

D. Kress (✉) · S. Meiswinkel
University of Siegen, Chair of Management Information Science, Siegen, Germany
e-mail: dominik.kress@uni-siegen.de; sebastian.meiswinkel@uni-siegen.de

J. Nossack
Center for Advanced Studies in Management, HHL Leipzig Graduate School of Management, Leipzig, Germany
e-mail: jenny.nossack@hhl.de

E. Pesch
Center for Advanced Studies in Management, HHL Leipzig Graduate School of Management, Leipzig, Germany

University of Siegen, Chair of Management Information Science, Siegen, Germany
e-mail: erwin.pesch@hhl.de, erwin.pesch@uni-siegen.de

H. Albach et al. (eds.), *European Cities in Dynamic Competition*,
https://doi.org/10.1007/978-3-662-56419-6_11

(e.g., 3D printers, autonomous cars, drones, quantum computers): the influences of digitalization are ubiquitous and awe-inspiring. Various fields in logistics, medicine, and agriculture have started to implement these new methodologies to cope with the challenges of globalization, but also in order to optimize work flows. To address the new complexity caused by globalization as well as the rapid and permanent change entailed by digitalization, disciplines have to share their means and knowledge in order to be sustainable, efficient, and competitive. It is, among others, the responsibility of Research 4.0 to support these developments and propose new concepts and models that should—in our opinion—focus on interdisciplinary approaches. In line with this argument, we present research concepts that combine scheduling problems from operations research with a game theoretic approach from economics in the area of intermodal transport logistics.

1.1 Challenges and Perspectives in Intermodal Transport Logistics

Bontekoning et al. (2004) and Macharis and Bontekoning (2004) define *intermodal transport logistics* as the movement of goods in standardized loading units (e.g., containers) by at least two transportation modes (rail, maritime, and road) in a single transport chain. The change of transportation modes is thereby performed at specially designed terminals (e.g., *megahubs* or *sea ports*) by transferring the loading units without handling the freight itself.

New challenges and perspectives in intermodal transport logistics at large city sea ports and megahubs arise mainly due to the ongoing increase of the container flow and the resulting need to make use of (semi-) automated systems. Danish Ship Finance (2014) reports that the world's container market demand in 2014 has increased by 2.7% in comparison to the demand in 2011. It is furthermore projected to increase by another 5.3% from 2014 to 2017. Moreover, the Institute of Shipping Economics and Logistics (2011) states a 9.5% increase of the size of the international container fleet compared to 2010. This development puts the entire logistic chain, and especially megahubs, under high pressure.

In order to cope with the increasing container throughput, megahubs automatize processes by using automated guided vehicles (AGVs) and (semi-) automated quay and stacking cranes (e.g., as implemented at Container Terminal Altenwerder (CTA) in Hamburg, Germany). Automatization, however, induces the need for smart software solutions that analyze, plan, and conduct the daily operations efficiently. Daily operations include, for instance, the allocation of container ships to berths, the loading and unloading of ships, and the intermediate storage of containers. Simulation studies and optimization techniques help to organize the container throughput and to reduce the ships' berthing time, which is considered the most expensive quantity and thus the main objective of a terminal's operator (Steenken et al., 2004). However, apart from this objective, megahubs also need to stay competitive and attractive to their customers. Topics such as quality of service, waiting times, sustainability, or waste minimization are increasingly important to the customers and have to be addressed. To ensure both, the efficiency of the megahubs and the consideration of the customers' preferences, new solution methods need to be developed.

A considerable amount of literature aims at improving the efficiency of megahubs from the perspective of the terminal operator. Vis and de Koster (2003), Steenken et al. (2004), and Stahlbock and Voß (2008) provide detailed surveys of recent literature. Solutions that take the customers into consideration require new solution methods that combine methodologies from different research fields. In this context, we will focus on situations where the operator, being the central decision maker for a specific scheduling problem (representing one of the aforementioned planning problems for daily operations at megahubs), is not equipped with all relevant data related to the problem because it is private information of selfish customers (also referred to as players or agents) who aim to influence the solution determined by some scheduling algorithm by submitting false information to the decision maker. In some cases, the decision maker can extract the true information by designing an appropriate algorithm that sets the right incentives for these players. This in turn enables the decision maker to generate "fair" solutions with respect to some *social criterion* that considers the interests of all players. The design of such algorithms is subject of a field of research that is usually referred to as *algorithmic mechanism design* (Nisan and Ronen, 2000).

A general introduction to the field of algorithmic mechanism design can be found in Nisan et al. (2007). Additionally, there is a fairly large amount of publications dealing with mechanism design in the context of scheduling problems. An excellent overview is given by Heydenreich et al. (2007). Basically, one can identify two streams of literature dealing with mechanism design in the context of scheduling problems. The first group of publications presumes that the machines are selfish agents (*machine agents*). These papers follow the seminal work of Nisan and Ronen (1999) and include Lavi and Swamy (2009), Archer and Tardos (2001), Christodoulou et al. (2009), and Koutsoupias and Vidali (2013). The second stream of literature assumes that the jobs are selfish agents (*job agents*), which is the perspective taken in this paper. Prominent examples of the latter stream are Suijs (1996) or Angel et al. (2006).

1.2 An Exemplary Problem Setting

We will consider the following exemplary scheduling problem throughout the remainder of this article (see also Kovalyov and Pesch, 2014). A service provider operates cranes in a megahub to load and unload trains or trucks. The service provider has service contracts with its customers. Each contract is related to a specific customer of the service provider and vice versa. Each customer requests a train or truck to be loaded or unloaded in a given planning period. These requests correspond to jobs to be processed by the service provider. The customers compete for quick execution of their jobs in the schedule determined by the service provider for the planning period. The processing time for each job is publicly known and assumed to be deterministic. Stochastic processing times, which address uncertainties in the runtime of a job, arise in real-life settings but are neglected in this paper. Jobs may incur additional costs to their owners if their completion time is too large, for example because of strict deadlines and corresponding contractual penalties. The related parameters are private information of the customers. The service provider's revenue for executing a job is fixed. Hence, the service provider seeks to determine a "fair" schedule that takes into account the interests of all customers. To generate this schedule, the service provider must know the private information of the players. Hence, the service provider must design an appropriate algorithm for scheduling the execution of the jobs.

1.3 Article Overview

The remainder of this article is organized as follows. In Sect. 2, we will introduce the problem setting described in Sect. 1.2 in more detail. Furthermore, we will present relevant definitions and introduce the notation. We will then turn our attention to related mechanism design insights in Sect. 3. The paper closes with a summary in Sect. 4.

2 Preliminaries and Notation

We will now formalize the problem setting described in Sect. 1.2 based on the illustration in Fig. 1.

There is a set $J = \{1, \ldots, n\}$ of $n \geq 2$ jobs (customer requests) and a set $M = \{m_1, \ldots, m_m\}$ of m parallel (identical) machines (cranes). Each job $i \in J$ must be processed exactly once by an arbitrary machine $m_j \in M$. The jobs are processed by the machines one at a time, starting from time zero, without idle time. Preemption

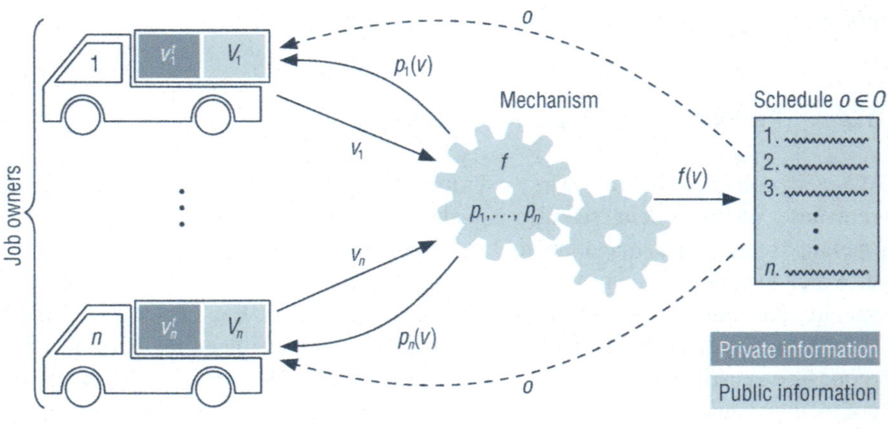

Fig. 1 Problem setting

of jobs is not allowed. We denote the processing time of job $i \in J$ by $t_i \in \mathbb{Q}_{>0}$. In addition to its processing time, each job is $i \in J$ is associated with a weight $w_i \in \mathbb{Q}_{\geq 0}$. The set of all feasible solutions of the problem of scheduling all jobs $i \in J$ on machines $m_j \in M$ is denoted by O. A feasible schedule $o \in O$ determines the completion time $C_i(o)$ of each job $i \in J$.

Each job $i \in J$ has an associated *owner* (*customer* or *client*). Moreover, each owner possesses exactly one job. Thus, in the remainder of this paper we can identify a job by its owner and vice versa. Each job owner $i \in J$ has a (true) *valuation function* $v_i^t : O \to \mathbb{R}$ that maps every feasible schedule of the considered scheduling domain to a real value. In our context, given a schedule $o \in O$, the scheduling cost incurred to job owner $i \in J$ is assumed to be linear in the job's completion time, i.e. the valuation function is $v_i(o) = -w_i \cdot C_i(o)$. Thus, the valuation function domains are one-dimensional.

Each job owner $i \in J$ reports a valuation function v_i, which may deviate from the true valuation function v_i^t, to a mechanism. v_i^t is private information of the job owner and is thus sometimes referred to as the job owner's *type*. Each valuation function v_i, $i \in J$, is element of a publicly known set V_i. We define $V := V_1 \times \cdots \times V_n$. Furthermore, we denote the vector of all valuation functions reported to the mechanism by $v = (v_1, \ldots, v_n)$ and the vector of all valuation functions reported to the mechanism except of v_i by $v_{-i} = (v_1, \ldots, v_{i-1}, v_{i+1}, \ldots, v_n)$. For the sake of notational convenience, we will use v and (v_i, v_{-i}) interchangeably.

The *mechanism* $(f, p_1, \ldots, p_n)$ itself is composed of a *social choice function* $f : V \to O$ that determines a (feasible) schedule and *payment functions* $p_1, \ldots, p_n$, with $p_i : V \to \mathbb{R}$ for all $i \in J$. The processing times of all jobs are assumed to be public information.

The *utility function* $u_i : V \to \mathbb{R}$ of player $i \in J$ is defined as $u_i(v_i, v_{-i}) := v_i^t(f(v_i, v_{-i})) + p_i(v_i, v_{-i})$. In order to be (dominant strategy) *incentive compatible* or *truthful*, the mechanism must guarantee that $u_i(v_i^t, v_{-i}) \geq u_i(v_i, v_{-i})$ for all $i \in J$, all $v_i \in V_i$, and all $v_{-i} \in V_{-i}$.

Table 1 summarizes the notation used throughout the paper.

One of the most important general results in the field of mechanism design is the *Vickrey-Clarke-Groves mechanism* (VCG mechanism), that was suggested by Vickrey (1961) and generalized by Clarke (1971) and Groves (1973). Basically, a mechanism is called a VCG mechanism, if the social choice function maximizes social welfare, i.e. the sum of all valuation functions, and if the payment functions $p_i(v)$, $i \in J$, are given by

$$p_i(v) = h_i(v_{-i}) - \sum_{\substack{j=1 \\ j \neq i}}^{n} v_j(f(v)), \tag{1}$$

where $h_i(v_{-i}) : V_{-i} \to \mathbb{R}$. Note that h_i, $i \in J$, is independent of the valuation function $v_i \in V_i$ reported by agent i. A VCG mechanism is incentive compatible, but a major drawback is the need for finding optimal solutions to the underlying

Table 1 Notation used throughout the paper

$\mathbb{R}, \mathbb{Q}$	Real (rational) numbers	
$\mathbb{R}_{>0}, \mathbb{Q}_{>0}$	Positive real (rational) numbers	
$\mathbb{R}_{\geq 0}, \mathbb{Q}_{\geq 0}$	Non-negative real (rational) numbers	
J	Set of jobs (owners, clients, customers, agents)	$J = \{1, \ldots, n\}$
M	Set of parallel (identical) machines	$M = \{m_1, \ldots, m_m\}$
V_i	Set of potential val. functions for client $i \in J$	
V	Cartesian product of sets $V_i, i \in J$	$V = V_1 \times \cdots \times V_n$
V_{-i}	Cartesian product of sets V_j, $j \in J \setminus \{i\}$	$V = V_1 \times \cdots \times V_{i-1} \times V_{i+1} \times \cdots \times V_n$
O	Set of feasible solutions of scheduling problem	
f	Social choice function	$f : V \to O$
v_i^t	True val. function of client $i \in J$	$V_i \ni v_i^t : O \to \mathbb{R}$
v_i	Claimed val. function of client $i \in J$	$V_i \ni v_i : O \to \mathbb{R}$
C_i	Completion time of job $i \in J$	$C_i : O \to \mathbb{R}_{>0}$
p_i	Payment function for client $i \in J$	$p_i : V \to \mathbb{R}$
u_i	Utility function of client $i \in J$	$u_i(v_i, v_{-i}) = v_i^t(f(v)) + p_i(v)$
t_i	Processing time of job $i \in J$	$t_i \in \mathbb{Q}_{>0}$
v_{-i}	Vector of claimed val. functions except $v_i, i \in J$	$v_{-i} = (v_1, \ldots, v_{i-1}, v_{i+1}, \ldots, v_n)$
v	Vector of claimed val. functions	$v = (v_1, \ldots, v_n)$
		$v = (v_i, v_{-i}), i \in J$

problem of maximizing social welfare, which may be NP-hard (see, for instance, Nisan, 2007). Hence, in the context of scheduling problems, VCG mechanisms are oftentimes not appropriate even if the objective function of the specific scheduling problem corresponds to maximizing social welfare. One must therefore make use of other theoretical results related to incentive compatibility that are suitable for approximate and heuristic algorithms. These results oftentimes turn out to "boil down to a certain algorithmic condition of *monotonicity*" (Lavi and Swamy, 2009).

3 Minimizing the Total Weighted Completion Time

We will now consider the (terminal operator's) objective of finding a schedule $o \in O$ that minimizes the total weighted completion time of all jobs, $\sum_{i=1}^{n} w_i C_i(o)$. This corresponds to minimizing the total scheduling cost and, hence, maximizing social welfare (i.e., generating a fair solution).

In Sect. 3.1, we will present the well known monotonicity condition of interest for one-dimensional valuation function domains. Furthermore, we will specify this condition for the class of List-Scheduling algorithms and analyze the corresponding payment functions. Based on these results, we will present a truthful polynomial time mechanism for an arbitrary number of machines in Sect. 3.2 and investigate specific payment functions of a VCG mechanism for the case of one machine in Sect. 3.3. We will sometimes denote v_i, $i \in J$, by $v_i^{w_i}$ to ease the notation.

3.1 Monotonicity and List-Scheduling Algorithms

In case of one-dimensional valuation function domains, it is well known that incentive compatibility is related to a certain *monotonicity condition* (see, for example, Krishna, 2010). In the context of the scheduling problem considered in this article, i.e. when each customer aims at minimizing the completion time of her job, the condition is as follows:

Definition 1 A social choice function f on a single parameter domain is called monotone in v_i, $i \in J$, if

$$C_i(f(v_i^{w_i}, v_{-i})) \geq C_i(f(v_i^{w_i'}, v_{-i})) \tag{2}$$

for all $v_{-i} \in V_{-i}$ and all $v_i^{w_i}, v_i^{w_i'} \in V_i$ with $w_i \leq w_i' \in \mathbb{Q}_{\geq 0}$.

Theorem 1 *A mechanism $(f, p_1, \ldots, p_n)$ on a single parameter domain is incentive compatible iff f is monotone in v_i for all $i \in J$ and the corresponding payment functions p_i are calculated as follows:*

$$p_i(v_i^{w_i}, v_{-i}) = p_i(v_i^0, v_{-i}) + w_i C_i(f(v_i^{w_i}, v_{-i})) - \int_0^{w_i} C_i(f(v_i^s, v_{-i}))\mathrm{d}s. \tag{3}$$

We will now characterize the monotonicity condition of Definition 1 for *List-Scheduling algorithms*. Any List-Scheduling algorithm is based on Algorithm 1, which generates a schedule S_j with a corresponding length τ_j for each machine $m_j \in M$ based on a list L_v of all n job-indices. We denote the i-th element of L_v by $L_v[i]$. It is easy to see that Algorithm 1 can be implemented to run in $\mathcal{O}(n \log m)$.

Algorithm 1 Greedy-List Algorithm

INPUT: List L_v of job-indices, number m of machines
$\tau_j := 0 \; \forall m_j \in M$
$S_j := [\,] \; \forall m_j \in M$
for $i := 1$ **to** n **do**
  $m_k \in \text{argmin}_{m_j \in M} \tau_j$
  $\tau_k := \tau_k + t_{L_v[i]}$
  $S_k := [S_k, L_v[i]]$
end for
OUTPUT: $S_1, \ldots, S_m$

Definition 2 A List-Scheduling algorithm is composed of two steps. First, it constructs a sorted list L_v of all n job-indices based on the vector of claimed valuation functions v. In the second step, it calls Algorithm 1.

Corollary 1 *Let $L_i(v)$ denote the position of job $i \in J$ in list L_v, i.e. $L_v[L_i(v)] = i$. A social choice function f that is established by a List-Scheduling algorithm is monotone in v_i, $i \in J$, if*

$$L_i(v_i^{w_i}, v_{-i}) \geq L_i(v_i^{w_i'}, v_{-i}) \tag{4}$$

for all $v_{-i} \in V_{-i}$ and all $v_i^{w_i}, v_i^{w_i'} \in V_i$ with $w_i \leq w_i' \in \mathbb{Q}_{\geq 0}$.

Proof Let $i \in J$ and $v_{-i} \in V_{-i}$ be arbitrary but fixed. We will show that (4) implies (2). Let $v_i^{w_i}, v_i^{w_i'} \in V_i$ with $w_i \leq w_i' \in \mathbb{Q}_{\geq 0}$ and $L_i(v_i^{w_i}, v_{-i}) \geq L_i(v_i^{w_i'}, v_{-i})$, i.e. reporting $v_i^{w_i'}$ results in a position of job i within L_v that is guaranteed to not succeed the position that results from reporting $v_i^{w_i}$. Algorithm 1 iterates over the jobs in L_v, starting with the first element of L_v. In each iteration, it determines a machine $m_k \in M$ with smallest length τ_k of the current schedule S_k and appends the corresponding job to S_k. Hence, the time instant at which a job $j \in J$ is started to be processed (starting time) by one of the machines is greater than or equal to the starting times of all jobs that precede j in L_v. Thus, reporting $v_i^{w_i'}$ results in a starting time which is smaller or equal to the starting time that results from reporting $v_i^{w_i}$ and, therefore, $C_i(f(v_i^{w_i}, v_{-i})) \geq C_i(f(v_i^{w_i'}, v_{-i}))$. □

Thus, a message of Corollary 1 is, that increasing the weight of a job $i \in J$ relative to the other jobs' fixed weights neither results in a worse position of i in the list L_v nor results in a larger completion time C_i. In other words, changing the weight of a single job $i \in J$ does not affect the relative order of the jobs $j \in J \setminus \{i\}$ in L_v.

To construct an incentive compatible polynomial time mechanism based on a polynomial time List-Scheduling algorithm that satisfies (4), we need to show how to calculate the payment functions (3) of Theorem 1 in polynomial time for a given $i \in J$ and $v \in V$ arbitrary but fixed. The first summand of (3) is independent of v_i. Hence, incentive compatibility is not affected by this term such that we may assume that it is a constant. The second summand can be determined based on a single call of the List-Scheduling algorithm. Moreover, note that $C_i(f(v_i^s, v_{-i}))$ is a step function, i.e. it is a piecewise constant function in s. Since v_{-i} is fixed and as a consequence of Corollary 1, the step function has at most $n-1$ discontinuities (see Fig. 2 for an illustration, more details on the example are presented in Sect. 3.2). Denote the set of the potential points of discontinuity by $Q_i = \{q_i^1, \ldots, q_i^{n-1}\}$, where $q_i^k \geq q_i^{k+1}$ for all $k \in \{1, \ldots, n-2\}$. Note that Q_i can be determined efficiently because the List-Scheduling algorithm is assumed to be polynomial and satisfies (4). Moreover, define $q_i^n := 0$ and $\hat{Q}_i := Q_i \cup \{q_i^n\} \cup \{w_i\}$. It is easy

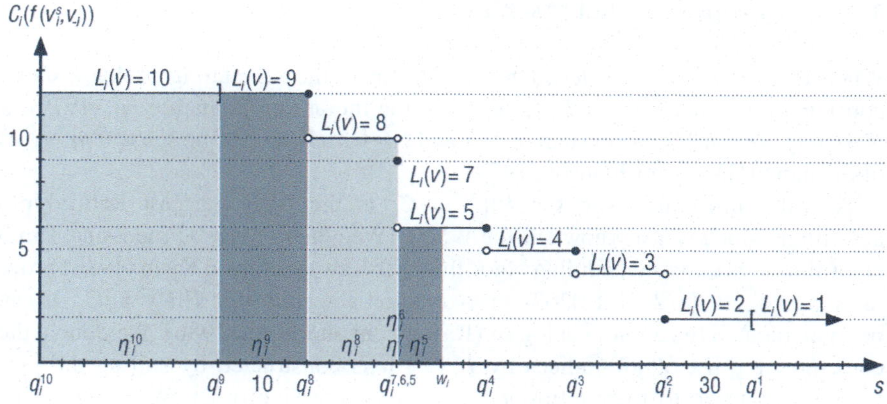

Fig. 2 $C_i(f(v_i^s, v_{-i}))$ for an exemplary instance with $n = 10$ and $m = 2$

to see that the evaluation of the third summand of (3) at a given w_i requires the computation of the areas of a finite number of rectangles, with the width of each rectangle being related to a (potentially open) connected subinterval of $[0, w_i]$ that is defined by two adjacent points of the set $\hat{Q}_i$ (see Fig. 2). However, because the value of $C_i(f(v_i^{q_i^k}, v_{-i}))$, $k \in \{L_i(v), \ldots, n\}$, may depend on a tie breaking rule applied by the List-Scheduling algorithm, we evaluate the step function at the centers of the connected subintervals mentioned above. We denote these centers by

$$\eta_i^{L_i(v)} := q_i^{L_i(v)} + \frac{1}{2}\left(w_i - q_i^{L_i(v)}\right),$$

and

$$\eta_i^k := q_i^k + \frac{1}{2}\left(q_i^{k-1} - q_i^k\right) \quad \forall k \in \{L_i(v) + 1, \ldots, n\}.$$

Then,

$$\int_0^{w_i} C_i(f(v_i^s, v_{-i}))\mathrm{d}s$$
$$= (w_i - q_i^{L_i(v)})C_i(f(v_i^{\eta_i^{L_i(v)}}, v_{-i})) + \sum_{k=L_i(v)+1}^{n} \left(q_i^{k-1} - q_i^k\right) C_i(f(v_i^{\eta_i^k}, v_{-i})). \quad (5)$$

Summing up, it is possible to evaluate $p_i(v_i^{w_i}, v_{-i})$, $i \in J$, with a linear number $(n - L_i(v) + 2)$ of calls of the List-Scheduling algorithm. Hence, because the List-Scheduling algorithm is assumed to be polynomial, the evaluation of the payment functions can be achieved in polynomial time.

3.2 Multiple Parallel Machines

When considering m parallel identical machines, the scheduling problem under consideration is denoted by $P||\sum w_i C_i$ in the literature (Graham et al., 1979). It is weakly NP-hard for a constant $m \geq 2$ and NP-hard in the strong sense if m is part of the input (Garey and Johnson, 1979).

A well known heuristic for $P||\sum w_i C_i$ is the LRF (Largest Ratio First) algorithm, which is also known as the WSPT (Weighted Shortest Processing Time) algorithm. It is a List-Scheduling algorithm that Kawaguchi and Kyan (1986) prove to be an $(\sqrt{2}+1)/2 \cong 1.0207$-approximation algorithm for $P||\sum w_i C_i$. It can be implemented to run in $\mathcal{O}(n \log n)$ (Kawaguchi and Kyan, 1986). We denote the corresponding list of job-indices by L_v^{LRF}. It is constructed by sorting the jobs $i \in J$ according to their ratios w_i/t_i in non-increasing order. We assume that ties are broken with respect to job-indices (smaller indices first), which results in monotonicity without influencing the performance of the LRF algorithm. The position of job $i \in J$ in list L_v^{LRF} is denoted by $L_i^{LRF}(v)$, i.e. $L_v^{LRF}[L_i^{LRF}(v)] = i$.

Theorem 2 *The social choice function established by the LRF algorithm is monotone in all* v_i*,* $i \in J$*.*

Proof Let $i \in J$ be arbitrary but fixed. Because of Corollary 1 it is sufficient to show that $L_i^{LRF}(v_i^{w_i}, v_{-i}) \geq L_i^{LRF}(v_i^{w_i'}, v_{-i})$ for all $v_{-i} \in V_{-i}$ and all $v_i^{w_i}, v_i^{w_i'} \in V_i$ with $w_i \leq w_i' \in \mathbb{Q}_{\geq 0}$. Let $v_{-i} \in V_{-i}$ be arbitrary but fixed. Then, for any fixed pair of weights w_i and w_i', $w_i \leq w_i'$, we obviously have $w_i'/t_i \geq w_i/t_i$ because the processing time t_i is a positive constant. Moreover, the jobs are sorted in non-increasing order of these ratios in L_v^{LRF}. The claim follows immediately. □

In order to compute the payments (3) of Theorem 1 in polynomial time, we need to evaluate (5). We observe that

$$q_i^k = t_i \frac{w_{L_v^{LRF}[k+1]}}{t_{L_v^{LRF}[k+1]}} \quad \forall k \in \{L_i^{LRF}(v), \ldots, n-1\}.$$

We note at this point that Fig. 2 relates to the example presented in Table 2. The weight $w_i = 18$ has been chosen such that five jobs succeed $i = 7$ in L_v^{LRF}. Hence,

Table 2 Example with $i = 7$, $w_7 = 18$, $t_7 = 2$, $n = 10$, $m = 2$

j	9	8	6	1	7	2	5	10	4	3
$k = L_j^{LRF}(v)$	1	2	3	4	5	6	7	8	9	10
w_j	32	42	24	20	18	32	16	24	12	8
t_j	2	3	2	2	2	4	2	3	2	2
w_j/t_j	16	14	12	10	9	8	8	8	6	4
η_i^k	–	–	–	–	17	16	16	14	10	4

there are five potential points of discontinuity in the interval $[0, w_7)$ that have to be taken into account when evaluating the integral (5). Each connected subinterval of $[0, w_7)$ defined by two adjacent points of discontinuity (or 0 and one point of discontinuity or one point of discontinuity and w_7) relates to one of six rectangles, the sum of the areas of which define the value of the integral. However, as can be seen in Fig. 2, only four rectangles have an area greater than zero.

3.3 One Machine

Consider a special case of the scheduling problem analyzed in Sect. 3.2 with only one machine, i.e. $m = 1$. This problem is denoted by $1||\sum w_i C_i$ in the scheduling literature (Graham et al., 1979). It is well known to be solvable in polynomial time by the LRF algorithm (see Smith, 1956). Furthermore, the objective function corresponds to maximizing social welfare. Hence, it is possible to implement a computationally efficient VCG mechanism $(f, p_1, \ldots, p_n)$. The payment functions $p_i(v)$, $i \in J$, specifying (1) are

$$p_i(v) = h_i(v_{-i}) + \sum_{\substack{j=1 \\ j \neq i}}^{n} w_j C_j(f(v)), \tag{6}$$

where $h_i(v_{-i}) : V_{-i} \to \mathbb{R}$.

It is possible to implement some desirable properties of the mechanism by choosing specific functions $h_i(v_{-i})$, $i \in J$, in (6). In the context of auctions, these properties sometimes relate to the mechanism never paying bidders and assuring that no player receives negative utility (see Nisan et al., 2007). A more closely related example is Duives et al. (2015), where the authors (amongst other things) consider truthful mechanisms that minimize the total payments made to the job owners in the $1||\sum w_i C_i$ setting with discrete one-dimensional type spaces. If we consider applications in intermodal transport as described in Sect. 1, it may be reasonable to design the payments such that the clients, on average, neither win nor lose money, i.e. $\sum_{i=1}^{n} p_i(v) = 0$. This is sometimes referred to as *budget balancedness*. The corresponding payment functions $p_i(v)$, $i \in J$, are derived by Suijs (1996). We revisit his result by explicitly characterizing the functions $h_i(v_{-i})$, $i \in J$.

Theorem 3 *Consider an instance I of $1||\sum w_i C_i$ with $n > 2$. Let C_j^{-i} denote the completion time of job $j \in J$ in an optimal solution after having removed job $i \neq j$ from the job set of I. If*

$$h_i(v_{-i}) = -\frac{n-1}{n-2} \sum_{\substack{j=1 \\ j \neq i}}^{n} w_j C_j^{-i} + \frac{1}{n-2} \sum_{\substack{j=1 \\ j \neq i}}^{n} w_j t_j,$$

then

$$\sum_{i=1}^{n} p_i(v) = 0.$$

Proof W.l.o.g. let $f(v) = o^*$ be the optimal schedule determined by the LRF algorithm and let $\frac{w_i}{t_i} \geq \frac{w_j}{t_j}$ for all $i, j \in J$ with $i \leq j$. As before, we assume that the LRF algorithm breaks ties with respect to job-indices (smaller indices first). Since job j is the j-th job that is processed by the algorithm, we have $C_j = \sum_{k=1}^{j} t_k$. Hence, $C_j^{-i} = \sum_{\substack{k=1\\k\neq i}}^{j} t_k$. For the sake of brevity we write C_i instead of $C_i(o^*)$.

$$\begin{aligned}
\sum_{i=1}^{n} h_i(v_{-i}) &= \sum_{i=1}^{n} \left(-\frac{n-1}{n-2} \sum_{\substack{j=1\\j\neq i}}^{n} w_j C_j^{-i} + \frac{1}{n-2} \sum_{\substack{j=1\\j\neq i}}^{n} w_j t_j \right) \\
&= -\frac{n-1}{n-2} \sum_{i=1}^{n} \sum_{\substack{j=1\\j\neq i}}^{n} w_j \sum_{\substack{k=1\\k\neq i}}^{j} t_k + \frac{1}{n-2} \sum_{i=1}^{n} \sum_{\substack{j=1\\j\neq i}}^{n} w_j t_j \\
&= -\frac{n-1}{n-2} \sum_{i=1}^{n} \sum_{\substack{j=1\\j\neq i}}^{n} w_j \sum_{\substack{k=1\\k\neq i}}^{j} t_k + \frac{1}{n-2} (n-1) \sum_{i=1}^{n} w_i t_i \\
&= -\frac{n-1}{n-2} \left(\sum_{i=1}^{n} \sum_{\substack{j=1\\j\neq i}}^{n} w_j \sum_{k=1}^{j} t_k - \sum_{j=1}^{n} \sum_{i=1}^{j-1} w_j t_i - \sum_{i=1}^{n} w_i t_i \right) \\
&= -\frac{n-1}{n-2} \left(\sum_{i=1}^{n} \sum_{\substack{j=1\\j\neq i}}^{n} w_j C_j - \sum_{j=1}^{n} w_j (C_j - t_j) - \sum_{i=1}^{n} w_i t_i \right) \\
&= -\frac{n-1}{n-2} \left(\sum_{i=1}^{n} \left(\sum_{j=1}^{n} w_j C_j - w_i C_i \right) - \sum_{j=1}^{n} w_j C_j \right. \\
&\qquad \left. + \sum_{j=1}^{n} w_j t_j - \sum_{i=1}^{n} w_i t_i \right) \\
&= -\frac{n-1}{n-2} \left(\sum_{i=1}^{n} \sum_{j=1}^{n} w_j C_j - \sum_{i=1}^{n} w_i C_i - \sum_{j=1}^{n} w_j C_j \right)
\end{aligned}$$

$$= -\frac{n-1}{n-2}\left((n-2)\sum_{j=1}^{n} w_j C_j\right)$$

$$= -(n-1)\sum_{j=1}^{n} w_j C_j$$

$$= -\sum_{i=1}^{n}\sum_{\substack{j=1\\ j\neq i}}^{n} w_j C_j$$

□

4 Summary

This research paper gives an introduction to challenges and perspectives encountered in intermodal transport logistics of large city sea terminals and megahubs. The enormous increase of the container throughput and the automation of megahubs induces the need for smart software solutions that support the terminal's operator to plan and conduct the daily operations. "Classical" solution concepts aim at improving the efficiency of megahubs mainly from the perspective of the operator. In order to stay competitive and attractive to their customers, solution concepts need to address the preferences of the customers as well. In this research, we design appropriate algorithms that take the interests of the customers into account. We concentrate on scheduling problems where the central decision maker (generally the terminal's operator) is not equipped with all relevant data of the specific scheduling problem because it is private information of selfish customers who aim to influence the scheduling solution by submitting false information to the decision maker. We propose algorithms for these scheduling problems such that the decision maker can extract the true information by setting the right incentives for these players in order to generate "fair" solutions that consider the interests of all customers. This solution concept requires a fast and frequent information transfer between decision maker and customers, which is supported by the ongoing digitalization in logistics that supports real-time tracing of goods and improves data interchange.

References

Angel E, Bampis E, Pascual F (2006) Truthful algorithms for scheduling selfish tasks on parallel machines. Theor Comput Sci 369(1–3):157–168

Archer A, Tardos É (2001) Truthful mechanisms for one-parameter agents. In: FOCS '01 - Proceedings of the 42nd IEEE symposium on foundations of computer science, Las Vegas, Nevada, 14–17 Oct 2001, pp 482–491

Bontekoning YM, Macharis C, Trip JJ (2004) Is a new applied transportation research field emerging? A review of intermodal rail-truck freight transport literature. Transport Res A: Pol 38(1):1–34
Christodoulou G, Koutsoupias E, Vidali A (2009) A lower bound for scheduling mechanisms. Algorithmica 55(4):729–740
Clarke EH (1971) Multipart pricing of public goods. Public Choice 11(1):17–33
Danish Ship Finance (2014) Shipping market review. Tech. Rep. November 2014, Copenhagen
Duives J, Heydenreich B, Mishra D, Müller R, Uetz M (2015) On optimal mechanism design for a sequencing problem. J Sched 18(1):45–59
Garey MR, Johnson DS (1979) Computers and intractability. A guide to the theory of NP-completeness. Freeman, New York
Graham RL, Lawler EL, Lenstra JK, Rinnooy Kan AHG (1979) Optimization and approximation in deterministic sequencing and scheduling. A survey. Ann Discrete Math 5:287–326
Groves T (1973) Incentives in teams. Econometrica 41(4):617–631
Heydenreich B, Müller R, Uetz M (2007) Games and mechanism design in machine scheduling. An introduction. Prod Oper Manag 16(4):437–454
Institute of Shipping Economics and Logistics (2011) Shipping statistics and market review. ISL, Bremen
Kawaguchi T, Kyan S (1986) Worst case bound of an LRF schedule for the mean weighted flow-time problem. SIAM J Comput 15(4):1119–1129
Koutsoupias E, Vidali A (2013) A lower bound of 1+ φ for truthful scheduling mechanisms. Algorithmica 66(1):211–223
Kovalyov MY, Pesch E (2014) A game mechanism for single machine sequencing with zero risk. Omega 44:104–110
Krishna V (2010) Auction theory. Academic Press, Amsterdam
Lavi R, Swamy C (2009) Truthful mechanism design for multidimensional scheduling via cycle monotonicity. Game Econ Behav 67(1):99–124
Macharis C, Bontekoning YM (2004) Opportunities for OR in intermodal freight transport research. A review. Eur J Oper Res 153(2):400–416
Nisan N (2007) Introduction to mechanism design (for computer scientists). In: Nisan N, Roughgarden T, Tardos E, Vazirani VV (eds) Algorithmic game theory. Cambridge University Press, Cambridge, pp 209–241
Nisan N, Ronen A (1999) Algorithmic mechanism design (extended abstract). In: STOC '99 - Proceedings of the 31st annual ACM symposium on theory of computing, New York, 31 May–03 June 2014, pp 129–140
Nisan N, Ronen A (2000) Computationally feasible VCG mechanisms. In: EC '00 - Proceedings of the 2nd ACM conference on electronic commerce, Minneapolis, MN, 17–20 October 2000, pp 242–252
Nisan N, Roughgarden T, Tardos E, Vazirani VV (eds) (2007) Algorithmic game theory. Cambridge University Press, Cambridge
Smith WE (1956) Various optimizers for single-stage production. Nav Res Logist Q 3(1–2):59–66
Stahlbock R, Voß S (2008) Operations research at container terminals. A literature update. OR Spectr 30(1):1–52
Steenken D, Voß S, Stahlbock R (2004) Container terminal operation and operations research. A classification and literature review. OR Spectr 26(1):3–49
Suijs J (1996) On incentive compatibility and budget balancedness in public decision making. Econ Des 2(1):193–209
Vickrey W (1961) Counterspeculation, auctions, and competitive sealed tenders. J Finance 16(1):8–37
Vis IFA, de Koster R (2003) Transshipment of containers at a container terminal. An overview. Eur J Oper Res 147:1–16

Dominik Kress is currently a post-doctoral research assistant at the Chair of Management Information Science at the University of Siegen (Germany). He received a diploma degree in business administration and engineering from TU Darmstadt (Germany), where he also worked as a research assistant at the Chair of Operations Research. He later received his doctoral degree in business administration from the University of Siegen, to which he is still affiliated. His current research interests include scheduling problems and algorithms, competitive facility location problems, and game theoretic problem settings arising in logistics.

Sebastian Meiswinkel is currently a doctoral candidate at the Chair of Management Information Science at the University of Siegen (Germany). He obtained a diploma degree in mathematics from TU Dortmund University (Germany), where he also worked as a research assistant at the Institute of Transport Logistics. His main research interests include discrete optimization problems and mechanism design in the context of scheduling problems.

Jenny Nossack studied mathematics at TU Berlin (Germany) and worked as a research assistant at the Chair of Management Information Science at the University of Siegen (Germany), where she also received her doctoral degree in business administration in 2013. She currently works as a senior research fellow at the Center for Advanced Studies in Management (CASiM) at HHL Leipzig Graduate School of Management (Germany). Her research interests lie in mathematical modelling, combinatorial optimization, logistics, and scheduling problems.

Erwin Pesch studied mathematics and computer science at TU Darmstadt (Germany). He was employed as a software engineer and a research assistant at Commerzbank AG and the Business Institute of TU Darmstadt, respectively. He worked as an assistant professor at the Faculty of Economics and Business Administration at Maastricht University (Netherlands) and as a professor at the Institute of Economics at the University of Bonn (Germany). Currently, he is a full professor at the Faculty of Economics and Business Administration of the University of Siegen and is the Director of the Center for Advanced Studies in Management at HHL Leipzig Graduate School of Management. He holds a doctoral degree in mathematics and a habilitation in business administration, both from TU Darmstadt. His research areas are logistics, decision support, project management, personnel planning and scheduling, many of which are closely related to different industry projects.

Printed by Printforce, the Netherlands